TEACHING/DISCIPLINE

A Positive Approach For Educational Development

THIRD EDITION

Charles H. Madsen Jr.
Clifford K. Madsen
The Florida State University
Tallahassee, Florida

ALLYN and BACON, Inc.
Boston London Sydney Toronto

To our parents—lifelong teachers,
unwitting behaviorists,
wonderful people

Portions of this book first appeared in Teaching/Discipline: A
Positive Approach for Educational Development, Expanded Second
Edition for professionals by Charles H. Madsen, Jr. and Clifford K.
Madsen, Copyright © 1974, 1970 by Allyn and Bacon, Inc. and in
Parents/Children/Discipline: A Positive Approach by Charles H.
Madsen, Jr. and Clifford K. Madsen, © 1972 by Allyn and Bacon, Inc.

Library of Congress Cataloging in Publication Data

Madsen, Charles H   1933-
    Teaching/discipline.

    Includes bibliographical references and index.
    1. Classroom management.   I. Madsen, Clifford K., joint author.
II. Title.
LB3011.M25 1980   371.1'024   80-19772
ISBN 0-205-07228-3
ISBN 0-205-07143-0 (pbk.)

Cover design: Leora Haywood

Printed in the United States of America

Printing number and year (last digits):
 10 9 8 7 6 5 4 3 2 1   85 84 83 82 81 80

Contents

Preface

This edition of Teaching/Discipline represents an expansion and re-organization of the Second Edition. It is written especially for teachers, prospective teachers, and other professionals who interact with students. It is specifically intended as a classroom discipline and subject matter presentation.

This edition is presented in four parts. Part I is organized in question and answer schemata designed to help clarify the central issues that have arisen from the authors' interaction with children and teachers in the schools. Part II represents a selected summary of scientific and professional practices deemed relevant, transferable, and directly applicable to classroom teaching. Over one hundred examples are arranged developmentally for the convenience of the reader. Part III treats the effect of teacher responses on student behavior in an attempt to help facilitate a positive approach. Part IV provides an observation manual, an introduction to behavioral terminology, and an introduction to workshops.

A glossary is included with explanations especially written for those with little background in behavioral research, to serve as a transition from this volume to the published research found in scientific journals.

We are deeply indebted to the researchers whose studies are summarized as Scientific Applications in Part II and more specifically to their unnamed scientific progenitors. We are hopeful that this edition will not only stimulate the beginning of greater efficiency in the classroom but will also provide an impetus for teachers to take fuller advantage of the benefits being produced through scientific research.

PART I

TEACHING AND DISCIPLINE

CHAPTER 1

Teaching
The Art of Discipline

A FIRST DAY?

As she approached the school, she wondered why all schools look the same. Why couldn't someone be imaginative enough to disguise the telltale landscape and those separate rows of windows that indicate the time-honored concept of individual classrooms? Why were all the buildings that didn't look as though they were designed by school boards called experimental? What about those experimental programs, anyway? Were there communities that really cared enough about education to pay for all that? It was obvious this wasn't one of them. Notice the dull color of the paint; that quonset hut must be new, but what a poor excuse for an education site. Oh yes, that must be a "portable classroom"—a nice euphemism for lack of planning or no money. Money—this job didn't pay that well. Why was she here? Parkside had a better program, or perhaps she should have stayed in school. The graduate assistantship could have come through, and why even teaching? But, then, why think about all that nonsense anyway? This is the day, the first day for the students. She felt her stomach skip and her throat tighten. Was it this bad for everyone? As she walked into the building she wondered why those other people looked so calm? She stopped at the restroom. Wasn't this the third time since getting up this morning? Her eye caught a limerick, and she wondered why students were not as creative in class as they were on bathroom walls. Why were all these wild thoughts so vivid this morning? "Okay, face it—you're scared. Just plain scared!"

Her mind wandered back to a discussion with her father. There was a teacher—fifty years in the public schools. She had gone home especially to talk to him those two weeks before the planning session. She remembered her father smiling as she asked him many questions. She remembered getting no answer day after day until the last evening before she was to leave. "But Dad, what makes a good teacher?" After a long silence his brow furrowed, and his bright eyes narrowed.

"Every teacher goes out with a golden apple of knowledge he wants to share, but some students don't want that knowledge, and their attitude becomes, 'Teach me if you can, but I'll make it as difficult as possible.' Remember two things. When it is as difficult as it can be, don't give up. You might think that it can't get worse, but it does when you give up. The second thing—*you can't even get started without discipline.*" As she looked in the mirror after washing her hands, she became suddenly angry with her father and that discussion. Clichés, clichés, that's all she needed now—two more clichés: "Don't give up. Discipline." She remembered her professors—more clichés. "Motivate the students, captivate their interests, recognize individual differences." Great, great, but how? No one ever says how. As she approached her room, she felt guilty about her thoughts concerning her father. Sure, he *was* a fine teacher—years of compliments, awards, letters, everything a teacher could want. Then she suddenly realized that even her father didn't know why. The art of teaching—is it really that elusive?

When she got to the door, she stopped for a long moment. "Please, please let me be a good teacher." Then it happened. The door knocked against her face as a student ran out. She watched the boy run down the hall as the students inside started laughing. She wondered quickly if she should go after him. "No, I'd better stay with the class." She had rehearsed an opening joke; that wouldn't work now. She felt her face flush as she tried to decide what to do. After a long pause she muttered, "Good morning," but instantly realized that it was a mistake when one boy softly mimicked her. Again, laughter. Why, oh why couldn't she start all over again? She looked over the sea of faces. Where was a friend? She quickly picked up a piece of chalk and began writing her name on the board. With her back turned, she tried frantically to think of some way to gain control. She heard some small noises, then a girl's louder voice, "Quit it." Was it this way everywhere? From kindergarten through twelfth grade, was this what teaching was all about? Finally she spoke. "Students, please take your seats so we can get started. As you notice on the board, my name is . . ." Two boys were standing in the back. "Would you please take a seat?" The class turned around to see. One boy shrugged "OK, OK, OK." The class burst out laughing again as he dropped into a chair. The other boy started to move, but then stopped as the class laughed louder. "Would you please sit down!" The class grew quiet. She felt her heart pounding and mustered the sternest look she could. Student and teacher were now staring at each other. The class-room became not only quiet but also electric as students looked from teacher to troublemaker and back again. After these thousand years of silence, she heard herself say angrily, "Now, you sit down this instant." Nausea came into her stomach as she watched the muscles tighten in his face, his lips curl sarcastically. "Are you goin' to make me?"

A first day?—A large majority of teachers who leave the teaching profession do so because of what they term "inability to discipline."

WHOM DO WE DISCIPLINE?

Many teachers and parents have drawn an artificial line between love and discipline. Some make a point for love; others for discipline. The wise think they solve the problem when they say it must be both, and all are perhaps equally naïve. The essential point is that we as teachers must understand precisely what we mean by love and/or discipline before we begin. The major thesis of this book is that we must be concerned with how people *act* in order to assess behavior or to define terms. How should one know that he is loved but by the way people act toward him: what they say, how they look, how they touch, in a word, what they *do*? Attention, praise, kind words, and physical contact have been demonstrations of love for years. Who cares if someone loves them if they never receive evidence through attention, contact, or by the spoken word? While it may be possible for love to exist in total abstraction, most people are not content with such little personal involvement, especially over an extended period of time. One often hears the phrase "I'll love you no matter what." This is a good example of a meaningless cliché. Indeed very few, if any, really believe it. "No matter what" remains an abstraction that has little meaning until it is violated. That is, I'll love you until you desert me, find someone else, treat me cruelly, violate my trust, and so on. Most people do stress overt behaviors. A more fitting phrase would be, "I'll love you if you love me," or "I will act in certain ways with you if you reciprocate."

If such statements as "I will love you no matter what" were left to idle verbalizations, there would be little problem. When they are taken seriously, they pose a very serious problem, especially for the teacher. The teacher is led to believe that teachers should "love" everyone; and, if this were not damaging enough, the teacher actually may believe that one should continuously *act* as though one loves all students "no matter what."

One behavioral principle that we try to teach all youngsters is simple. "When you do nice things, nice things happen to you. When you do bad things, bad things happen to you." Even allowing for slight inconsistency, if we truly believed and taught in a manner conducive to this end, we would shortly have many "nice children." Yet we violate this principle regularly by teaching a child the exact opposite. This simple principle has several perversions: (1) when you do *bad* things, *nice* things happen to you; (2) when you do *nice* things, *bad* things happen to you; (3) no matter what you do, *bad* things happen to you; and (4) no matter what you do, *nice* things happen to you (i.e., I'll love you no matter what). Perhaps the saddest ramification of this last distortion is that while we treat the child, for a time, as though all behavior deserves nice consequences, we finally give up on the child at that precise point when he has finally learned exactly what we have taught him: No matter what he does, nice things happen to him. We often crown this educational achievement with statements such as: "I've tried everything with that child and nothing works," or "I just can't get through to that student."

Discipline is a process whereby certain relationships (associations) are established. It is a way of behaving, conducive to productive ends. First, it must be taught; secondly, it must be learned, i.e., internalized. Love, if it is to transcend mere rhetoric, is a way of feeling and acting conducive to productive ends. Most teachers enter the teaching profession because they truly love children (care about students) and desire to help each child achieve his greatest potential. Sometimes, people are paid to care about children, that is, to teach.

The most difficult aspect of human interaction based upon love is to develop the ability to withhold overt acts of love (ignore or disapprove) to help the child learn appropriate ways to behave. When love responses have been previously established, we can then respond in similar kind to the child's behavior. Thus, when a child demonstrates inappropriate responses and we actively withdraw our overt responses of love, we teach the child that his behavior is not deserving of love responses from us. The most tragic mistakes of the teacher occur when the courage to act in this way is absent, and the teacher succumbs to "giving in." The child learns a perverted association: "When I do bad things, nice things happen to me." In the long run everyone suffers, but mostly the child. The authors call this teaching behavior "mistakes of love." More appropriately it might be classified as "naiveté" or "lack of courage." It is amazing, although apparent, that some people actually believe that all responses should be regarded with overt acts of love. The teacher who really loves a child will have the courage to teach him proper associations. We discipline only those people we care about; others we leave alone.

Whom do we discipline?—We discipline those we love.

WHY DO WE DISCIPLINE?

Discipline is necessary if a child is to function properly. All teachers have had the unfortunate experience of observing either children or adults who are "undisciplined." We usually refer to such people as lacking motivation, apathetic, rowdy, or even mean, spiteful, or deceitful. But why are children so classified? How do they become this way? If self-discipline is to be internalized, then how is the child to achieve this attribute? The answer is obvious—*it must be learned.* Teachers often "beg the question" by stating that it must come from *within* the child. Yet how does motivation or proper attitude get "in"? Even if some of it is "in," will it continue to serve in the future? These are questions with which the teacher must deal.

Particular patterns of responses are learned from the external world (external stimuli). If a student is "motivated," it is because he has learned to associate certain behaviors with certain outcomes. Motivation does not exist in a vacuum; it is a way of behaving. If the teacher wants a student to behave in a certain way, the teacher must structure the student's external world (i.e., control his environment) to insure that the desired behavior will be learned. The disciplined child is a child who (1) has learned to behave socially in appropriate ways, and (2) evidences proper patterns of responses to academic work. If either one of these two general categories of behaviors is absent, we usually say the child "has a problem."

We must be very careful, however, not to designate many behaviors into one or two artificial categories and believe that we have solved the problem because we have arbitrarily classified it or given it a name. People react differently to various situations (stimuli). It is very interesting to take a pencil and paper and write down one's own responses in different situations. How do we act in the classroom, in church, at a football game, in faculty meetings, swimming, buying shoes, driving a car, getting out of an invitation, giving a speech, eating dinner, listening to beautiful music, listening to an argument? Yes, we act differently, we dress differently, we talk differently, we even smile differently in these diverse situations. If we were brave enough to list our most secret behaviors, we would probably shock those very people who believe they know us the best. It is unwise to classify behaviors into artificial categories that have to do with only a few situations. Perhaps some justification can be made for general attributes (e.g., apathetic, aggressive, boisterous, unmotivated), but such classification is extremely deceptive and at best provides only partial information.

When learning is defined as a change or modification of behavior, then three things are necessary: (1) experience, (2) discrimination, and (3) association. For instance, a child is presented with a color (*experience*). After a time the child *discriminates* the color from other colors or the absence of the color. Through repetition, an *association(s)* is made with the color, for example, red. The child may then evidence in some behavior, most often previously learned, (e.g., pointing, matching, speaking, thinking) that he has learned the color. The preceding definition of learning based on reinforcement theory does not quarrel with mediational processes in learning or with the material to be learned. It proposes a method to promote or expedite this learning. In short, it asks, "How should we go about teaching the color red in the best possible manner to insure correct association?" If the child responds favorably to teaching, we assume the external stimuli are associated in a way that functions as a reward for the child. But what if the child does not respond? Then we must restructure the external environment so that the child does receive proper motivation.

How, then, are we to get the student to learn the many behaviors that will provide him with the necessary skills to achieve a productive life? Within the complexity of his many responses to his external environment, we must structure his external world to provide proper relationships to be learned. We should not sit back and hope that motivation will somehow "get inside." We must structure the environment to provide the student with proper associations. Discipline must first be external; it must come from *without* before it can be from *within*.

If learned relationships to external stimuli are conducive to productive ends, the child will have a repertoire of responses that will serve him well as he meets the constant challenges of life. If he is capable of following rules, acting enthusiastically regarding new learning experiences, staying on task during work periods, relating well with other children, knowing when to be assertive and when to acquiesce, indeed, if the student has learned to respond appropriately to many specific situations, then we say he is well disciplined.

Why do we discipline?—We discipline to provide for social order and individual productivity.

WHY DEVELOP TECHNIQUES FOR DISCIPLINE?

Mother has just finished teaching and expects her seventeen-year-old son to pick her up from school at approximately 4:00 P.M. Four arrives, no son; the woman begins to pace a little and thinks about a hectic afternoon and a ruined supper. At 4:15 she becomes a little angry and thinks about her inconsiderate offspring. Four-thirty P.M. arrives, and, in spite of trying to do something else, she begins to worry about his whereabouts. Between 5:45 and 6:00 (while many transportation invitations are turned down) he is imagined dead in a car wreck, attacked by someone, unconscious in the hospital, picked up by the police, drunk in an alley, and sundry other things, all of which are negative (she has even lost her concern for transportation). Is it not strange that during these times most people do not imagine that the son happened to get involved with a classmate and forgot the time while having a wonderful talk, enjoying a pleasant stroll, meditating by oneself while looking at flowers in the park, or perhaps shopping for a surprise gift for this mother.

What, in reality, is the problem in this case?—the mother who is "fretting and worrying" about possible catastropic events or a seventeen-year-old-son who is late? One real problem is the worry. When pickup time arrived, if mother had waited a reasonable amount of time and then arranged other transportation, there probably would have been much less of a problem.

Unfortunately, it happens frequently that many people reinforce in themselves (substitute spouse for son and reread the above example) and others the very worst. We often train ourselves to worry unnecessarily about terrible things that only might happen, such as potential loss of loved ones or inability to succeed in the future, for example. The problem is actually the worry itself, especially when nothing is done to change behavior. Many people manage systematically to increase their worrying and, in addition, convince themselves that it is being done because of sincere concern for themselves or others.

It would seem that every person should be trained explicitly to prepare for foreseeable emergencies. We should teach ourselves and our our students specific actions to deal with emergencies (what do you do when a stranger tries to pick you up; if the school is on fire and smoke is coming from somewhere; if you are hurt on the playground; if you are offered narcotics, etc.). Potential situations should be handled by these procedures with extensive role playing. Correct responses may then be based on the values of teachers and should clarify just what "normal" routines ought to be in emergencies. When values *and* techniques are specified and practiced, then if worry occurs, it is definitely not conducive to happiness. When we are waiting for errant progeny it is too late to do any teaching, and if some accident has occurred there is nothing to be done until we are notified.

Worry, or "depression," usually represents nothing more than statements to oneself or others indicating that we "feel sorry for ourselves" and as such are definitely unproductive. Frequently as we interact with each other and begin to spill our tale of "worry and woe" the "significant other" listens intently, nods his head, exhibits a "sad" face, and asks questions. Generally, as he performs for us this disservice, we pretend he "understands" which further reinforces our "depression." Teachers might tell friends, each other, and especially their students that if one wants to feel sorry for oneself and waste precious time instead of *deciding* what to do and then working on the problem, he had better find someone else with whom to talk. Often those students who "forget" or refuse responsibilities just want to spend time complaining. The only negative or similar comments we might allow are comments that honestly report the facts of a situation and are followed by an attempt to give a statement about what behaviors are being planned to alleviate the problem. "Tell me what you intend to do; do not give me your problem." It is astounding to find how fast "depression" and "worry" are relieved in children (and even adults) when no one pays attention and the negative verbal behavior is either punished or ignored while positive solutions are praised. "Is that what you will do next time? That's excellent. Let's pretend that I'm the other person and you show me what you will do."

A teacher might also be careful not to reinforce young children for crying following refusals and thereby reinforce the self-fulfilling prophecy that if only one could cry it out of his system, he would feel better. The teacher might focus on delineating the problem without reinforcing emotional responses and, at the same time, take the responsibility of planning a program with the student that will lead to behaviors incompatible with feeling sorry for oneself (doing something about the problem when possible or engaging in a "fun" activity when it is not possible to structure other responses).

Worry, anger, and other responses are expected in human beings of all ages. These responses might be acknowledged immediately, and then followed by behavioral techniques to change the emotion. They should not be reinforced or worried about. Young people should be trained to deal with a problem immediately, rather than receiving reinforcement for extended periods of worry. Hence, the focus becomes one of solving the problems that have produced the worry, anger, or crying (depression) and thus of acting one's way into a new way of thinking.

Why develop techniques for discipline?—To stop worrying and start acting.

WHAT DOES DISCIPLINE TAKE?

In his book *Profiles in Courage,* the late President Kennedy stated the problems of the politician in facing the demands of continued popularity as opposed to having the courage to act on his convictions. Politicians are not alone in this dilemma. Few people realize the pressures placed on the teacher for conformity and popularity. This pressure comes not only from community, administration, and parents, but also from colleagues and students. It is much easier to go along, not to rock the boat, to reevaluate one's position, especially in relationship to touchy problems. It is difficult to discipline the principal's daughter, to face the disapproval of a colleague, or to face an irate parent who insists his child has been dealt with unfairly. It is difficult to explain a simple behavioral approach that rests on direct immediate consequences and not on intriguing deceptions. It is difficult to explain to a parent that *the question of discipline is not one of strictness or permissiveness but one of cause-and-effect relationships.* It is difficult to help a child when the behavioral interactions required may be different from those the teacher and the child are used to, or to show parents how they can help their child when the teacher's instructions to them require opposite parent/child interactions than those previously established. It is difficult to live through the first day of a new program in discipline without giving in. It is most difficult to lose, for a time, the favorable response of a child.

Every teacher is faced with the problem of wanting to be liked. In our society, being liked is an admirable goal. It is indeed easy to demand a little less, hoping to be liked. Some people's desire to be liked is so great that they will suffer mild contempt for the privilege. Furthermore, even though most adults do not hesitate to have a young child suffer momentarily for long-term gain (medical inoculations, drudgery of learning hard concepts), many teachers do not have the courage to initiate a program of discipline that, although it might cause temporary disruptions in classroom routines, would in the long run really benefit the child. In addition, most teachers come to realize that even the most sophisticated students often evaluate a teacher's worth in terms of entertainment: "Here I am; what do you have for me today?" The value of discipline is not likely to be cherished immediately. "Why didn't I have anything fun to do today?" Students may even respond negatively when entertainment is not forthcoming. Nevertheless, it should be remembered that the *teacher's approval* is probably more important to the student than vice versa. The teacher's personal approval is one of his most effective rewards. *It should not be given indiscriminately.* Indeed, one never does a person a favor by letting him get away with anything, especially anything he does not like about himself. If the teacher really knows in what he believes, then he is much less likely to succumb and give in to pressures.

What does discipline take?—It takes courage.

WHAT IS EFFECTIVE TEACHING?

It has been suggested that so long as the teaching profession could not effectively demonstrate that it could insure specific educational outcomes few seemed to care a great deal about specific aspects concerning curriculum, who should teach, and so on. Now it would appear that advances in technology might renew interest concerning all aspects relating to teachers, students, and what educational experiences ought to be.

It seems apparent that no teaching technique can be effectively divorced from the person who uses it. This point, however, makes a case for more rigorous screening of prospective teachers, not for the abandonment of effective techniques. It is a curious argument that maintains that effective techniques must be kept from teachers because then teachers may actually teach more efficiently. Because of the effectiveness of certain procedures it seems that the profession may now address the truly important issues?

What specifically should be learned? Or more importantly, who will decide what is to be learned, both socially and academically? What values and accompanying behaviors evidencing selected values should be learned? When, where, and by whom?

Who should be given the responsibility to interact purposefully in the learned process, that is, to teach?

Should society require any objective evidence for this learning, that is, data from observation or other formal means?

If continued research demonstrates the efficacy of empirical cause-and-effect relationships (data based on observation), ought derived principles to be systematically implemented within the schools?

If so, then what should be the boundaries concerning choice and application?

It seems very unwise to mix the above value questions with questions relating to techniques. The choice of a particular teaching approach does not help the teacher decide why, what, and who is going to learn. These issues represent more important value choices. However, after questions relating to these values have been answered, effective techniques may be used to enhance learning. Of course, the choice of a particular technique as opposed to other approaches represents a value choice. In addition, if certain approaches are implemented, selection of specific procedures (e.g., discovery versus errorless discrimination), as well as choice of potential student/teacher interactions approval versus punishment) represents another value issue.

It would seem that initially we should address the more important issues concerning learning rather than extol or condemn a technique by alluding to many ancillary values or detriments that we feel might ensue from its application.

Figure 1 might be useful in illustrating this point. Fill in three or four of the most important values you think should be learned by students (academic, social, or both). For example, reading, writing, consideration for others, self-actualization—whatever *you* consider to be positive. Now list some things you consider to be negative (e.g., lying, stealing). It is obvious that many different techniques might be used to teach "negative" as well as "positive" values.

The purpose of this exercise is to indicate that effective methods, much like any human product (atomic energy, jet propulsion, governments), may be used either to the benefit or detriment of other human beings. Scientific techniques are characterized by definitions of behavior that can be observed (pinpointed) and then measured (recorded and counted). These techniques include the isolation of specific cause and effect relationships and thereby provide a scientific methodology for the evaluation of learning.

Nonobservable techniques are much more difficult to explain or measure, but they may be extremely important in teaching/learning situations where "scientific techniques" seem inadequate. It should be remembered that there is no absolute agreement concerning almost any aspect of education. It might be wise to develop a tolerance for ambiguity while deciding which particular instructional procedure is appropriate for each situation, student, time, or place.

What is effective teaching?—That which implements selected values.

STUDY GUIDE FOR CHAPTER 1

Questions:

1. What is suggested as an important variable in being an effective teacher?

*2. State the behavioral principle that we try to teach children and the "perversions" of the principle. If you disagree with this, state why.

*3. What does "discipline" involve?

4. State specifically to what discipline and motivation refer.

5. What is a general attribute?

6. Paraphrase the gist of the paragraph beginning, "When learning is defined. . . ." (see page 8).

7. How is self-control or self-discipline acquired?

*8. Why is discipline neither "strictness" or "permissiveness" but related to cause and effect?

*9. What is one of the most effective rewards a teacher can use?

*10. How is worry (depression) reinforced?

*Using the preceding questions indicated by an asterisk(*), transfer the concept dealt with in the question to specific content area classroom teaching situations—in chorus, band, orchestra, art, physical education, social studies, language arts, special education, arithmetic, English, history, algebra, geometry, science, modern languages, forensics, dramatics, football, track, chemistry, literature.

LEARNING ACTIVITY 1—
VALUES-TECHNIQUES DICHOTOMY

Behavior modification represents the use of a series of techniques that have been scientifically verified in an attempt to promote more effective learning for both social and academic subject matter (see Part II). A behavioral approach does not help the teacher decide why, what, and who is going to learn. But behavioral principles may be used to enhance learning of appropriate behavior after questions relating to values have been decided.

Study the Values-Techniques Dichotomy Chart shown here and fill in three or four of the most important values—academic, social, or both—you think should be instilled in the students you are going to teach. Do the same for values that you feel should not be taught to your students under any circumstances. In addition, your instructor may require that you write a short paragraph on how behavioral techniques could be used to teach both negative as well as positive values.

The purpose of this exercise is to demonstrate that behavioral techniques, much like any human product, may be used either to

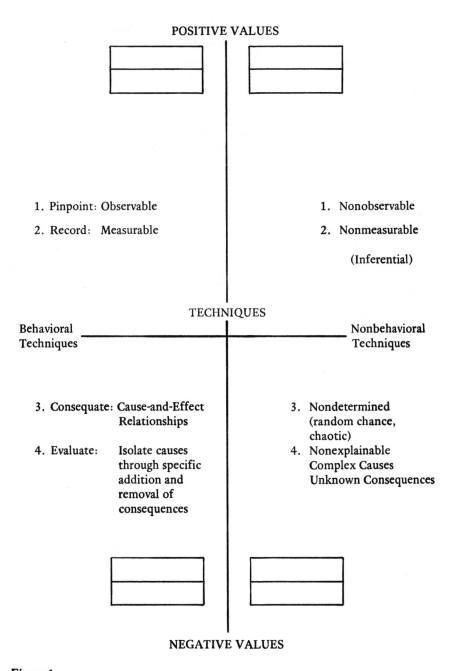

POSITIVE VALUES

1. Pinpoint: Observable

2. Record: Measurable

                       1. Nonobservable

                       2. Nonmeasurable

                          (Inferential)

TECHNIQUES

Behavioral   Nonbehavioral
Techniques   Techniques

3. Consequate: Cause-and-Effect
                  Relationships

4. Evaluate: Isolate causes
                through specific
                addition and
                removal of
                consequences

                       3. Nondetermined
                          (random chance,
                          chaotic)
                       4. Nonexplainable
                          Complex Causes
                          Unknown Consequences

NEGATIVE VALUES

Figure 1

the benefit or the detriment of other human beings. These techniques can be used to isolate specific cause-and-effect relationships by affecting the consequences of behavior and thereby providing a scientific methodology for the evaluation of learning.

LEARNING ACTIVITY 2–
VALUES-TECHNIQUES DIFFERENTIATION

Many values (implicit or explicit) are reinforced by teachers without a clear understanding of the difference(s) between values and techniques. The following list of values is derived from actual observations of classroom teachers. Any values may be reinforced using either approval or disapproval techniques.

1. In the blanks provided, fill in specific consequences (see example) including both approval and disapproval techniques (see pp. 181–211).
2. Circle all teacher values which you do not value (i.e., behavior inconsistent with your value system).
3. Go back and review your lists of consequences and change ten examples to consequences which you would not prefer to use (i.e., consequences inconsistent with your value system) that you have either observed or read about.

Teacher Values	*Example of Specific Consequences Following Behavior*	
1. Following classroom rules	A(pproval)	teacher's praise
	D(isapproval)	———
2. Working (staying on-task)	A	———
	D	———
3. Academic achievement (learning to read)	A	academic grades
	D	———
4. Working quietly	A	———
	D	———

5. Working well together (cooperation)   A ——————

                                          D ——————

6. Respect for teacher (not being sassy)   A ——————

                                          D ——————

7. Waiting quietly (patience)   A ——————

                                 D ——————

8. Doing extra work (industry)   A ——————

                                  D ——————

9. Effort   A ——————

             D ——————

10. Raising hand to get attention   A ——————

                                     D ——————

11. Completing assignments on time   A allowed to work
                                          on own project

                                       D ——————

12. Staying in seat while working   A ——————

                                     D ——————

13. Following directions   A ——————

                            D ——————

14. Walking inside building   A ——————

                               D ——————

15. Taking responsibility for own materials   A ——————

                                               D ——————

16. Liking school and school work   A ————————
    (positive attitude)
                                           D ————————

CHAPTER 2

Discipline
The Way to Learning

WHAT DO STUDENTS BRING?

At any time in the chronological development of a child, we are prone to look back into the child's history to explain his present behavior. Thus, we have a never-ending spiral that assesses blame backwards (behavioral antecedents). Colleges blame the public schools, public schools blame the home, and the parents blame each other or the child's progenitors *ad infinitum.* If we must stop somewhere, let us stop at birth, although some theoreticians would impute motives even before the child's first breath.

Let us consider three oversimplified, but rather characteristic, views of the child at birth: (1) the child is born good, (2) the child is born bad, and (3) the child is born neither good nor bad. If, as some believe, all children are born basically good, then the child's only impairment is the corruption of living. The teacher's goal would be not to corrupt his basic nature. This would not be difficult in a Utopian world. Perhaps it would not be difficult in the world in which we live, if all behavioral responses were predestined to be ideal. A problem arises, however, when "good" is specifically defined; each person's idea of the "good" does not always coincide with another's. A second problem arises for the teacher if the child has somehow been previously corrupted, for now the child evidences both "good" and "bad" behavior.

The second view proposes that children are born bad. In this case, the teacher's job would be to correct the basic "badness" so the child could be "good." Again we have a problem with definition of "bad," especially without reference to specific overt behaviors.

It is curious that many people who believe in this "badness" theory assume quite readily that children's good behavior is *not* learned, while insisting that all bad behavior (usually referring to moral transgressions) must be eliminated. Regardless, if the child has learned any "goodness" at all, he will still present a mixture of both "good" and "bad."

The third position postulates neither good natures nor bad and, therefore, assumes that all behavior is learned. The teacher's job in this situation simply would be to teach the child correct responses. Nevertheless, in all probability the child will have picked up some "bad" behaviors. Therefore the same situation will be evidenced as with the other two positions. The important question regarding the foregoing is: What should the teacher do? Regardless of philosophical orientation, should the teacher's responses to the student be any different? Indeed, *is it possible to start teaching at any other place than where the student is?* Suzy, Sam, and Fred all cry out in class— Suzy because her sweet nature has become corrupted, Sam because he was born bad, and Fred because he learned some wrong associations. Does it really matter what their personal history or the teacher's philosophy has been? The important question seems to be: What does the teacher do? Even if we could solve the philosophical problem or know the particular individual reinforcement history of the individual children, they are still crying.

All too often, we pretend that we have solved a problem because we can find some explanation for the behavior (e.g., high score on "problem child tests," family depravity, "bad seed," terrible first-grade teacher). Unfortunately, the children will continue to cry out in class until we do something to change their behavior. During the very first processes of interacting with the child, the teacher should be able to find out just *where the student in both socially and academically* and assess the extent of any specific problems. These first encounters with the student provide all that is needed to determine where the student is. The teacher then can begin to do something concerning the student's behavior. A long involved analysis of the child's "personality" is generally both unproductive and unnecessary.

What do students bring?—Does it really matter?

WHAT DO TEACHERS BRING?

Most individuals working in education seem convinced that the learning environment should be a relatively positive place where students learn "to be nice people and take joy from learning." In fact, many teachers, administrators, counselors, and others have been asked to respond to the question of whether or not they believe the classroom atmosphere should be predominantly positive (approving) or negative (disapproving). Responses overwhelmingly indicate that school personnel believe that teachers should be predominantly positive. Over 99 percent of respondents, more than 25,000, "strongly agree" or "agree" on questionnaires that teachers should have a positive classroom environment. Ninety-seven percent also agree that a strong indicator of a positive environment would be where more approving than disapproving comments and non-verbal behaviors are directed by the teacher toward student behavior. However, this human self-report data is in sharp contrast to results based on actual classroom observations.

Interaction patterns based on definitions of approval and disapproval between students and teachers observed by trained personnel show an entirely different distribution of results. Less than 10 percent of teachers (kindergarten through high school) actually dispensed more approval for appropriate than disapproval for inappropriate social behavior. This difference between verbally stated values and actual behavior seems even more disparate when it is realized that trained observers used the teachers' own definitions of appropriate and inappropriate student behaviors.

It is amazing that actual interaction patterns of teachers with students are so different from the intended outcomes. Results indicate clearly that there are definite differences between the verbal reports of values and actual in-class overt behaviors. Computations indicate that the approval ratio is less than 50 percent in 92 percent of the cases. It should be noted that many teachers are not as negative in dealing with academic behavior (34 percent do give more approval than disapproval to appropriate academic behavior). The computation for the approval ratio is based upon the amount of approval dispensed relative to all reinforcing behavior and does not depend upon the absolute frequency of reinforcing behavior. Thus the approval ratio is based upon the percentage of approval teachers give independent of the total frequency or amount of behavioral interaction. It has also been observed that, the higher the grade level, the more time the teacher spends questioning, stimulating, or explaining rather than reinforcing appropriate social behavior.

The extent to which successes or failures occur in pupils' learning can probably be attributed to the degree of success the teacher achieves in arranging the total school environment. It is also assumed that successes or failures concerning teacher effects should be demonstrated in observable classroom results. Therefore, precise methods could be assessed as to effectiveness and durability. Specific effects should be demonstrated concerning environmental change as well as documented procedures used in the interaction between those who learn and those who teach. A systematic analysis of some of the variables within the learning situation that could bring teacher experiences in line with their own values appears needed. The premise of these experiences is that through learning effective techniques teachers will be better at their jobs—better able to insure academic and social improvement and better able to prevent potential problems that might interfere with learning.

What do teachers bring?—It really does matter.

WHO HAS THE RESPONSIBILITY?

Teacher X has a problem child. In almost every situation when he should be acting one way, he is acting another. His behavior gets constantly worse in the classroom until the teacher can take it no longer. The teacher passes the point of feeling frustrated and, if honest, may even admit dislike toward this source of constant irritation. The teacher decides to find out just what the student's problem is. The student is sent to the school counselor; and, after an extensive battery of tests, social reports, and time-consuming investigation, the teacher gets an answer: "Johnny is a problem child." On every one of the "problem child tests" (personality scales), he scored extremely high. Not only did all the tests indicate that he was indeed a problem child (exhibited deviant associations), but the report concerning his home life was even worse. Teacher X cannot help feeling pity when learning of his terrible home situation and begins to wonder how he survived as well as he did. Teacher X discusses his home situation with a close colleague, and both of them marvel anew how bad life for some children can actually be. Johnny continues to be a problem child, but now his teachers *"know why"* (high test scores—bad home). He may not even finish school; he will probably grow, continually harassing society, and end up in other more stigmatized institutions. "How tragic, but what can a teacher do with a home situation like that?" Obviously nothing—the end?

Johnny is a complex organism. Among his many attributes is an ability for exceptional discrimination. All of his empirical senses provide a basis for remarkable differentiation. At an early age (approximately six months) he could even discriminate among people. He learned what to touch, what not to touch; he learned a complex language system; he learned auditory and visual discriminations; he learned to yell at playtime and *not* to sit quietly during individual study periods. He even learned to "put on" a teacher when he could get away with it.

Of course Johnny is a "problem child." This is precisely why he was sent to the counselor. And how unfortunate that there are many "diagnosticians" whose major purpose is merely to confirm the prognosis of the teacher—if their terminology can be understood. Johnny will continue to be a problem child until someone teaches him different responses. He has learned a repertoire of responses to deal with his world—the more antisocial his home environment, the more deviant his responses.

The truly pathetic situation is that no one will teach Johnny and change his behavior. The only place in which there is some hope for Johnny is the school. Yet many teachers quickly abdicate responsibility once his history is known. *Johnny can discriminate.* He can be taught new responses to deal with the other world outside the home. He can learn to read, write, spell; he can learn new rules of social interaction and thereby break the cycle of his past. If cooperation with the home is not possible, he can even learn these responses *in spite of a bad home.*

It is not easy to deal with the Johnnies. They take time, energy, and a disciplined teacher. All the Johnnies do not change for the better or even survive; yet for these children, *the school is their only hope.*

Who has the responsibility of discipline?—The teacher.

WHY DON'T THEY LEARN?

Many questions have been raised in relation to why Johnny does not learn. Too often criticism comes from proponents of these questions who do not support their queries with long-term constructive encouragement or positive alternatives. Instead, scathing indictments are directed toward those very teachers who spend a great deal more time worrying about why Johnny does not learn than do most of their critics. In every aspect of learning, continued educational research is needed to ascertain and remediate learning difficulties. Yet at present, the teacher must strive to do the best job possible.

Education is stressed in many ways in our culture. Quite naturally we often assume that everyone wants to learn. We even assume that they want to learn what we want them to learn. Some children do not want to learn. Others do not want to learn what we think they should learn. The reaction of the teacher should not be amazed bewilderment (the teacher's reinforcement history includes values established through 16 years of learning) but a basic question: *Why should they want to learn?* Children must be taught to be motivated, curious, or interested, that is, to establish their own goals. Some children are just too comfortable to learn. Why should one learn to speak, let alone properly, if all desires are met without this particular mode of verbal symbolization? Why should one learn a difficult mathematics system if gazing out the window passes the time better? Why should one practice spelling if one finds that more attention is received when one wanders around the room or writes a "special note" or plays at the pencil sharpener or does any number of things more fun than spelling?

The desire to learn must be taught. Appropriate learning behaviors, such as good study habits, paying attention, or working for long periods, must be established that provide some reward for the child. No thinking adult wastes time in idle pursuits that are difficult and meaningless. How can the teacher expect everyone automatically to want to learn, especially when it may represent work?

Why don't they learn?—Because the rewards of learning have not been established.

WHAT IF IT'S WORK?

Most people assume the responsibility of work. We speak often about work: working on a project, going to work, getting work, finishing our work, yet we have a burgeoning conspiracy to turn work into play. Most teachers realize the importance of making work as palatable as possible. If students get excited about work they consider it play, and everyone is much happier. The ingenious teacher has striven for years to turn work tasks into play. The great teachers are those who are able to elicit a pleasurable response toward the most rigorous pursuits and make the most difficult task pleasant.

Unfortunately, our highly technological society has turned many work tasks into play without a corresponding discipline toward those tasks that entail "work-work" as opposed to "play-work." The young boy's delight in finally building his very own plane wanes appreciably when he is confronted with a common battery-propelled toy that flies instantly and can be purchased for a fraction of his allowance. Most adults will testify with pride to those endeavors that represented, for them, hard work and true discipline. Patience, repetition, and arduous industry are still required for long-term achievement and happiness in almost every activity of life. Yet we have more and more "instant avenues to success." The problem for today's teacher is not only in structuring "play-work" (technology is providing wonderful aids in this regard), but also in teaching the necessary discipline for *long-term* rewards as well (i.e., establishing maturity). If behaviors conducive to long-term goals are not acquired early, it is much less likely that they will be acquired at all. If a child does not learn early in life to work hard and long for specific goals, then he is not likely to change as he grows older.

Today's schools provide many extracurricular activities with almost as much turnover as there are activities. The possibilities for diverse activities become greater and greater for the growing child. Almost all his time can be spent changing from one activity to another. Consider specialized fields such as music, art, and creative writing. How many times have we said as adults, "I'd give anything to play like that, or to paint like that, or to write like that?" Of course, we would not. We know what it would take in time and effort. The irony is not that we do not often have such skills; it is that we do not have enough understanding concerning the importance of long-term skill acquisition to appreciate the skill evidenced in others and to insure that our students stay with an activity or task long enough to master it.

This should not indicate that the teacher ought to take pride in being a punishing taskmaster. It is extremely unlikely that students will want to continue learning, past formal experiences, if their true "reward" for learning (working) has been merely to have the gruesome experience stop. The secret for developing the capacity for work is to stretch the length of time between *rewards* so that the student will strive through some misery to seek long-term goals, for example, a college degree, writing skills, continued reading of great literature, ongoing enjoyment in listening to music materpieces, or an insatiable desire for scientific precision.

Thus, the problem for the teacher is not only to make work tasks pleasurable but also to develop the capacity for work. *This constitutes a process of teaching for delayed rewards over an ever-increasing temporal span.*

What if it's work?—Then work it must be and the capacity for work must be developed.

WHO DECIDES WHO DECIDES?

Power, by whatever name, is one of the most contingent of all behavioral interactions. When referring to physical objects in motion such as a moving automobile, few people question the power of the car to damage a person's body; only the intent, skill, or responsibility of the driver. Some people seem to assume power over other people; others manifest power that is thought to be given to them, such as the power of elected officials to enforce laws. Literary sources often portray individuals seeking power—others avoiding it. Most of us, however, choose either to relabel power (especially in this age of the euphemism) or to pretend that power actually does not exist. We prefer, instead, to talk about responsibility, duty, or rights, as in the discussion in this chapter. Perhaps most of us would like to believe that no one has power over us and that anything we might say or do would be only by choice. Often it frightens us to realize the power that does exist—especially the power we, as teachers, have over our students. Not only are teachers often bigger, at least for a little while, but most of us also think faster than youngsters and, therefore, are able to "snow" them. We work through a problem quickly, we know many important facts, we answer a difficult question—*the awe and respect of students is very reinforcing.*

Often we use our sophistication to manipulate students into doing something that they do not think about: "Would you like to put your materials away before lunch?" We do not ask them, "Do you choose to be messy?" It seems that most often we do about "everything in our power" in order to impose our value systems on them: "Choose any story your wish . . . then we will take a vote on it . . . you must take turns . . . now we do want our room to be clean don't we . . . of course you don't take money from another student without asking . . . etc." It would appear that most of what we just assume to be the correct thing to do represents the imposition of our value system on the student. Probably almost all of our "acculturating process" actually represents the imposition of values, whether these values come from home, school, community, church, or elsewhere. Who decides a child should read, write, spell, not steal, or finish school? Teachers who have not thought about these activities as an "imposition of their values" sometimes become extremely upset and state, "Well, how do you expect the child to live a happy life or get a decent job or anything else!" "I can't sit by and watch that child hurt himself." Do you expect me to be silent when I know she's ruining her life by quitting school now?" At the same time, teachers may say, "I do want my students to think for themselves and I want them to establish their own values. . . ."

Teachers who do not make clear differentiations in their own thinking about who decides who decides, probably will have many problems. Teachers are charged legally with the imposition of certain values concerning students' behavior; many would say that ethically teachers ought to be responsible for much of the student's behavior, and some would say, that is precisely what being a teacher is all about; to instill within each child the selected best from the cultural heritage in order that, following school, the young adult will function productively. Regardless, *who decides* is not nearly as difficult a question as *who decides who decides,* for most teachers truly want their students to be able to make decisions for themselves. Teachers therefore decide to allow their students to decide certain innocuous things; *When* do you choose to clean up your materials? *Where* can you be reached in case we need you? *Which* assignment do you choose to do? *Who* is it you will be leaving with? *Where* do you want to do your work?

Teachers who start early to teach students precise definitions and specific allocations of power will be better able to deal with apparent inequities as situations arise. Some teachers refer to this structuring as "defining limits" or specifying acceptable behavior regarding such aspects as social relationships, propriety, honesty, and so on. If a person is taught early that a teacher is not always right or an all-knowing genious; that teachers do not always evidence perfect taste, heal all wounds, or even "understand" some of the latter ones, then the child might not have to be so disenchanted when he discovers our feet of clay. If a teacher states precisely what power resides with the teacher and what decisions rest with the student, perhaps the student will continuously strive to earn more privileges rather than feel sorry for himself because he is not permitted to do something. Issues regarding power are not easy to think through nor are their behavioral contingencies easy to establish. Much like issues concerning "fairness," problems relating to power rest on the values of all individuals concerned. Even some adults have not established who decides who decides in regard to major issues concerning themselves and their employees or even spouses. Also, in the upper grades teachers and students must often decide to *agree to disagree* if harmony is to prevail. Anger is not reinforced in relation to those decisions that we definitely believe are not ours, only with those decisions that we believe ought to be within our own and not someone else's control.

Who decides who decides?—As far as the student is concerned, the teacher.

STUDY GUIDE FOR CHAPTER 2

Questions:

*1. List the three states in which children are considered to be born. Explain the teacher's role in each. What is your position?

2. Why is a traditional analysis of a child's problem behavior often unproductive?

*3. Why do you think there is such a disparity in what teachers' desire to do and what they actually do in classroom settings?

*4. What does it mean to "arrange the total school environment?"

*5. Why do teachers give more approval to academic behavior than they do to social behavior?

6. Describe why some children may not *want* to learn. Explain why they are not just "born that way." Provide an explanation of what can be done.

7. Where does this analysis put the notion of motivation? Since motivation is typically referred to as an "inner" state, explain why unmotivated behavior is not explained this way.

8. Why is the capacity for work necessary?

9. How is the capacity for work developed? Some people are industrious and some are lazy; how is this difference analyzed?

*10. What is meant by "who decides who decides?"

*Answer these questions within your subject matter area (e.g., Language Arts, Social Studies, Physical Education).

LEARNING ACTIVITY 3–HUMAN ECOLOGY AND REINFORCEMENT: POTENTIAL SPHERES OF BEHAVIORAL INFLUENCE

1. Write or discuss what the teacher can realistically expect to accomplish based upon the following diagram. Keep in mind the question "Who has the responsibility?" for specific behaviors, and that the student is subject to many potentially contradictory sources of reinforcement, but also the student possesses abilities to learn discrimination and therefore behave differently under different conditions. Discuss your ideas with other participants.

2. List different behaviors that adults exhibit under the following conditions: (a) sports events, (b) in church, (c) eating in a restaurant, (d) watching TV and, (e) playing tennis.

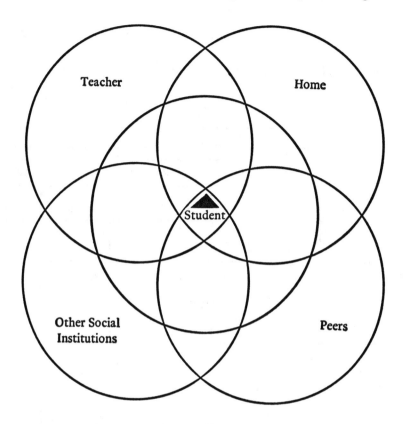

LEARNING ACTIVITY 4—HOW POSITIVE AM I: INTERACTION ANALYSIS FOR GROUPS

Participants should be separated into small groups of approximately four to six and will discuss human relations problems while keeping records of group interactions.* Prior to discussion, the group should determine the period of time that each record keeper will maintain the record, list each participant's name on the form, decide upon topics to discuss, set the timer, and begin discussions. Following each discussion period, the record keeper should tally the number of positive and negative comments and approving and disapproving bodily expressions and report totals for all group members prior to beginning the next discussion session. The same procedure should

*Rotate record keeper approximately every five minutes. A kitchen timer with a bell is most effective as it reminds the group to stay on-task as well as indicates the time to change record keepers.

INTERACTION ANALYSIS FOR GROUP DISCUSSIONS

Date _____

General Topic _____ (Time: Start _____ End _____

Number in Group_____ Observation Interval _____

Names of Participants	APPROVAL		DISAPPROVAL	
	Words*	Expressions**	Words†	Expressions††
Bob Complainer			ᵗᴴᴸ ᵗᴴᵗ /	ᵗᴴᴸ ///
Jane Ambivalent	ᵗᴴᴸ /	///	ᵗᴴᴸ /	///
Sam Kindly	ᵗᴴᴸ ᵗᴴᴸ ᵗᴴᴸ ᵗᴴᴸ	ᵗᴴᴸ ᵗᴴᴸ ////		
Suzy Average	////	/	ᵗᴴᴸ /	//

*Words-Approval are positive comments, defined as specified solutions to specific problems

**Expressions-Approval are bodily or facial expressions of an approving nature

†Words-Disapproval are negative comments, defined as the statement of problems with no specified solutions

††Expressions-Disapproval are bodily or facial expressions of a disapproving nature

be repeated either until the time is used or until all members of the group have had the opportunity to be recorders.

The previous form is an indication of how the record will look after each recording session.

Note: An extension of this activity has proved to be very effective in reducing negative comments in teachers' lounges, principals' offices, homes, and work areas. Construct a large chart with the name of each person written down the side of the chart and whenever any other person in the vicinity hears either a positive or negative word or comment from any other member of the group that person goes to the chart and puts a mark under either the positive or negative half of the sheet. This procedure has increased approving statements and decreased disapproving statements.

CHAPTER 3

Learning
The Modification of Behavior

WHAT IS BEHAVIOR MODIFICATION?

Behavior is a common word that is used casually in referring to many things. The term *behavior,* as used in this book, refers to *anything* a person does, says, or thinks that can be observed directly and/or indirectly. Besides referring to specific cause-and-effect relationships, behavior modification includes techniques for changing behavior. A well-behaved student is one who behaves in ways that the teacher and/or student thinks are appropriate to the situation.

Principles for teaching (shaping appropriate behaviors) should not be confused with other issues. It is important that techniques of behavior modification not be confused with the use of these same techniques to implement specific values. Many teachers regard the questions concerning *why, what,* and *for whom* as certainly more important than *how.* Therefore, after teachers have decided what is to be learned and why it is to be learned (i.e., chosen their values), a behavioral approach will help them go about teaching it. Also, we encourage teachers to involve their students in these decisions whenever possible. There is a simple rationale to explain the efficacy of behavioral approaches. Simply stated, *behavioral change must be based on a reason:* people work for things that bring pleasure, people work for approval of loved ones, people change behaviors to satisfy desires they have been taught, people avoid behaviors they associate with unpleasantness, and people act in similar ways to behaviors they have often repeated. The behavior modification approach actually comes from science and represents nothing more than simple cause-and-effect relationships.

The scientific study of human behavior, or the study of cause-and-effect relationships, should not be confused with other value choices.

As was stated in Chapter 1, it is generally useful to distinguish between values and techniques. For example, a positive value that many teachers hold is to teach youngsters to read (even if the desire to read is *not* present in the child). Once this value, and perhaps its imposition, has been determined, then the teacher may choose various techniques to effect the desired reading behavior. Application of a behavioral technique to establish this value would be concerned with the effects of academic feedback and/or other reinforcements to the youngster concerning shaping desired responses in relationship to the target goal (reading). It is important to realize that many values other than reading might be decided on by the teacher as well as other techniques to effect whatever values the teacher may choose to teach. Some teachers choose to have students raise hands for teacher attention, some do not. Some teachers specify "quiet time," others prefer the "hum of industry." Some teachers choose "communication" as a value and spend a great deal of time in verbal interaction, others spend more time helping students interact with subject matter. Behavioral techniques can be used to implement any or all of these values. Students may be taught (reinforced) to raise hands, not to raise hands, or any combination depending upon the situation. The "hum of industry" can be implemented as can "quiet time" or any combination thereof depending on the circumstances and activity of the teacher. Students can be taught to communicate or to remain silent or to alternate during various time periods.

Techniques also can be used to implement what many teachers consider extremely negative values. Children can be effectively taught to cheat, lie, hit, steal, and even to "hate school." Of course, the selection of any techniques represents a certain value choice; also, if one chooses a behavioral technique, then the determination of appropriate "reinforcers" represents an important value choice. However, basic social and academic values to be taught to students should not be confused with issues concerning techniques for implementation. It is assumed that Jesus, Socrates, and Moses were effective behaviorists. So was Hitler.

Some teachers might say, "Yes, but isn't that a cold approach?" Certainly not. Even though behavior modification is based on scientific principles verified in the laboratory, it is largely the nature of material to be learned that represents important value choices. Actually, because of its consistency and simplicity, behavior modification effected and applied by means of contingent reinforcement (approval-disapproval) represents a very kind and understandable system to students of all ages. The behavioral scientist who observes a classroom activity can behaviorally classify almost everything that goes on, regardless of how well the teacher may understand principles of reinforcement.

Cause-and-effect behaviors are always present. For example, some teachers do not realize the effects of their own behavior on their students. Some do not understand the effects of their own approval or disapproval and do not realize when they are being sarcastic: "Why don't you just stand up and tell the *whole class,* Jimmy?" Whereupon Jimmy does. In such a situation teachers may unwittingly reinforce a wrong behavior, and problems are created because the student is not really sure of the teacher's meaning. Being taken literally is the price one pays for using sarcasm. The applied behavior analyst could demonstrate how teachers might be more effective in the application of the teacher's own values through the judicious use of behavioral principles. Many teachers are actually surprised to learn how closely they approximate a fairly comprehensive behavioral approach. After being apprised of behavioral principles, many teachers exclaim, "Why, that's what I've been doing all the time!"

What is behavior modification?—Techniques for implementing values.

IS BEHAVIOR BEING MODIFIED?

A high school teacher stops by a student working on math and checks correct/incorrect responses. This teacher has observed that most students learn more efficiently when they are given prompt *academic feedback.* He is using a principle of behavior modification to improve academic performance.

He goes back to his desk to correct assignments. It is important to him that he finish by the end of the day. He has discovered that, by randomly picking out a different day of the week for students to receive corrected papers, he can dramatically increase their academic performance. Again, behavior modification.

The same teacher seeks another student engrossed in his work assignment. He moves quickly to this student's seat, smiles and whispers in his ear, "It's good to see you working on your assignment." He has noticed that if he can praise him while he does his work *without the other students noticing* the student works much more. When the teacher recognized him while he was not working this student used to be the "class clown." Both situations represent behavior modification.

An elementary school teacher goes to her desk to correct assignments. A little boy comes quickly to her desk and asks a question. She ignores him completely and calmly goes about correcting her papers. He stays about 15 seconds and then goes back to his work. The teacher smiles to herself as she checks a chart designed for this particular boy. She has almost extinguished his habit of running to her desk (only once this week; initially he did it 28 times a day and that was *after* she started recording it). The teacher sets her handkerchief on her desk as a reminder to go to this child after he has been in his seat for a few minutes. She hopes that his question was not a really important one, that it can wait two or three minutes.

She waits for a few minutes and then takes the time to check on the child who came to her desk—he wanted to know if he could get a book from the library—she returns to her seat. She hears Suzy starting to talk to her neighbor. The teacher immediately gets up, goes to Suzy, and firmly tells her that she should stop visiting until her work is done. The teacher notices that Suzy appears a little sad. She is a sensitive child, and the teacher has long since discovered that a bit of teacher disapproval will halt her inappropriate behavior. Behavior modification.

As two students fight instead of quietly visiting, the middle school teacher thinks about the token system the school counselor is trying to establish in some of the rooms. She has read many reports about "token economy" systems and understands that they represent an effective application of behavioral principles, but she does not choose the technique for her class. She has never liked material rewards for learning (except for herself) and prefers to use other things instead. Besides, she cannot imagine how her class could be much worse than it is. She really is discouraged. She knows also that the counselor sometimes uses very strong disapproval as well as a special "time-out room" for some students. The effects of his procedures are well documented and consistent with behavioral approaches, but she prefers not to use them. She tries to reason with her students but actually ends up yelling nearly all day long. She uses disapproval (almost 80 percent of the time) in efforts to modify social behavior, but generally with little effect. Although she knows that this interaction is about the same for most teachers, she sincerely wants to be more positive. Principles of behavior modification are indeed operating within this classroom but the teacher's behavior, regardless of her intent, is not producing the desired effect.

Across the hall, another teacher interacts quietly with her students. She also does not like the counselor's particular token system. She has decided to become more contingent with her verbal behavior alone. At first it was difficult, not "natural." She had to learn to use effectively techniques of behavior modification in order to reinforce certain academic and social behaviors. Now, when she hears the loud adult voice in the adjoining classroom, she thinks about the discussion of honesty she had with a colleague. Should a teacher be honestly disapproving most of the time because it is a "natural" response? She had decided no.

She stands in front of her class. "Students, I would like your attention. Suzy's looking at me. Good Sam. Now David's looking at me. Now I have everyone's attention. Thank you." (Again, behavior modification.) "You may all stop your individual work and visit now until it's time for music. . . ." (When the students helped make class rules earlier in the year, they expressed a desire for individual talk time. Establishing rules with student help has *nothing* to do with behavior modification.)

The above paragraphs describe procedures whose efficacy or non-efficacy has been documented in behavioral research. In essence, this research shows that behavior is maintained and shaped by its consequences. (Strange, isn't it, that so obvious a truth should be so badly used in practice?) It should be apparent from the above that behavior modification represents the use of a series of scientifically verified techniques that may be used to promote more effective learning of both social and academic subject matter. A behavioral approach does not help the teacher decide why, what, and who is going to learn. These issues represent important value choices. However, after questions relating to these values have been answered, behavioral principles may be used to enhance learning of appropriate behavior.

Is behavior being modified?–Always, but not necessarily in the direction we choose.

ARE VALUES IMPORTANT?

Techniques of reinforcement can be so effective that every teacher ought to choose the important values (ideas) to be implemented within the classroom. Yet even though many teachers believe in positive ideas, it becomes more difficult to specify the observable behaviors that students engage in when being in harmony with an ideal. It is therefore useful for teachers to structure commonly used words that represent "ideas" or abstractions into specific, overt, demonstrable behaviors. (It should be noted that even though all "words" may merely be symbolic representations, some words seem specific in their elicitations and, therefore, are preferred in describing empirical relationships. Thus, "verbalizes facts" appears more quantifiable than does "honest.") For example, most teachers believe students ought to be kind, communicative, cooperative, and sensitive. Yet for these ideas to be effectively taught, they must be described in greater specificity such that they can be counted, that is, follows rules, helps others, talks with others, looks into eyes, shares materials, asks for help, and so on. Thus, we must define our values (ideas) so that the way a student acts provides some overt evidence as to whether the student is developing the particular patterns of responses that we desire. Every teacher usually demands this type of behavior in reference to academic responses (assessments, questioning, tests, etc.) yet does not specify as accurately concerning social behavior.

A specific behavior is anything a person does that can be observed and measured. Ideas are generally made more and more behavioral as behaviors are specified in observable and measurable terms. This is obviously the first step in structuring any learning sequence: to define values so that the behavior of the student provides some indication that learning is taking place.

Specificity is the key to behavioral analysis; the teacher must deal with each specific situation in order to teach proper associations. Differentiating in terms of one specific behavior that occurs in a particular situation is the key to effective teaching. In academic work, most teachers would not begin to classify children into all-inclusive categories. Because May is excellent in spelling does not mean that she is exceptional in geography. Similarly, because she does not constantly disrupt the class does not necessarily indicate that she is "well-behaved." Is it not curious then that when referring to the many social skills necessary for any student we tend toward greater classification with much less justification considering the magnitude of individual responses to social stimuli? These classifications are even more undesirable if we consider that in our complex communication, we have developed a certain "shorthand" for descriptive purposes. Words such as "love," "motivation," and "discipline" are used as though these words had meaning apart from specific situations. Of course, it would be extremely difficult "to communicate" without using such a "short-word system." We should remember, however, that each situation is different. Every particular word refers to many different behaviors, and each association merits specific consideration. We must remember to deal individually with each behavior. When speaking of the "value of discipline," we should specify both the nature of each situation and the response. We must specify exactly *what* happens as well as *when* it happens. We must specify the nature of the situation (antecedent), the response, and the consequences that follow. When we use the word "discipline" as an abstraction referring to many separate behaviors, we must realize that definitions of discipline must be specific to certain behaviors if the teaching of proper associations is to take place. Disciplining a student, therefore, means something different in each situation if procedures are to be effective.

Are values important? —Important enough to be specified.

IS SUBJECT MATTER DISCIPLINE?

The recent impetus for behavioral theory, or reinforcement theory, or whatever one chooses to call behavioral principles, substantially grew from the works of B. F. Skinner. Programmed instruction is the best-known result of this initial work, as are many other "systems" relating to teaching, treating mental illness, behavioral research, and clinical psychology. Indeed, the entire rationale concerning behavior modification is that behavior is *learned.* What behavior? *All behavior, including knowledge of subject matter.* Behavior thusly defined includes emotional responses, attitudes, reading, listening, talking, looking into the mirror, liking a person, wanting to talk out a problem, hitting, being frustrated, staying "on-task," getting "off-task," responding appropriately to the desires of a teacher, not responding to the desires of a teacher, all "good" behavior, all "bad" behavior, disturbing the class, being well behaved, being excited about learning, hating to learn, and so on—and so on—and so on.

The most basic reductions of reinforcement theory as an explanation to assess a person's responses at any given time are: (1) a person has *not learned,* (2) he has learned correct associations, or (3) he has learned *incorrect associations.* Exactly the same principles are used to teach subject matter as are used to teach appropriate social skills. If the teacher wishes that children have a real desire to learn a particular subject matter, then the teacher must structure the external environment so that children will seek the structured contingent rewards for their academic work tasks. After initial manipulation, the rewards for learning will often come from the reinforcement of the learning material itself. Incidentally, this is precisely what most teachers do when they initially make a "game out of learning." The children become enthused concerning the game *per se,* not realizing that it is a subtle hoax to stimulate effective learning. Curiously, some teachers who try desperately to make learning "fun" also say they reject any "manipulation techniques." The teacher's job is to structure learning experiences. This structuring process involves manipulating the environment conducive to effective learning, whether the goal be simple word associations, complex problem solving, or concept formation. It would seem that the teacher should structure as widely as possible. One should know the subparts necessary to any complex academic task (e.g., English, reading, algebra, history) and structure the situation in order that each child have a "rewarding learning experience." It can be seen that even in reference to our most cherished clichés, we allude to behavioral manipulation. It appears paradoxical for the teacher to reject manipulation when this is indeed the essence of the teacher's work.

Behavioral research demonstrates that if subject matter can be: (1) geared to the student at his own level, (2) presented in logical sequences, with (3) appropriate feedback concerning correct/incorrect responses, and (4) contingent rewards given for successive approximations toward defined goals, then *learning will certainly take place.* Exactly the same principles apply to teaching subject matter as apply to teaching social skills.

Is subject matter discipline?—Yes.

ARE GOALS NECESSARY?

Traditionally, teachers have been instructed to prepare goals for the classroom. This usually represents at best a vague effort, often after the fact, to state formally what the learning experiences are aimed toward, that is, what should be the learning outcome. The major problem regarding goals is that they are usually stated in euphonious clichés: "preparation for life in a democracy," "to develop language skills," "to understand the different cultures of the world," "to develop an appreciation for music." What do such statements tell us? How will we know if we have achieved our "goals"? Some educators try to solve the problem by proposing even greater hierarchies, including ideals, objectives, attitudes, and so on. The problem is easily solved, however, if the teacher states goals that represent overt behavioral changes. How else, incidentally, will we know that a student "understands" or has "learned"? The teacher must also decide whose goals are to be effected in the classroom: students', parents', administrators', and/or what combination.

Goals stated in behavioral terms are not only manageable, they are also clear in defining the behaviors to be learned: "to be able to verbalize the Constitution, giving dictionary definitions to all words found therein," "to recognize on a map the separate nations of the world," "to differentiate between ten musical compositions," "to have a reading, writing, and spelling vocabulary of three hundred selected words." If concepts such as appreciation, understanding, or attitudes are to have meaning, these meanings should be defined in ways conducive to assessment. It is very easy to hide behind such generalities. *If children are to learn, then we must know precisely what it is they are to learn, how to teach it to them, and also how to determine if they have learned it.*

Are goals necessary? —Certainly

CAN BEHAVIOR BE MEASURED?

The most critical difference between a behavioral approach that pinpoints specific observable and measurable behaviors and other approaches to teaching is the keeping of behavioral records. Evaluation of any procedure instituted to induce learning (behavioral change) is virtually impossible without records. Formal and informal tests have always provided indications of academic behavioral change. Other indices of measurement, especially relating to social skills, have previously seemed to defy classification. It is possible, however, for the teacher to learn to assess social behaviors. Most individuals are not content to rely on a "feeling" concerning their bank balance, and the bank is even less likely to honor an overdrawn check because the depositor "feels" his balance is sufficient. Is it not then curious that when we deal with the social behavior of human beings (who are more important than bank balances) that we change rules, reinterpret contingencies, and fail to follow through because we "feel the behavior is really not that bad" or "feel" that the student *really* understands the regulations or perhaps "feel" that we may lose the student's respect? Measurement and specific records are crucial for accurate evaluation. The only difficulty regarding these classification procedures is that they take a little extra effort. Behavior *always* occurs in time intervals. If teachers are to know whether a particular social behavior is getting worse, better, or staying the same, the frequency of behavioral occurrences must be recorded *across time within specific time intervals.* Recording procedures are not difficult; one needs only paper, pencil, and some measure of time (clock).

For example, what if undesirable behavior in a particular classroom is defined as standing up? Instead of doing work at their desks, many students walk around the room. The first procedure would be to know precisely how much standing up is taking place (baseline). If this recording does not take place and the teacher first takes remedial steps, then it will not be known if the undesired behavior is getting better, worse, or staying the same. It may seem that this procedure is not necessary. "Why not just tell them to sit down and see what happens?" The problem, however, arises *in time;* that is, some children will sit down immediately, but in the *long run* more children may stand. Even if the standing students do sit immediately, the problem is not solved; it continues with the other students across time. To conduct this type of recording, the teacher might assign a work task and then sit so as to see every student and count the number of children standing in a number of time intervals. After a few days of recording the number of such behavioral occurrences on one individual or on many, the teacher has some idea of the *frequency of the behavior.* A checklist at the students' desks also can be very effective.

The same basic procedure may be used for speaking out, talking, playing at desk, looking out the window, cheating, hitting, sharpening pencils, disturbing others, crying, or any other conceivable behavior (adaptive or deviant). It is important for the teacher to have a record for *social behaviors* as well as for academic behaviors. A general "all right" or "satisfactory" will not accurately assess a student's academic progress over a period of time; neither will it accurately assess his social behavior. The time these behaviors take to record does not compare to the time a teacher spends repeating instructions (nagging). It is interesting that one of the author's experimental teachers who absolutely refused to "waste my time with all that book work" was recorded by experimental observers saying, "Now stop that talking," 143 times in one morning session. Checklists for assignments of any kind can be developed by the teacher with a minimum of effort. This process represents nothing more than extending principles of record keeping across time within a specific time interval (for example, twenty minutes, A.M., P.M. during rest time, one day, one week, playtime, lunchtime, ten seconds, ninety seconds, or any other time period).

Can behavior be measured?—Easily.

STUDY GUIDE FOR CHAPTER 3

Questions

*1. What does the behavioral approach represent?

2. Why is it possible to teach different values using identical techniques?

*3. What types of behaviors are learned? Are any of these types amenable to change through behavior modification?

*4. At any given time, a person's responses may be thought of as coming from one of three explanations. List these three explanations.

*5 Why is it that some teachers do not realize that they are using principles of behavior modification?

*6. What is specificity?

7. How is it possible to specify values?

*8. Be able to present the argument for specifying in detail the goals of education. Be able to analyze one of the generalities listed.

9. Why is it necessary to record behavior?

10. How might you record talking out, looking out the window, or a similar activity? (Remember, the first step is to define the behavior specifically, then to count it in some time interval such as the number of occurrences per 45 minutes, class period, hour, day.)

*Transfer the above questions to your subject area (e.g., Algebra, Art, Home economics).

LEARNING ACTIVITY 5–TRANSLATING IDEAS (VALUES) INTO BEHAVIORS

The objective of Learning Activity 5 is to structure commonly used words that represent ideas (values) concerning social behavior into specific overt demonstrable behaviors. As has been previously stated while all words may merely be symbolic representations, some words seem specific in their elicitations and, therefore, are preferred in describing empirical relationships. Thus "looks into eyes" appears much more quantifiable than "communicative."

Read the two examples under each idea and note How Observed and Counted Across. Next add two additional behaviors. Then fill in how they would be observed and the observational time intervals. Remember that the period of time a behavior might be measured across depends upon the urgency of dealing with the behavior, and the logical amount of time needed to determine whether or not the behavior is stable or infrequent (marriages are measured in years while eye contact would be recorded across seconds).

You may prefer to actual behaviors that have been demonstrated in classrooms or to behaviors you may wish students, or even yourself, to acquire.

Idea: Honesty

Behaviors	How Observed	Counted Across
1. Returns materials	visually	A.M./P.M.
2. Verbalizes facts	visually/ aurally	days
3.		
4.		
5.		
6.		

Idea: Dishonesty

Behaviors	How Observed	Counted Across
1. Steals others' materials	visually	days, weeks
2. Fabricates experiences	aurally	days
3.		
4.		
5.		
6.		

Idea: Appreciation

Behaviors	How Observed	Counted Across
1. Says thank you	aurally	A.M./P.M.
2. Expresses positive words	aurally	hours
3.		
4.		
5.		
6.		

Idea: Democratic

Behaviors	How Observed	Counted Across
1. Votes	visually	months
2. Follows rules	visually	minutes, A.M./P.M.
3.		
4.		
5.		
6.		

Idea: Kind

Behaviors	How Observed	Counted Across
1. Helps others	visually	A.M./P.M., days
2. Interacts with others	visually	days, weeks
3.		
4.		
5.		
6.		

Idea: Communication

Behaviors	How Observed	Counted Across
1. Talks with others	visually	minutes
2. Looks into eyes	visually	seconds
3.		
4.		
5.		
6.		

Idea: Good Human Relations

Behaviors	How Observed	Counted Across
1. Touching	visually	seconds
2. Talking with others	visually/ aurally	minutes, seconds
3.		
4.		
5.		
6.		

Idea: Cooperation

Behaviors	How Observed	Counted Across
1. Shares materials	visually	A.M./P.M., days
2. Asks for help	visually/ aurally	A.M./P.M.
3.		
4.		
5.		
6.		

Idea: Sensitivity

Behaviors	How Observed	Counted Across
1. Appropriate talking	aurally	seconds, minutes
2. Not talking	visually	seconds, minutes
3. Picks up nonverbal motor cues	tactually	seconds
4.		
5.		
6.		

Idea: Creativity

Behaviors	How Observed	Counted Across
1. Writes using new word organization	visually	weeks, school term
2. Nonverbal expression in new media	visually	weeks
3. Divergent solutions to school, social, or building problems	aurally, visually	weeks
4.		
5.		
6.		

LEARNING ACTIVITY 6—YOUR BEHAVIOR CAN BE MEASURED

As stated previously the most critical difference between a behavioral approach that pinpoints specific observable behaviors and less systematic approaches to human interactions is the keeping of behavioral records. Evaluation of any procedure instituted to induce behavioral change is virtually impossible without records. Measurement and specific records are crucial for accurate evaluation. The difficulty regarding these classification procedures is that they take extra effort. Behavior always occurs in time intervals. If we are to know whether any particular behavior is getting worse, better, or staying the same, the frequency of behavioral occurrences must be recorded across time and in specific time intervals.

One important aspect of learning record keeping is for a person to develop the self-discipline necessary to keep individual records representing his own behavior. A good place to start is with the time spent on this course or workshop. Each participant is urged to maintain an individual time log indicating amounts of time spent engaged in learning activities. Each week one time log should be completed. (Academic instructors may require that the log be turned in weekly, workshop directors daily.) A model time log is provided.

The time log is divided into four mutually exclusive categories— Reading, Discussion, Writing, and Other—since two or more behaviors

TIME LOG

RATING KEY

1	2

1 = Time in Minutes
2 = Rating

A = Very Worthwhile
B = Some Value
C = Little Value
D = Wasted Time

Class _____
Name _____
Week No. _____
Dates _____

Days A - Readings								Wkly. Total	Last Cum. Total	New Cum. Total
Texts										
Behavioral Articles										
Others Related										
B Discussion										
Class Attendance										
Class Members										
Other (Specify)										
C - Writing										
Learning Activities										
Summaries (Behavioral Articles or Texts)										
Other Assignments										
D- Other										
Observing										
Supervising Practicing Mini - Teaching										
Course - Related Thinking										

Comments on Back   Grand Totals _____ _____ _____ cannot occur at precisely the same time (although discussion and/or writing and reading may be closely interspersed). Any class preparation or learning time which is not covered in the Reading, Discussion, and Writing categories may be recorded under Other. This category includes classroom observations, supervision behaviors, or any activities assigned but for which no category exists. These should also be listed on the back of your log.

Keep accurate records and, each time you engage in an activity, log the amount of time in the upper half of each square which is diagonal (round up or down to fifteen-minute time periods). The number of hours are important in order to ascertain how much time one is spending on the course or workshop. It is critical to record time spent as immediately as possible. Few people have a good enough memory to record time spent after even a one-day interlude. After recording time spent, record a subjective rating in the lower half.

CHAPTER 4

Behavior
The Contingent Result of Life

WHO HAS THE PROBLEM?

Perhaps one of the most challenging tasks for today's teacher is to know what literature to believe and what to reject, which authority to respect and which to discount. In our multimedia world we seem to have experts by the score with almost as many admonitions as we have experts. Presumably many teachers are saying, "What don't they get together; one says that what is right today was wrong five years ago; what we got when we were growing up was wrong, or another says right, depending on whom you read." The authors are sympathetic to this situation, especially since we are constantly dealing with children's problems. It is our strong belief, however, that many problems may be "caused" by reading and acting on some of the pronouncements of these articles. Teachers come to us constantly with "students' problems" that did not exist before an article was read. We are reminded of the man who worried for twenty years about latent fear until the day he decided he didn't have to worry about it as long as it was latent.

It would be less than honest for the authors to presume that we are not admonishing, we certainly are. Foremost, *severe problems should be referred to a professional.* It is our hope, however, that teachers will rely on their own honest assessments concerning most teaching. Honesty, we believe, is the key to behavioral assessment by teachers, even if students are being advised by professionals. If teachers are honest, they will not *give their problems away and absolve responsibility.* The attitude of giving a problem away is perhaps best illustrated by a graduate student in psychology who was presenting to a graduate seminar the case of his first interview with a client. He was apologizing to the other members of the seminar, "I guess I fouled up, about the only thing that I established was that the client had a studying problem." One of the older supervisory clinicians rose to his feet, smiled at the young man, picked a little at his pipe, and addressed the group, "As some of you know, I was an obstetrician before I changed to clinical work and I didn't learn much from my previous medical specialty that had immediate transfer. I did learn one thing, however, and that concerns *who's pregnant!* You know, the very first time a patient came to me, the one thing I tried to firmly establish was who's pregnant. 'No *we're* not going to have a baby, your *husband's* not going to have a baby, your *mother's* not going to have a baby, your *family's* not going to have a baby—you, *you're* the one who is going to have a baby.' It was always amusing to me to see some of the expectant mothers trying to give their problem away. Of course, it was they who had to eat properly, receive proper supplements when needed, go through the entire pregnancy, and so on. Son, if within that first session with your client you established *who* had the problem, you succeeded. If your client left realizing that her studying difficulty was not her roommate's problem or her professor's problem or her mother's problem or her counselor's problem, then you are well on your way."

Assessing who has the problem requires a teacher to decide if the problem really belongs to the student or to the teacher. Often both have a problem: the child, an inappropriate behavior that needs to be changed; the teacher, the responsibility to do something about changing it. Many times, however, problems are not real. The only problem extant is in the head of the teacher. After reading some article, the teacher begins to worry about a potential problem, sometimes to the extent that interaction with the student actually creates the very problem suspected. Certainly, these self-fulfilling prophesies should be avoided, especially when the suspected problem cannot be specified as a behavior(s), but refers only to an idea such as inferiority, lack of love, need for expression, need for individual achievement, or other non-specified ideas.

Even though the teacher is advised to be self-reliant in behavioral assessment of childrens' problems, the teacher also should be careful not to believe that deviant behavior is *just a stage* the youngster is going through. If by "stage" we mean precisely the length of time that a child exhibits incorrect responses until something is done to insure improved behavior or if by "stage" we mean those behaviors quite proper for one age but not for another, then there is no cause for concern—still no reason for alarm. If, however, we refer to "stage" in an attempt to *give away our problem* hoping that in some mysterious manner a day will come (perhaps next year) when the problem magically goes away, then perhaps we should reevaluate. The very young child's occasional "disrobing" should not be equated with his occasional "lie." The social contingencies operating within his environment will probably modify his clothes wearing behavior, but probably not his lying. The student who occasionally "has severe temper tantrums" should not be equated with the student who occasionally "forgets to clean his desk." The younger who occasionally "refuses to share" is not comparable to one who "plots to put himself up by secretly bringing physical harm to another." Classifying problems into "normal stages of development" should be done with great care.

Teachers should realize that even seemingly innocuous behaviors probably change because something or someone in the student's environment interacts to modify specific responses—that is, some problems will extinguish when the older students' environment sets up different expectations; other problems will intensify. The extent to which these problem behaviors change is determined by the cause-and-effect relationships interacting within the student's world, not by magic or by just growing older. There are many old liars, adults who constantly lose their temper, and teachers who scheme in putting down other colleagues, workers, or even friends to get ahead. Being honest, there also are adults who are exhibitionists, extremely messy, and even stingy.

Who has the problem?—You decide.

WHAT IS THE PAYOFF?

A traditional viewpoint prevalent in education is to focus on many antecedent events (reinforcement history) leading toward a particular goal, rather than to focus on the manipulation and control of the present environment. This procedure of looking backward is both unproductive and unnecessary, especially when it absolves the responsibility of solving the current problem. When the teacher wants to change a specific inappropriate behavior, the teacher must first *find the payoff* and eliminate it if possible. *Behavior that goes unrewarded will extinguish.* The teacher must watch the student carefully to determine the payoff. The teacher must also recognize individual differences; the payoff is often different for each child. For example, students A, B, and C talk in class. After many warnings the teacher finally sends them to the principal's office. This is just exactly what student A wanted; he finally managed to goad the teacher into "punishing" him. Student B just liked to make the teacher angry. Every time she got stern it just "broke him up." He knew he was bothering her, and he enjoyed her distress: "Wow! She gave me such *stern* looks." Student C did not care about the teacher or the principal. He did care about students A and B. Everytime he talked, they listened. On the way to the principal's office, student A filled the others in. "Listen, the principal sits you down and comes on with all this 'You've got to be a good boy' stuff. Man, the last time I was in there I really had him snowed. Besides, he never checks to see if you go back to the class, so we're out for the day." When students A, B, and C return to class, they will continue to talk even more.

Teachers who have simple monolithic explanations for all maladaptive behaviors will be generally ineffective. "All those children need is a little love." "The thing they need is a good, hard paddling." "Get them out in the world; then you'll see how they do." "They need a decent place to live." "They need someone who truly understands them." The problem with this type of analysis is that it is neither differentiated nor individualized. There are some children who may fit one, none, or all of the above categories, plus countless others. The one thing that children exhibiting inappropriate responses *do* need is a teacher who can find the payoff. What is maintaining the problem, keeping the behavior alive? If the payoff can be found and completely eliminated, then the behavior will gradually extinguish—*if consistency is maintained.*

A word of caution is important. One significant result of eliminating the payoff is that the undesired behavior will get initially worse before it gets better. The teacher must remember that the student has learned a behavior to get what he wants. When the "reward" is abolished, he tries even harder (i.e., the inappropriate behavior increases) before he comes to realize that there is no payoff. After this initial surge the behavior will extinguish. The initial rise is extremely important to remember. Many people give up during the storm before the calm, "Oh, I've tried ignoring, but the baby cried even louder."—Of course.

Finding the payoff can be difficult, and sometimes the payoff comes from a source that the teacher cannot control (parents, peers, physiological reactions, internal imagery, etc.). Nevertheless, many problems can be solved by cutting out the "reward."

What is the payoff?—That which keeps the behavior alive.

P.S. Give student A a task much less desirable than talking in class, preferably where he cannot talk to anyone—isolation. Smile at student B when he is not talking; absolutely ignore him when he is. Move student C to the other side of the room away from students

A and B, or make him apologize in front of the class, or perhaps even punish students A and B and tell them it's not their fault but student C's.

WHAT CONSTITUTES REWARD?

After a teacher determines the payoff for a particular behavior and eliminates it, the teacher will soon observe a decrease in undesirable behavior. Sometimes this alone is all that is needed. Yet more often other things in the students' environment (stimuli) must be controlled; that is, other contingencies must be structured in order to discipline. It is better to start with just one behavior and not try to eliminate everything simultaneously, unless the teacher has a great deal of help and can initially devote available time just to social behavioral problems. If many undesired behaviors are prevalent throughout the classroom, the teacher is advised to establish a priority and start with the inappropriate behavior that most interferes with learning. It is extremely important that teachers deal with overt behaviors, not ideas (for example, "getting to work on time" as opposed to "a bad attitude about math"). It is also advisable to make up a set of easily understood rules for each activity. In making up the contingencies (i.e., structuring the rewards) the new payoff for *desirable* behavior (following the rules) must be known, tangible, and close enough to the student's own behavioral responses to motivate the student to seek it. Initially it is far better to give too much reward than not enough. The idea is to get the student "winning" as soon as possible. For general control in the early elementary years, words, contact, and expressions are highly effective; group activities and peer group approval provide powerful rewards for the adolescent years (middle school, junior high, and high school); material things and individual activities for young adults (junior high, high school, college). Various "token systems" are generally effective at all age levels and come closest to representing our own monetary system. For young students correct responses can earn "tokens" that are exchanged for tangible goods (e.g., most young children enjoy things such as toys, trips, playthings, or food). Tokens may be chips, papers, check marks, or anything convenient. Rewards earned for tokens should have specified values (i.e., colored paper equals five points, a ruler equals eight points, a commercial game equals ten points) so that students can receive tangible credit for exhibiting appropriate behaviors, such as following specific rules (written on chalkboard). Each student could have a small notebook marked by teacher, students, or both. At appropriate intervals (after study, before lunch, following discussion, etc.) the teacher marks the students' points. The teacher may begin a program by displaying rewards and asking the students which one they are working toward. Then the teacher may go over the rules. The rules should be written down in a conspicuous place and explained daily— at a time other than when they have been violated: we sit quietly during individual study. We raise our hand before we interrupt to talk. We stay at our own desk during study time unless given permission to leave. We respect others' rights, and property, etc. At opportune times, the teacher circulates and writes down the points. The very act of recording may be used as an effective control. It is critical for the teacher to try very hard to *catch the child being good* and reward him with points paired with words and expressions of praise instantaneously.

In the initial stages of control it is important to have the student achieve success quickly, after which the time between behavior and reward can be stretched for longer periods while continuing to pair appropriate personal responses from the teacher (words of praise, expressions such as smiling, and closeness such as positive touching). In time the personal approval of the teacher, and later, the student's approval of himself will probably be all that is needed for proper motivation.

This is certainly what most teachers desire; but in order to achieve this level of sophistication, one must start where the child is. Some children enter school with response expectations amenable to smiling, pleasing teachers, being obedient, etc. Other have to learn appropriate responses through more tangible rewards. Token systems may be set up at all levels of sophistication in preparation for adult employment.

One extremely effective technique for small children is the use of food (candy, juice, flavored cereal) as contingent reinforcement. The teacher may start the very first day of the new program with a "goodie" party. The teacher gives the students a treat and while the students are eating the teacher says, "We will have another "goodie" party if you are quiet while I count to ten." (The teacher then counts aloud quickly, making certain they win.) After giving the candy the teacher says, "If everyone is quiet for five minutes we will have another party, but if someone talks we will not get to have one." Now the teacher sits back and waits; in all probability someone will talk, whereupon the teacher says, "Oh, I'm *very sorry.* Mary talked before our time was up; now we will not get to have a party. Maybe tomorrow we may have one if everyone is quiet." (Some children will think this is not "fair"). *Because the teacher does not get angry at Mary, Mary cannot give her problem to the teacher.* Mary receives the disapproval of the group so there is no payoff from the other children. Instead of interacting directly with Mary, it may be better to use vicarious reinforcement and modeling. To use this technique the teacher chooses one of the most well-behaved children and says, "I surely like the way Sheila is sitting so quietly. If everyone behaved like Sheila, we could have our party." Sometimes the teacher may wish to give rewards to those children who were quiet and not give anything to those who were not. (Mary may not think this is fair.)

The use of group approval-disapproval is very effective, particularly with older students. When activities are given or denied contingent on the behavior of all concerned, the children themselves will take the responsibility for discipline, and discipline will start to evolve from within the group. *Peer approval* is extremely important to teenagers. This is precisely the reason for such high "esprit de corps" in many group organizations such as band, athletics, social clubs, and gangs.

When teachers as well as the other students are taught to cut out the payoff for a particular individual's inappropriate behavior, the undesirable behavior will generally decrease. Of course, students may indeed be embarrassed after receiving such responses from their peers—so be it. It is precisely this contingent embarrassment that solves the problem. If students do not care what others think of them, then withholding of approval or verbal disapproval is not effective. It is the teachers' value system that determines what contingencies are to be used. Contingencies, in both approving and disapproving ways, that the teacher *can* use include:

1. Words (spoken and written)
2. Expressions (facial-bodily)
3. Closeness (nearness-touching)
4. Activities and privileges (social-individual)
5. Things (tokens, materials, food, playthings, money)

Other than the rewards of the activity itself (sometimes there are none), these categories constitute the *entire resources* that the teacher has for structuring. Teaching should develop them well. (Study the examples and lists in Parts II and III.)

What constitutes reward?—That which the student will work toward.

IS THE WORLD FAIR?

For years, teachers have been advocating the uniqueness of every student. "All children are not alike," they say. "Each child has had many different experiences." "Children come from many different backgrounds." "They need individual attention." One would assume from this dedication to individual difference that teachers would teach differently and meet the discipline problems of each student in a unique manner; but this does not seem to be the case. Most teachers also seem preoccupied with an *undifferentiated* concept of "fairness."

Children do not have a problem with undifferentiated "fairness" until someone teaches it to them. Usually it is taught by their parents, who manifest the same thinking as some teachers. With little hesitation, parents will talk at length about how different their children are. Equally without hesitation, they try as hard as possible to be "fair." Fred and Jane are different in many, many ways. They like different things, they respond differently, and one child is almost always older. Yet, when Fred gets to go, Jane gets to go; when Jane gets candy, Fred must have candy. If Fred receives a toy, Jane must, also. Fred and Jane learn quickly "Why can't I stay up late?" "Why don't I get to go?" "How come I don't get a present?" "Why does she always get the biggest apple?" Thus Mother and Dad spend a great deal of time and energy trying to be "fair." They also create much anxiety for themselves by not admitting that they do treat the other children differently and from time to time may actually even like one child more than another. These are all unnecessary attempts designed to solve the problem of undifferentiated fairness they have created for themselves. "But Fred, your bithday will come next month." "Jane, you see Fred is older than you; that's why he stays up later." "OK, if you're going to fight over who gets the biggest apple, neither one of you can have one."

People *are* different. Some are extremely different, particularly if they have physical or mental handicaps. It would seem that the kindest teaching behavior would be to instruct students in this regard—let them know that the world is not always "fair." Prepare them for the suffering they will endure because of others' mistakes. Let them realize from the beginning that their efforts are not always evaluated fairly. Help them understand that in a democracy the group often suffers from the actions of a few. Let them realize that occasionally they will be punished for things that they do not do. Teach them to understand that justice is an ideal, less often a reality. *Yes, and also instruct them to be just in their own personal behaviors, but not always to expect it from others.* Some of the gravest problems encountered by students come from an undifferentiated concept of "fairness."

Fairness is not a simple matter. People have labored for centuries to ascertain "what's fair" in relationship to many different situations (laws). Within the academic realm, the teacher also works hard at differential assessment. Grades are assigned differentially as are special projects, reports, reading groups, and so on. Thus, *the teacher establishes rules of academic discriminations (fairness?).* How naïve, then, to equip the students with one special response the teacher knows will cause him problems as he matures. The teacher also loses a most effective technique (group approval-disapproval) when refusing to use the group in "shaping up" individuals, for to punish the group because of the actions of one individual or vice versa does not seem "fair." Ideally, proper interaction patterns will eventually evolve from within the group. Students will help discipline each other, not by punishing, or tattling but by ignoring, attending to what is proper; not talking or listening to each other when they should not be, and generally *staying on-task.* Discipline, however, will not evolve from the group unless the teacher uses the group to bring particular individuals "in line."

No one wishes to be punished for another's actions. In cooperative societies, however, this goes on continuously. If elected officials in a representative government decide to enter a war they do not ask the individual student. If a student in the bud of maturity fights, and subsequently dies in battle, then who suffers? Why not prepare students for the world in which they live, where everyone's life is affected by the acts of others? Let them realize early that if we are to function socially then we must take the responsibility and the results of interacting with others—we do not stand alone. Help students understand that "what's fair" is a big question relating differentially to almost all aspects of life. Do not prepare them for certain disillusionment with one undifferentiated response. Help them discriminate between the many issues of fairness and be prepared to deal realistically with these discernments. Students may then come to accept life's inequities while doing something to change many of them, rather than feeling sorry for themselves because they find some aspects of interaction "unfair." When the teacher deals with fairness, optimism need not suffer—only naïveté.

Is the world fair?—Sometimes.

CAN CONTINGENCIES BE STRUCTURED?

The basic premise of reinforcement teaching is to arrange the stimuli of the external world to shape the behavior of the students—to structure the environment so that the student receives approval-disapproval reinforcements contingent on appropriate/inappropriate behavior. Therefore, *reinforcement teaching is the structure of approval and*

*disapproval reinforcers, across time in precise intervals, to shape de-
sired behavior toward specific goals.* Experimentation in learning
demonstrates that: (a) If a student knows specifically what is expected
of him and (b) he wants to do it, then (c) he probably will. The necessity for specific measurable goals (expectations for students) has
already been mentioned. The crux of the problem rests with (b):
arranging the contingencies of reinforcement so that a student will
want to do what the teacher expects.

Five techniques used in structuring contingencies are:

1. *Approval* (rewards)

2. *Withholding of approval* (withholding rewards—hope)

3. *Disapproval* (punishment)

4. *Threat of disapproval* (fear)

5. *Ignoring* (not attending in any manner, verbal or nonverbal)

Approval is easily understood. Approval is anything that is generally
thought to be related with "happiness": *Words* used as praise: *expressions,* such as smiling; *closeness,* such as embracing or touching;
activities that are enjoyable, *things,* such as games, badges, food trinkets,
etc. Teachers must be sure, however, that what they believe is functioning as positive reinforcement is truly positive (some children don't
like ice cream).

Withholding of approval (withholding rewards) is used when the
positive reinforcer functions to produce "hope" for the attainment of
a reward the next time when the behavior is improved. In a way, this
procedure functions as "punishment" (disapproval), although with
potentially greater effect for improvement and less wear and tear on
everyone concerned. Teachers may also place the responsibility for
improvement on the student and perhaps avoid negative emotional
reactions directed toward themselves following punishment. "I'm sorry
you didn't finish on time. Now you cannot go out to play. Perhaps
tomorrow you will finish on time. Then you may play."

Disapproval is also easily understood. Disapproval is generally
synonymous with what most persons term *unhappiness.* Disapproval
comes in such forms as *words* when one is getting yelled at; *expressions* such as frowning; *closeness* when one is being hit or placed in
isolation; *activities,* as when one is deprived of something he wants
or made to do an unpleasant task; and *things,* such as feared objects.

The teacher must also be careful not to conclude too easily what
constitutes disapproval. Students may often exhibit many inappropriate, maladaptive, and perverted associations. "I like to get spanked."

"I enjoy making my teacher angry." Extreme disapproval (corporal punishment) should be used very sparingly, if at all. Perhaps the most important thing to be remembered about physical punishment is that if teachers decide to use it, *it should be strong enough to stop the behavior immediately and eliminate the problem at once,* otherwise teachers may only insure that the student will engage in similar behavior in the future and, therefore, punishment will probably intensify, especially if teachers become angry and do not realize that they themselves are contributing to the problem. Many children have been gradually conditioned to endure severe beatings, usually *without* a decrease in maladaptive responses.

Threat of disapproval (fear) should be used rarely, yet it is profoundly effective once the knowledge of disapproval is established. Individuals learn how to behave in order to avoid disapproval (unpleasant consequences): "I am careful when crossing the road to avoid getting killed." "I don't play with guns because I could get shot." "I study so I won't fail." Even though fear is an extremely effective suppressant of much inappropriate behavior, it does little to establish the joy of learning and living. Children (or adults) who are completely negatively motivated are usually tense, unenthusiastic, quiet, shy, passive, and generally fearful. Some of these children do eventually succeed, although this negatively motivated "success" usually comes at the high price of guilt, compulsiveness, generalized anxiety, and perhaps later, even ulcers.

Ignore—just that—Ignore.

The formula in Table 4-1 represent interactions for behavioral shaping. The teacher is advised, if at all possible, to use primarily

Table 4-1

		Teacher Behavior				
		Approval	Withholding of Approval	Disapproval	Threat of Disapproval	Ignore
Student Behavior	Appropriate	Yes	No	No	No	No
	Inappropriate	No	Yes	Yes*	Yes	Yes**

*Unless payoff
**Unless dangerous

approval, withholding of approval, and ignoring in controlling behavior. There is some indication that these "positive approaches" can be more effective, but, more important, *much less damage can be done than through the use of extreme disapproval (punishment).* This does not mean the teacher should be permissive. It indicates that as teachers structure the students' environment contingent on appropriate be-haviors (that is, produce appropriate cause-and-effect relationships), they should diligently try to do so through the use of "positive" techniques and structuring incompatible responses. Withholding an overt love response seems much more kind than corporal punishment. Alternately, there are times when disapproval (punishment) might need to be used. Some maladaptive behaviors of children are much worse than the punishment it could take to eliminate them.

Can contingencies be structured?—They must.

ARE THOUGHTS BEHAVIOR?

Laura was in her third year of teaching high school English. She has just returned from Thanksgiving vacation and discovered that she was pregnant. Having tried repeatedly to achieve this state she was ex-tremely happy yet she "worried constantly" concerning how she was going to finish the school year. She was concerned about her classes, she worried about finances, she did not know just how she was going to tell her principal.

Laura's classes were just perfect as far as she was concerned. It had not always been that way. During the beginning of the school year she had had the normal kinds of problems until such time as she was able to develop her own *style* in a manner that the students re-sponded to her as she wanted them to. She had noticed that her verbal disapproval (even when she used it sparingly) was actually functioning as "nagging." After she had determined to use only verbal *approval* and had set up other consequences for student *mis*behavior she had settled down into a pleasant year.

Yet, as the Christmas holidays approached the problem of her pregnancy continued to bother her. Sometimes the ambivalence seemed to be unbearable. Even during the nicest parts of the school day when students were not just doing good work but were actually being tender to each other she felt preoccupied and distant. One day when she had students sincerely applauding the accomplishments of each other, her mind suddenly wandered to the yet dormant life within her and she felt that same old pang of uneasiness.

Laura decided that she definitely must do something about this problem as it seemed to be getting worse daily. She finally discussed it with a close friend who was also a teacher but became upset because her friend had suggested that she use one of those "behavioral programs" to deal with it. "How absolutely insensitive," she thought. How could any of the techniques that she was using in her classroom apply to her problem? She remembered asking sarcastically, "Am I supposed to give myself a token every time I don't think about it?" Her friend had answered, "Yes."

Laura thought about that conversation for some time. Then she decided to do exactly what her friend had suggested—not give herself a token but to engage in an incompatible behavior (a thought-stopping process) every time she found that she was thinking (actually worrying) about her problem. She also decided to apply some of the instructive advice she had been giving her class all year in settling their problems in a positive manner. She finally told her principal—and wished that she had done so earlier because her principal was so supportive. She then told her students who were even more receptive. More importantly, she taught herself to stop worrying about her condition unnecessarily by writing down on a small card several sentences (e.g., I don't want to waste my time worrying about this; this worrying is completely unproductive; I am going to put this card in my purse and stop worrying NOW!)

Like many others, Laura was very capable of applying principles of behavior modification to help students within her classroom, but she was not initially capable of applying those same principles to remedy her own problems. While it is always difficult to see one's own problems as being as simple as other people seem to think they are, it is still necessary to have some plan of action. It is also important to act in a positive manner conducive to effecting resolution of one's problems. Sometimes it is advisable to seek professional help, more often it is advisable to apply the same external reinforcements to control thought processes just as one would do to decrease or increase more "observable" behavior.

Most sophisticated people live in a "world of ideas." Sometimes these ideas are productive and pleasant; sometimes these ideas are destructive, even to the point of complete debilitation. A burgeoning field relating to "cognitive behavior modification" is attempting to sort out the variables, schedules of reinforcement, and the positive/aversive histories of people in order to help them to live more productively. While this area seems extremely complicated, it is beginning to demonstrate that thoughts can also be modified.

Are thoughts behavior?—Think about it.

STUDY GUIDE FOR CHAPTER 4

Questions

1. How does one decide who has the problem?

2. What point is made with the example of students A, B, and C? Explain why teachers should understand the analysis of students A, B, and C.

*3. How is the choice made about what competing or inappropriate behavior is to be eliminated first?

*4. What is vicarious reinforcement and modeling? Give an example. Why might it be used?

*5. What makes group approval-disapproval work effectively?

*6. How can you tell what will be rewarding? Can you predict in advance what may work?

*7. Should a teacher treat all children the same in academic and social situations? Explain.

8. Should a child be taught that the world is unfair? Why or why not?

*9. Which three techniques should be employed most in structuring contingencies by teachers? Why?

10. Are thought behavior? List some thoughts that you might change with principles of behavior modification.

*Transfer these questions to your specific situation (e.g., Vocational-Technical Education, English).

LEARNING ACTIVITY 7—LEGAL, MORAL, AND ETHICAL RESPONSIBILITIES FOR THE TEACHER

Write an essay dealing with the issues relating to the legal, moral, and ethical responsibilities in regard to teaching. Be sure to include such aspects as: What is fair? What behaviors should be referred to professionals in other areas? What type of potential approvals/disapprovals will be ethically and morally correct? What aspects of discipline represent legal considerations?

The following questions might help stimulate ideas for writing an essay (or facilitating class discussion).

1. Can humans modify their behavior to be more free?

2. Can humans really avoid controlling others (through the ongoing exchange of rewards and punishments) even if they wish to?

3. Under what circumstances and for what types of behavior is negative reinforcement and/or punishment appropriate/necessary?

4. In what ways can behavioral techniques be abused? Is the potential for abuse greater for the behavioral approach than other approaches?

5. Should behaviorists be allowed to "experiment" with humans? What criteria should be established to determine the permissible areas of behavioral intervention? Should some populations (institutionalized mentally ill, the mentally retarded, or prisoners) be immune from experiments? Should they have less right to informed consent because of diminished capacity or status?

6. What limits should we place on the teaching of others? Can an acceptable standard be developed that allows for the proper treatment of chronic problems while somehow preventing "brainwashing" and unwarranted deprivations of rights and freedoms?

7. Should parents be granted the right to informed consent before a student is admitted to a behavior modification program? When do behavior modification practices (deliberate or unwitting) constitute a "program" subject to special consideration?

8. What kinds of reinforcers are really proper for the school environment (for "adjusted" or "maladjusted" children)?

9. Are structured techniques such as token economy system too mechanistic to be used in the schools? What better alternative, if any, is available for dealing with reluctant learners?

10. How might behavioral principles be employed to improve or reform the educational system (increase motivation, reduce disruption, promote individuality and creativity, provide instructional alternatives, promote racial harmony)?

LEARNING ACTIVITY 8— INTERPERSONAL EXTENSIONS

1. Pinpoint 15 specific problem behaviors discussed in class, small group sessions, or from your own experiences that relate to inter-

personal behaviors. Develop and outline sequential consequences based upon behavioral principles that would alleviate, remediate, or prevent additional or similar problems in the future.

2. Discuss solutions in small groups with continued recording and reporting of positive and negative comments.

CHAPTER 5

Life
The Structure of Activities
in Time

IS TIME IMPORTANT?

Thank you, reader. Thank you for what? Thank you for reading the next paragraph. You have not read it yet? Oh.

Why is the preceding rather absurd? It is because the "thank you" comes before the fact. Therefore, it has little meaning and even less significance in modifying your behavior (except perhaps in creating confusion). In all research concerned with behavior, no one has ever been able to teach anything through the use of antecedent rewards. *Rewards must come after the fact.* Thus, we enter the most elusive aspect of teaching—time. All events take place in time. Benjamin Franklin has this maxim: "Dost thou love life? Then do not squander time, for that is the stuff life is made of."

One of the most basic differentiations of the growing child comes in his progressive sophistication regarding time. Even adults cannot really tell time, as evidenced by the chronoscopes we strap to our arms. Our temporal span is exceedingly short, and our assessment of ongoing time becomes humorous (try to estimate a minute without counting to yourself)! Even with a minute you must "fill it up with something" in order to approximate the passage of time. Now consider these foolish temporal contingencies: One-year-old; "Baby knows I'll pick her up after I finish my work." Three-year-old: "Tomorrow we will go out to play." Six-year-old: "Be good, next week is party time." Nine-year-old: "When you get to eleven, you may join the scouts." Thirteen-year-old: "If you pass all your classes, you may have a car when you're sixteen." Sixteen-year-old: "You must graduate from high school if you expect to have a good life." College freshman: "Study diligently and you will be a good teacher." If these sequences sound

long, try a few out on yourself just to see how close a contingent reward or punishment must be in time to motivate you." "One more
drink and tomorrow morning, wow!" "You don't have the money—
why not just charge it?" "Better stop this late discussion—8:00 A.M.
comes early." "Better start studying—final exams in just two weeks,"
As you can see, your temporal motivation is not long at all. Of course
you realize the necessity of working toward or avoiding all those things,
but they are up there in time somewhere—not now—not close enough
in time really to motivate *you*.

If contingent rewards/punishments for behavior are to be most
effective, they should take place immediately; and *the teacher must
always know, before the fact, just what the contingencies are to be.*
With small children this is tremendously important. "Daddy's going to
spank you when he gets home" is a typical example of a ridiculous
contingency.

It is also important to correct any inappropriate behavior before it
becomes full-blown—to nip it in the bud. The teacher who believes that
a small disturbance "will get better" is right. It will get better and
better and *better* and BETTER! Full-blown disorder is usually encouraged by hesitation and caused by self-deception. *Initial stages of
control are the most important.* As the child matures, his temporal
span will increase if he is taught proper behaviors while progressively
lengthening the time between action and consequence. If the bag of
oats is too close to the horse, he eats the oats; if the bag is too far
away, he does not move. Time and the control of reinforcement schedules across time is imperative. Reinforcers can be delivered on many
different schedules depending on the circumstances (fixed time, fixed
interval, variable time, variable interval, or mixed). The job of the
teacher is to meet the student where he is and then progressively take
him to the point where he will be content to wait for longer and longer
rewards while still exhibiting proper behavior (e.g., structuring progressive work tasks toward final grades). Actually, many people guard
time more jealously than anything over which they have control. *The
art of living evolves from the structure of meaningful activities in time.*
Is time important?—Time is life.

HOW SHOULD WE SCHEDULE ACROSS TIME?

Schedules of reinforcement concern events across time. They provide
extremely important information when analyzing human behavior.
Schedules are generally considered as either fixed or variable and an
analysis of these schedules provides the understanding one needs in
order to determine teaching/learning contingencies. For example, if

one desires higher work productivity, it is possible from an external or outside consideration to structure schedules such that another human being would work much harder than previously thought possible because of efficient external structuring of reinforcement schedules. However, the differentiation between structuring from an internal point of view and having a structure imposed upon us remains the most important aspect if we are to gain clear understanding of the efficacy of reinforcement schedules. This is difficult, as are many temporal concepts, because people react negatively to many of these concepts precisely because of the aversive schedule to which they have been previously subjected. A good example of this point concerns financial remuneration. It has been demonstrated many times that one's pay is made much stronger as a contingency when put on some kind of variable or piece-work schedule. Most of us do not like to receive pay in this manner because it takes away our "security," (that is, acts as a weaker contingency). This is but one example that must be understood if one is to gain a clear perception concerning schedules of reinforcement.

Schedules of reinforcement can be given on an intervallic or time schedule (fixed or variable) and also on the basis of a work product ratio. *Ratio* schedules whether they are fixed (every problem completed) or variable (pop quizzes) are best conceptualized as schedules of reinforcement concerning feedback or payoff after certain responses have occurred. This is in opposition to intervallic or temporal scheduling relating to periods of *time*. An example of *fixed interval schedules* would be days, months, weeks, minutes, and so on. *Fixed ratio schedules* might refer to reinforcement given after every two times, every five times, six times, or any other aspect that would refer to a fixed feedback after certain amounts of behavior. *Variable interval schedules* have to do with variations in time and vacillate across time in some manner of predetermined order or on a random basis. *Variable ratio schedules*, alternately, include a payoff having to do with a variation after certain responses.

The most easily understood *variable ratio schedule* concerns gambling. Many times the topic of gambling is used to teach the concept of variable ratio scheduling. Obviously, if one knows that one is going to lose every time, one will not gamble. If one were to win every time, someone else would have to pay the price of the gambler's winning. Therefore, as far as the "manipulator" is concerned the idea is to have the gambler win enough in the short run in order to lose money in the long run. This is not a difficult thing to do if the manipulator is keenly aware of the effectiveness of certain schedules of reinforcement. Initially, the notion would be to get the gambler winning or to get the gambler "hooked on gambling," as it were, such that a pattern of expectancies would keep the gambling frequency high whereby the gambler gradually loses money to the one in control.

Gambling is not only an interesting example illustrating variable reinforcement, it is probably the most common aspect of life's schedule that contributes to depression and mental illness. Partial schedules (variable ratio schedules) of reinforcement are generally operating constantly in our lives. The effect of these schedules is to teach one to go for longer and longer periods of time exhibiting fewer inappropriate (that is, maladaptive responses) as well as more appropriate responses. Therefore, as with other principles of reinforcement, the entire issue of values needs to be predetermined so that we can teach or structure consistent with the value hierarchy previously determined. Variable schedules of reinforcement will be dealt with later, but to understand the beneficial as well as the devastating effects of variable schedules we must also understand aspects of fixed scheduling.

Measured or ongoing time is assessed in fixed intervals. As has been previously mentioned, these fixed intervals for the most part concern seconds, minutes, hours, days, weeks, months, years, and so on. We have developed tremendous sophistication in this measurement and most of life is structured around certain fixed interval schedules. Fixed interval schedules also provide the most emotional security as well as the most precise measurement of time. Many of life's activities have been structured around fixed intervals and the most common is the circadian schedules that have to do with daily life. Other common examples of fixed interval schedules are birthdays, fixed pay periods, school holidays, and work schedules across hours that are regular. Most aspects of life about which we rarely think are structured within fixed schedules. A contingent or cause-and-effect relationship between fixed schedules and the behaviors that these schedules presumably are intended to reinforce, however, appears to be quite weak. While a fixed interval schedule provides the most security it also provides the least motivation in modifying or changing student behavior. That is, it represents the weakest form of increasing or decreasing certain responses. For example, most people who have been conditioned to a fixed interval schedule concerning pay rarely develop a contingent relationship between the money that they receive for their work and the job itself. Thus, the contingencies that do operate concerning money have to do with more direct behaviors, for instance, paying one's bills. Consequently this pay schedule has little to do with our on-the-job behavior. It is of course possible if we do not make enough money to pay our bills that we may work harder, that is, engage in extra work for overtime or take another job part-time such that more money can be made. However, even in these endeavors if the pay comes on a fixed schedule the relationship between what is done and how one is rewarded for same is still weak. This same solution often exists with report cards. Sometimes the fixed schedule whereby parents receive feedback is not connected to ongoing *student study*.

Fixed ratio schedules are the next most effective. That is, when "effective" is defined as the application of a reinforcement schedule in order to increase or decrease some behavior. An example of a fixed ratio schedule would be payment for piece-meal work where every correct problem or finished assignment received certain remuneration. It is obvious that this represents a stronger contingency because it has to do with *quantities* of production as opposed to set time intervals (i.e., fixed interval schedules). Some parents prefer to use a fixed ratio schedule in their giving of allowance. Other parents prefer to give allowance to children on the basis of a fixed interval schedule, that is, for growing so many days older. Variable schedules are generally thought to be much more effective than fixed schedules. A variable interval schedule is concerned with events happening in some erratic or randomly determined temporal period. A common example of a variable interval schedule might concern receiving mail, where one is not really sure what day a response will come and eagerly waits for letters. It should be noted, however, that bills also arrive by mail although a simple distinction is made by most people concerning bill receipt as opposed to more happy correspondence. Furthermore, bills are generally considered aversive. They are most often saved until some *fixed interval*, whereby they are paid or manipulated in some other way. Receipt of happy mail or any other mail that comes at a variable interval is generally dealt with more immediately or at least on some kind of variable schedule as opposed to a fixed schedule. Of course, the above example does not represent the case when people write to each other or receive mail everyday. In this case, receipt of mail everyday would again be on a fixed as opposed to a variable schedule. Receipt of mail precisely at the same time every week would also represent a fixed schedule, although even if one receives mail on the average of once a week, the mail generally does not come precisely the same day. Other common examples concerning variable intervals have to do with receipt of company, visits, good and bad news over periods of time, and many other events that keep us in anticipation of further happenings. Obviously, this anticipation can be defined as both good and bad. It can provide some variety, but it may be too costly in relationship to other issues.

Variable ratio scheduling is generally considered to be the most effective. In this regard certain behaviors as opposed to temporal increments are paid off or reinforced over an erratic period of time, for example, gambling in which the particular behavior under question can be maintained for longer and longer periods of time in anticipation of a reinforcement that is never quite "fixed." Variable schedules are used in many ways to motivate and to increase or decrease certain behaviors. Precisely because variable schedules are so effective they are capable of creating the most anxiety. In laboratory experiments it is possible to get lower animal forms to exhibit many behaviors of "mental illness" by carefully controlling schedules of reinforcement. If we wish to act responsibly as teachers, it is essential that we understand the subtle and sometimes the not so subtle reinforcement schedules that are operating within the learning environment. This is especially important for the detrimental aspects of life that we desire to bring under control.

How should we schedule across time?—very carefully.

IS CONSISTENCY DIFFICULT?

If one were to take the principle *"Behavior that is partially reinforced is the most difficult to extinguish"* and asked to devise a system whereby he could make a million dollars through its use, one might come up with gambling. As has been previously stated, gambling is an activity that represents partial reinforcement at its best. If a gambler knows he will always lose, he will not gamble. Obviously he cannot always win, so the trick is to structure the environment so that he *wins* often enough to *lose* his money in the long run.

Such is the case with other behavior for many students have been taught to gamble. The child does not remember the 1,321 times he went to bed at 8:00 P.M. He remembers the two times he got to stay up. The third grader does not really believe that the teacher will send him to "the time-out room (isolation) for ten minutes." This is already the sixth time the teacher has threatened and nothing has happened yet. The ninth grader cheated before and didn't get caught; why should he get caught this time? The college student has turned in late papers before; why should this professor be such a "hard nose?"

Inconsistency teaches just that—inconsistency. At best it produces gambling children, at worst large-scale mental illness. *The most difficult task for a teacher is consistency!* The teacher should plan how the contingencies are to be structured, make the rules, and *follow through.* The only thing that you teach a child when you break the rules is just that—to break the rules. How pathetic it is to observe children who have many severe maladaptive behaviors that have paid off and therefore allowed to fester for longer and longer periods because of partial reinforcement. It is much like *favorable* responses; we stretch the temporal spans between reinforcement to provide longer periods of productive activity. The reinforcement history of some children's maladaptive responses contains so much partial reinforcement that they will fight for weeks and months before giving up their learned behaviors.

Is consistency difficult?—It is the most difficult aspect of discipline.

IF AT FIRST YOU DON'T SUCCEED?

If behaviors can be learned, they can also be unlearned or relearned. Sometimes in our zeal to get through to our students, we make mistakes. Sometimes regardless of zeal, we make mistakes. The effectiveness of behavioral techniques with severe problem behaviors within mental hospitals and institutions for the retarded and handicapped should give us the courage to move forward. Behavioral techniques have demonstrated that even severely handicapped children can learn much faster and a great deal more than we previously believed possible.

Since it is impossible for the student to maintain two contradictory responses at the same time, the skillful teacher will program to elicit responses *incompatible* with inappropriate behavior. "Count to ten before you get angry; think before you begin your work; raise your hand before you talk; take three big breaths before you cry; speak softly so we can have a soft argument; now we are practicing good grammar; let's take a break so we can begin with freshness; I'll close the curtain so the outside will not distract us; let's put our other materials away before we begin the new activity," and so on. Severe disapproval (punishment) alone may stop inappropriate behavior, but it will not necessarily teach a correct association. The child who is hit with his spoon because he cannot use it properly will not necessarily learn proper etiquette. Similarly, the student who is punished for his faulty reading will not necessarily learn to read efficiently. The one child might shun the spoon; the other student may stop reading. Teaching the incompatible responses is perhaps the most effective behavioral technique because it constitutes a double-edged approach. Not only is the inappropriate behavior eliminated, but it is replaced by a correct response as well. Thus the student unlearns and relearns at the same time. It should be obvious that in this case appropriate responses are directly proportional to decreases in inappropriate responses. This procedure eliminates the need for much disapproval (punishment) and at the same time teaches correct associations. However, the teacher must deal with overt behaviors. *It is much easier to act your way into a new way of thinking than to think your way into a new way of acting.*

Four principles for the teacher are:

1. *Pinpoint:* It is necessary to pinpoint explicitly the behavior that is to be eliminated or established. This takes place at many different levels relating to many differentiated behaviors. It leads to a hierarchical arrangement of skills and behaviors based on expected specific behavioral goals. Do not deal with intangibles or ideas. If the behavior cannot in some way be both *observed* and *measured,* then you can never know if it has been either established or unlearned.

2. *Record:* List the specified behaviors in time intervals (seconds, minutes, hours, AM., etc.) and thereby establish a precise record from which to proceed. Keep the record accurate. Do not guess; be scientific. As maladaptive responses are eliminated, or decreased, more time can be devoted to more productive learning.

3. *Consequate:* Set up the external environmental contingencies (including primarily your own personal responses) and proceed with the program. Contingencies include: approval, withdrawal of approval, disapproval, threat of disapproval, and ignoring. Reinforcement techniques can be: words (spoken or written), expressions (facial or bodily), closeness (nearness or touching), activities (social or individual), and things (materials, food, playthings, awards). Remember that when you ignore, behaviors often initially increase (sometimes for long periods) before they are eliminated.

4. *Evaluate:* Be prepared to stay with a program long enough to ascertain its effectiveness. Compare records after consequating with records taken before. Is the behavior increasing, decreasing, or remaining the same? Learn from your mistakes. And:

"If at first you don't succeed . . ."—Well, you know.

WHEN WILL STRUCTURE END?

It is clear that the final goal of the education process is to provide the student with behaviors necessary for self-discipline. Indeed, persons whom we as teachers have the privilege to instruct and teach at some future time must be able to be independent. This is, perhaps, the end for which the beginning was made. The goal is achieved less often than most teachers would desire. Students sometimes graduate in ignorance, because of age, to find a job, to get out, but generally not because they have developed sufficient "love" for themselves and others to achieve a state of "independence." We hope that when they must leave for other reasons that then they will be independent. It seems important to insure that this goal is achieved, for when other conditions impinge on the youngsters' environment they must be prepared.

When an individual has learned from his past reinforcement history to arrange his values hierarchically, when he is able to work productively over long periods of time, when he is able to delay gratification, when he is able to be content with his own company and refrain from haphazardly seeking other individuals, when he is able to modify and control the environment that, in turn, controls him, then perhaps he has achieved an appropriate level of independence. Many problems arise in interpersonal relationships because one or more of the individuals are unable to exhibit any independent behavior. Additionally, some teachers are concerned with vague concepts of "togetherness" that somehow are supposed to develop positive values automatically. Like many ideas (as opposed to overt behaviors), these concepts are highly elusive. When teachers sincerely believe that children will turn out all right if only the child graduates or spends time with "good" companions this can be devastating.

It is necessary to specify both the overt behaviors that the individuals value in terms of "independence" and the precise amount of time necessary to effect goals (e.g., honesty, kindness, creativity, sensitivity, communication, spontaneity). Before structuring training for independence, teachers should: (1) assess specific values that they cherish and arrange these values in a hierarchical order from the most to the least important. The next step is to (2) define specific behaviors that relate to each of the abstract values, and then (3) teach these behaviors (values) following the behavioral model. The amount of time to be devoted to teaching as well as the time important to spend with certain individuals (alone or in groups) should be outlined.

"Independence," or lack of it, becomes a problem when individuals are unable to be happy when alone or sometimes even when with others. It would seem that everyone should learn to be happy under each condition, as both situations are considered important. Therefore, structuring specified temporal intervals is important. Individual students should be helped with programs that increase both independent activity and joint activity. Truly happy people seem to be those who are happy to be alone, perhaps even for extended periods of time when necessary (vacations, military service, etc.) and also very happy when with others. This condition is not accomplished by students becoming dependent on others to provide a little more life into an otherwise dull existence. Regular routines to occupy one's time can be developed in advance and be readily available when a person needs to be self-reliant.

When will structure end?—With independence.

TEACHING—ART OR SCIENCE?

The question will continue to be asked: "What makes a good teacher?" We have all known some great teachers as well as others who wane by comparison. Analyzing teaching behavior is really no different from analyzing student behavior. Earlier it was stated that students must know what is expected of them and want to do it. Most teachers have at least a general idea of what is expected of them and also want to be good teachers. However, if they do not structure the behaviors to be learned, practice techniques of effective classroom control and subject-matter presentation, and maintain consistency, then they fail. Every principle relating to student behavior throughout the preceding chapters also applies to the teacher. It is more important, however, for the teacher to realize that *it is the teacher's responsibility* to insure that proper learning actually takes place—not the student's. How easy it is for some teachers to give *their* problem to the students. "They don't want to learn." "I can't wait to get out of this chalkboard jungle." "Why should I care if the students don't?" Perhaps the extreme of this attitude is manifested by some college teachers who judge their academic prowess by how many students they fail. The teacher who really cares will persevere. Through trial and error, the teacher will find better ways to stimulate students toward their optimum potentials. With or without a full understanding of behavioral principles, the teacher will come to find better methods of behavioral control and subject-matter presentation.

The ability to recognize individual differences and to structure a class environment with meaningful contingencies relevant to specific situations represents an outstanding accomplishment. However, good taste is also of major importance. The authors know of one seventh-grade teacher who controlled her class by having the most deviant children "participate in a mock wedding ceremony if they were very bad." When the children evidenced proper behaviors, they were then allowed to "get divorced." This disciplinary procedure was tremendously effective and used behavioral principles. However, it raises serious questions regarding the teaching of other associations.

Another teacher told of a technique she used with second-grade boys. "When a boy misbehaves, I make him wear a girl's ribbon in his hair." Does it work? Very well, but again we question the advisability of such insensitivity. It is ironic that this same teacher thought it "terrible" that parents were asked to send some children to school without breakfast occasionally in order to effect proper behaviors through *rewards* of cereal and milk.

It is readily apparent that regardless of how many "behavioral recipes" are available, the insensitive teacher will still be found wanting. The art of being a good teacher seems directly contingent on the behaviors of the teacher as a person. Modeling effects assimilated through the influence of an outstanding individual are still some of the most powerful and far-reaching. Most teachers will allude to a special teacher in their past who influenced them tremendously, even to the point of going into the profession. The truly effective teacher will combine the science of behavior with the art of living to create that exceptionally rare atmosphere—an environment in which children not only take excitement from discovery but also learn to be nice people.

Teaching—Art or science?

SUMMARY

Teaching—The Art of Discipline

Many teachers leave the teaching profession because they have not developed effective techniques of classroom control and subject-matter presentation. Even though some teachers believe that discipline refers to a continuum from permissiveness through strictness, it is easily observed that this is not the case. Effective discipline ensues from direct cause-and-effect relationships. Therefore, concepts such as spanking versus loving, classroom freedom versus dictatorship, expression versus subjugation are extremely deceptive. Indeed, we discipline only those we love; social freedom can exist only within defined parameters; and self-expression, much like everything else, must be *learned*. The reason we discipline is to provide each child with behaviors necessary for individual productivity. Realizing that decisions determining what constitutes these basic behaviors (curriculum) are our responsibility, we should structure wisely and not deceive ourselves by stating that children are deciding all things for themselves. When we teach children to think (i.e., establish values, decide), we should do so with the express purpose of insuring logical mediational sequencing and not use the euphemism "thinking" as a rationalization to eschew the responsibility of our job. Every teacher should initially realize that the teacher's primary responsibility is to acculturate the child. Teaching a child to spell, read, write, as well as to be well behaved, represents the *imposition* of social and educational values that do not originate with the student. The teacher who states, "Oh, but that's not what I mean," obviously needs some personal remediation in thought processes to differentiate between those aspects of life that are definitely mutually exclusive and those that are not. Every teacher should know precisely what decisions are to be the student's and what decisions are to be the teacher's. If a teacher accepts this responsibility and does not try to "give the problem away," then children will acquire the basic learnings necessary to develop their own values. Regardless, one should realize that it takes a tremendous amount of courage to act on the basis of one's value orientation, whether he be student or teacher.

Discipline—The Way to Learning

Learning necessitates experience, discrimination, and association. The first aspect of learning both socially and academically is to determine just *where the student is.* That is, to determine what behaviors currently are present and, therefore, to know precisely where to start. *Academic learning* involves structuring subject matter in easily attainable sequential steps beginning at the student's own level. In assessing *maladaptive responses,* the deviant behavior itself is the foremost concern. An involved history of how the student got that way is both unproductive and unnecessary. Academic assessment should take several days, social assessment several minutes. All too often, knowledge concerning a terrible home life, bizarre past experiences, or personality test scores provides the opportunity for some teachers to give up on the child because the teacher discovers a "reason" for the deviant behavior. If students are not "motivated to learn," then motivation must be taught before the teacher should expect it to be internalized; it must come from without before it can be from within. Desire for learning (motivation) is taught by establishing *rewards* for learning, first extrinsically, later intrinsically. Realizing that at some point learning usually represents work, the teacher must stretch the ratio of previously established rewards to motivate students through the difficult times. This represents a process of partial reinforcement to teach for long-term goals, that is, establish maturity. The teacher also defines limits of acceptable behavior by initially deciding which decisions are to rest with the student and which with the teacher.

Learning—The Modification of Behavior

Behavior modification is a process for structuring both social and academic learning experiences to provide both fine discriminations and correct associations. It seems amazing that there are some teachers who cannot imagine students being able to learn *academic* behavior without receiving feedback (e.g., math) and yet cannot imagine why they should give any feedback for *social* behavior. The teacher must deal with specified overtly demonstrable behaviors, however, if the teacher expects to know what has been learned. It has been demonstrated that if a student knows precisely what is expected of him and if he wants to do it, he probably will. Preparing expectancies for students necessitates the structure of goals. Instructional goals should represent definable overt responses that are realistic, manageable, and, above all, measurable. All behaviors, both social and academic, must be measured *in time intervals.* Precise and accurate records must be kept.

Behavior–The Contingent Result of Life

Behaviors are learned in time through contingent reinforcement. Therefore the teacher must structure the student's life experiences if effective learning is to take place. How much control is to be exercised depends on the values of the teacher (deciding who has the problem). *Reinforcement teaching is the structure of approval and disapproval responses, in time, to shape desired behavior toward specific goals.* Deviant behavior is often eliminated by cutting out the payoff; wholesome learning is established by instituting a payoff. The teacher must observe the student closely–paying particular attention to what happens immediately before and after a specified behavior–to become proficient in behavioral analysis. It should be remembered that when the teacher begins to structure or restructure environmental contingencies, problems of "fairness" arise. The teacher then must discriminate between many separate and related social and/or academic issues to decide what is to be done, that is, what's fair. Approval-disapproval techniques for shaping desired behavior include every available personal response as well as all objects at the teacher's disposal: subject matter, words, expressions, closeness, activities, and things. Personal responses should be overtly practiced. Merely reading, discussing, and thinking about responses is not enough to develop these tools effectively.

Life–The Structure of Activities in Time

Everything happens in time; indeed, *life is time.* Temporal aspects of life are not only extremely important but highly elusive as well. Therefore, precise timing in delivering responses cannot be overemphasized. While temporal consistency is the single most important aspect of discipline, it is also the most difficult. In order to discipline effectively, the teacher must structure everything *in time*. Structural manipulation of the external environment is based on these steps: (1) *Pinpoint*—defining the *problem* behavior to be eliminated, the *new behavior* to be learned, or both (teaching incompatible responses). Pinpointing regarding *subject matter* is accomplished by structuring specific measurable goals; pinpointing *maladaptive social responses* necessitates defining deviant responses specifically in overt categories and observing the child carefully. These observations not only establish what stimuli are presently reinforcing undesired behavior but also provide clues for selecting effective reinforcers that can be used to establish other responses. (2) *Record*—assessing behavior quantitatively. It is imperative that accurate records be kept. Otherwise the teacher can never ascertain the relationship between the frequency and magnitude of the *old* social/academic, adaptive/deviant behaviors and the new. Records must be precise and recordings must be done *in time intervals*. (3) *Consequate*—controlling the external environment through the use of approval-disapproval reinforcers delivered contingently on time schedules to teach desired behaviors. (4) *Evaluate*—measuring the frequency of behavior to see if the behavior gets better or worse. Most often, thoughtfully prescribed contingencies decrease objectionable behaviors from the original recorded level and/or increase desirable responses. If selected reinforcers are not effective, a new structure may be required and other contingencies established. Indeed, restructuring regarding all aspects of instruction should represent a continuous process toward greater refinement and increased teaching effectiveness aimed toward student independence.

Effective teaching takes much practice. Similar to other pursuits in life, the rewards of teaching seem both proportional to, and contingent on, thoughtful involvement, structured action, and continuous learning and evaluation. Hopefully, the end product of this teaching will be a person who is informed, who is individually productive and socially responsible, who has the ability to analyze, criticize, and choose alternatives, and who has a compelling system of values whereby he may actualize his life in a manner consistent with ever-increasing knowledge—in a word, a person who evidences discipline.

STUDY GUIDE FOR CHAPTER 5

Questions:

1. Explain how time is important in relating to life.

2. What is meant by the statement that rewards must come after the fact if they are to be effective?

*3. Explain the various fixed and variable schedules using your own examples.

*4. What is meant by the statement, "Partial reinforcement is the most difficult to extinguish?"

*5. Why do you think consistency is the most difficult task for a teacher? Give an example.

6. Explain why it is much easier to act your way into a new way of thinking than to think your way into a new way of acting.

7. List and describe the four steps teachers can use in modifying classroom behavior.

8. What elements contribute to independence?

9. How would you teach independence behaviorally?

*10. Why is teaching an art as well as a science?

*Transfer these questions to your own teaching situation (e.g., Music, Preschool).

LEARNING ACTIVITY 9—TIME AND BEHAVIOR MODIFICATION

1. Write an essay on: How is time important in modifying behavior? Make certain you concern yourself with the issues of (a) when the reinforcement is delivered, (b) increases in the success rate of material learned, (c) partial reinforcement effects, and (d) the learning of a reinforcement schedule.

2. Discuss, in groups or in writing, how gambling is an illustration of the effects of partial reinforcement.

3. Using the pinpoint model, indicate:

   a) How you would reinforce someone in order that they become a constant gambler

   b) How you would reinforce someone in order that he become a person who will never gamble

   c) How you would teach an adult illiterate to learn to read, using the same consequences in a and b above

Read and discuss other participants' essays and indicate how you would apply the same principle to academic responses (reading, mathematics, obeying classroom rules) by substituting actual academic behaviors for the gambling activity.

LEARNING ACTIVITY 10–
SELF-MODIFICATION

Principles are generally more useful after one has used them on oneself. Therefore, include all four aspects of the teaching principles (pinpoint, record, consequate, and evaluate) and develop some specific procedures to change one of your own behaviors:

1. An inappropriate behavior you choose to decrease in yourself
2. An appropriate behavior you choose to increase in yourself
3. A behavior either appropriate or inappropriate you desire to change in another person: child, supervisor, spouse, roommate, fiance. It is assumed that any attempt to change behaviors of others will be discussed with the person involved and consent obtained prior to beginning any program.

Remember to pinpoint the precise behavior(s) that will be recorded and set up an observational recording system with specific time intervals and specific times of the day when recording will take place. Record the occurrence of the behavioral pinpoint for at least five observational periods (in some instances more than one can occur on the same day) so adequate recording (baseline data) can take place prior to institution of the consequences. Consequences should be honestly applied and recorded for at least five days or longer before evaluation takes place. If the behavior does not change in the desired direction with the contingencies as applied, then "Try, try again" by implementing additional consequences.

General Objectives: The student will conduct a behavioral change project on a child, another student or friend, or him/herself. Any project on another person must be preceded by a signed permission form by that person or, in the case of a child, by the child's legal guardian. This permission form must include the behavior to be changed and a brief description of the method.

Project Description: The project is to include at least 15 days of data taken at least once per day. Five days of "baseline" data is to be recorded before any program of contingencies is instituted and at least 10 days of data are to be obtained after the contingencies are begun. If possible, there is to be at least one "reliability check,"

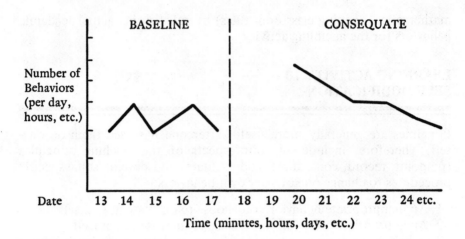

that is, another person independently taking data at the same time in the same place, and so on.

Contents of Final Report: The report will consist of four sections: (1) pinpoint, (2) record, (3) consequate, (4) evaluate. Each part will contain the following information.

Pinpoint: A. A brief description of the subject including age, sex, major (if appropriate), and so on. B. A brief description of the history of the problem. C. A behavioral description of the problem to be changed. D. The desired direction of change.

Record: A. The unit of behavior being recorded. B. The unit of time of observation. C. The precise observation procedure, that is, exactly what was done to record the behavior. D. How the reliability check was made.

Consequate: A. A precise description of what the subject must do to earn the rewards of punishers, and so on.

Evaluate: A graph of the 15 days of data, the baseline data separated by a vertical line. The occurrences of behavior should be on the ordinate, that is, up and down on the vertical axis and the units of time on the abcissa, that is, across on the horizontal axis. See the example above.

BEHAVIORAL PRINCIPLES APPLIED

CHAPTER 6

Changing Wrong Associations

The preceding essays comprising Part I were not presented to express maverick points of view. These issues were developed to prepare the teacher to deal with human behavior more objectively. It is extremely easy to make-believe, to pretend that behavior is mystical and that somehow children will learn the opposite of what they are taught. Are the fine, gifted students direct products of our inspired teaching, whereas the slow, mischievous, or dull students products of someone else? If we are honest, we must take our share of the grief as well as the joy. Perhaps the most frightening aspect of teaching is that behavior is most certainly learned, and, for this, we as teachers must take full responsibility. Pretending is easier, for discipline is an awesome challenge. We prefer to believe that the deviant child will somehow change—that his bad behavior is just a stage, or if only he could work it out of his system everything would be all right. We hope, but hope wears thin without positive signs of improvement. We struggle, we wait, we often become discouraged, and finally we realize that it is indeed a cause-and-effect world—in the long run we do "reap what we sow." After myths are laid aside; after the teacher stops worrying and starts acting; after personal beliefs, consistency, and individual responsibility are all in harmony—the teacher begins to teach. Subsequently, behavior becomes more predictable and effects of specific actions assured. As behavioral principles are practiced and applied, the teacher becomes confident that *wrong associations can indeed be changed.*

The following examples represent selected scientific and professional applications of behavioral changing. These excerpts are
presented in a form that should be easily understood by teachers.
Scientific Applications are summaries of scientific studies that have
been published in journals or presented by researchers at scientific
conventions. Sources for these reports are noted in the reference
section with the example number preceding the reference. *Professional Applications* represent the attempts of "ordinary" teachers,
parents, counselors, and others to deal with specific problems systematically. These examples are selected from the authors' files.

This format does not begin to do justice to the original reports.
The thoughtful reader will not only seek other professional examples
directly applicable to his own teaching situation but will also begin to
read original scientific literature while trying to study carefully the
cause-and-effect relationships obviously evidenced in behavioral
research and writing. The Introduction to Behavioral Terminology
pp. 260–283 is designed to help in this transition. It is important
for the teacher to understand the principles underlying discipline
before choosing specific techniques.

It is important that as you progress through the following examples you make the discriminations necessary for implementing an
effective program in relationship to your own values. Some of the
pinpointed behaviors may seem very "wrong" to you. Additionally,
some of the procedures used to effect change may appear extremely
questionable. It is mandatory that you differentiate amount the many
examples in order to select both behaviors and procedures that are
appropriate to your own value system and personal teaching style.
As has been stressed repeatedly, just because something is behaviorally
effective does not indicate that it ought to be done. The following
examples include many different behaviors and procedures that are
not school related intended to stimulate thought toward greater understanding and sensitivity. There are several examples (that while
effective) are not within the value system of the authors. *Each
person must discriminate.* Processes and principles are of much greater
consequence than is the choice of reinforcers. When processes of
education are fully understood, fanciful gimmicks become sound
pedagogy.

The examples are structured to start with simple applications
and progress to more difficult and complex issues with some devia-
tion for variety. The following is a list of examples in relationship
to developmental areas.

PINPOINT REFERENCE GUIDE

Preschool Examples

Example number	Pinpoint
1	Fear in young children
2	Fighting over toys
3	Crying when parents leave child at nursery
4	Low-frequency talking
5	Crawling during school
6	Discriminating rules for visiting children
7	Assessing truth
8	Physical aggression
9	Aggressive hitting
10	Isolate behavior
11	Walking in street
12	Repeated crying
13	Sex-role behavior
14	Mistreatment of animals
15	Screaming, yelling, fighting between siblings
16	Temper outbursts
17	Determining effective rewards to increase learning
18	Breaking household rules
19	Self-help behaviors
20	"Disobedience" and "aggression"
21	Children manipulating parents

Lower Primary Examples

Example number	Pinpoint
22	Show-off
23	Fear of going to school
24	Increases in speaking about oneself

Lower Primary Examples (cont.)

Example number	Pinpoint
25	Talking, standing, blurting out, noisy inattention, turning around
26	Child asks about sex
27	"Off-task" during individual seatwork
28	Striking children with objects
29	Following instructions
30	Inappropriate behaviors
31	Failure to eat "nourishing" foods
32	Hyperactivity
33	Writing vulgar words
34	Standing up, walking around
35	Using subject matter to reinforce low-level subject matter
36	Arson
37	Rest time disruptions
38	Teaching beginning reading
39	"Bad attitude"
40	Thumb-sucking
41	Unfinished assignments, bothering neighbors, playing
42	"On-task" attention, academic accuracy

Upper Primary Examples

Example number	Pinpoint
43	Bothering teacher at desk
44	Teasing other children
45	Child interfering with other child's play
46	Overactivity
47	Littering
48	Disruptive classroom behavior
49	Positive piano practice
50	Disruptive noise
51	Reading "bad" literature

52	High noise level—lunchroom
53	Arithmetic achievement
54	Excessive dawdling
55	Teaching lying behavior
56	Inappropriate oral hygiene
57	Classroom "out of control"
58	Negative comments and high intensity "screaming" among family members prior to evening meal
59	Volunteering answers
60	Bed-wetting (enuresis)
61	Academic underachievement
62	Talking out, standing
63	Tardiness following recess
64	Remediation of mutually aversive interactions between a problem student and four teachers

Middle School/Junior High School Examples

Example number	Pinpoint
65	Homework study time
66	Low-level skill achievement
67	Noisy transition changing classes
68	Chewing-gum vandalism
69	Off-task individual study
70	Constant talking out and disturbing others during study time
71	Fighting during recess
72	Vandalism
73	Disruptive behaviors—talking, fighting, out of seat, throwing objects, noisy
74	"Joy riding"
75	Disruptive social talking
76	Juvenile offender
77	Teaching contractual agreements
78	Academic failure
79	Rebelliousness, disagreements, and refusal to talk to parents

Middle School/Junion High School Examples (cont.)

Example number	Pinpoint
80	Increasing math responses
81	Low arithmetic achievement
82	Obesity
83	Negative verbalizations
84	Physical abuse of mother
85	"Off-task," low-achieving students

High School/Adult Examples

Example number	Pinpoint
86	School failure
87	"Love-note" passing—boy-girl talking
88	Homework study
89	Boredom
90	Guffaw laughing
91	Positive verbalizations about oneself and positive social interactions
92	Noncooperation
93	Use of illegal drugs
94	Fear of failure, worrying
95	Rehearsal effectiveness
96	Using adoption to control adults
97	Garbage removal from kitchen
98	Embarrassment
99	"Inappropriate" sexual advances
100	Lawbreaking
101	Excessive local directory-assistance telephone calls
102	Low-level English achievement
103	Academic "apathy"
104	"On-task" versus cluttered communication
105	Developing a study routine
106	Dishonesty

PRESCHOOL EXAMPLES

Example 1

Pinpoint: Fear in young children (separate studies concerning 600 children, infants and school age)

Record: Overt signs of fear exhibited whenever children confronted fearful situations. Procedures reported from parent interviews and classified according to effectiveness.

Consequate: Following procedures reported effective by parents: (1) *Incompatible response.* Feared object or situation gradually introduced into child's presence while child engaged in fun activity; (2) *Gradual approach.* Child led by degrees (over a number of days) to come closer and closer to feared object or participate in feared activity; (3) *Modeling.* Feared activity or object made readily accessible to child while other children participated enjoyably.

Evaluate: *Incompatible responses, gradual approach,* and *modeling* eliminated about 85% of children's fears, according to parents.

Note: The following procedures were *not* successful: disapproval, social ridicule, scolding, verbal appeals, punishment, forcing child to participate, or changing the child's activity whenever he was afraid. When any fearful situation is forced on a child, fear may be *increased.*

Scientific Application (p. 306)

Example 2

Pinpoint: Fighting over toys (2- and 6-year-old boys)

Record: Children fought as to who owned particular toy (four times in A.M.); mother admonished children to share.

Consequate: Program instituted to teach children: (1) ownership and (2) sharing. Children told "ownership is when a toy belongs to you, and you can do anything you want with it," and "sharing is when you let somebody else use something that belongs to you." Children given separate toys (some for John, some for Marc, some for both), again admonished to share, and praised when they did.

Evaluate: Children initially hoarded their own toys (two weeks), then began to trade (three occurrences, two days), then to share (sixteen instances over four days). Fighting over toys diminished to an average of less than one per day.

Professional Application

Example 3

Pinpoint: *Crying when parents leave child at nursery* (18 children, infants through 6 years old)

Record: Parents recorded children crying and clinging an average of 9 to 12 times and also commented on "general upsetness" when parents ready to leave child (15 minutes prior to leaving, two to six observations).

Consequate: Parents "proved" to child they always come back (building hope in the child). Parents kissed child goodbye, ignored clinging, left immediately, walked around nursery, came back in the door. (Parents instructed to always wait until crying ceased before reentering.) Parents again left following same routine (hug and kiss), promising to return shortly. (Any hesitation at door reinforces crying; it is even worse to comfort child after he begins to cry, which teaches him that if he is upset enough he can delay parents' exit.) This same procedure followed for varying lengths of time (ten seconds, two minutes, thirty seconds, four minutes, one minute, six minutes, etc., the technique is then expanded to longer periods of time). About every third time a special little treat is given to the child for being nice when parents arrive.

Evaluate: Goodbyes became happy times as children anticipate parents sometimes coming back with special small toys or treats.

Note: It is suggested to parents that when they begin this program for the first time, they begin at least one hour prior to normal departure time.

Professional Application

Example 4

Pinpoint: *Low-frequency talking* (4-year-old girl)

Record: Verbalization occurred only during 11% of all 10-second intervals observed (trained observers).

Consequate: Teacher attention to child contingent on talking; when child did not talk, she was ignored by teacher. Child also required to answer questions when requesting materials before receiving them (materials contingent on question answering).

Evaluate: Talking increased to average 75%.

What would happen if . . .

Consequate II: Teacher attention to child contingent on nonverbalization; when child talked, child ignored by teacher. (Reversal of contingencies.)

Evaluate II: Talking decreased to 6%.

Consequate III: Again teacher gave attention for verbalizations, but stopped requiring talking before providing requested materials.

Evaluate III: Child's talking increased to 61%, dropped to 28% when questioning and further talking eliminated.

Note: Authors indicate that since talking dropped when teacher discontinued the questioning as requirement for receiving materials, it is clear that it was not the teacher's social approval alone that was responsible for the high rate of talking. They report that questioning the child and requiring several responses before allowing access to materials is crucial.

Scientific Application (p. 306)

Example 5

Pinpoint: Crawling during school (nursery school, girl 3.4 years)

Record: Girl spent 75% of time (observed two weeks) in off-feet position. Also avoided contacts with other children and adults.

Consequate: Nursery school teachers *ignored* girl when not standing; approached, praised, displayed interest when girl on feet. Disapproval techniques such as anger, shame, disgust, or disappointment not used.

Evaluate: Girl stood 75% of time during first week. During second week, up as much as other children.

Consequate II: Contingencies reversed. Teachers approved *off*-feet behavior.

Evaluate II: First day of reversal, girl off-feet 75% of time; second day 81.9%.

Consequate III: Return to praise for standing.

Evaluate III: First hour of first day, on-feet 75.9%; first hour of second day, 62.7%; by second hour, 100%. *No relapses observed.*

Scientific Application (p. 306)

Example 6

Pinpoint: Discriminating rules for visiting children (13 children, 2 to 9 years old)

Record: "Total bedlam" (three visits from other children) reported by one parent who said, "If I have to put up with those neighbor's children again, I'll even stop letting their parents visit." Another parent, "I can't do anything with that child after she comes from Grandmother's."

Consequate: *Difficult* program to teach parents to have enough courage to enforce their own rules with other children and also with visits to grandparents. *Simple* program to teach visiting children discriminations. "In this house you must follow (different) rules." Visiting children told when entered house about expectations and consequences: "If you play nicely, you may have a treat, and if you break our rules (carefully explained), you must leave."
    Own children told "when we are home from grandparents' we have different rules."

Evaluate: Children learned to discriminate (rowdy, undisciplined, only in situations where allowed) and followed rules in orderly house after being sent home twice (average) first week. Own children took average of one day to "shape up" after visit to grandparents.

Note: Only adults' behavior presents problems in these situations. However, an initial strong positive approach with other parents, especially one's own, usually solves the problem. When adults do set strong limits with neighbor's children (especially if they pay off from time to time, children's good behavior), their house will usually be the one all the children "love to visit." When grandparents visit it is wise to give them a set of the child's rules when they arrive, making sure to correct grandparents' deviations immediately and gently. Children also learn different rules in different classrooms.

Professional Application

Example 7

Pinpoint: *Assessing truth* (12 children, all under 6 years old)

Record: Children suspected of wrongdoing, that is, in this particular case parent entered room of two children after younger brother started to cry (parent's self-report).

Consequate: "Annabelle story" (or masculine counterpart name) instituted. Child given story paradigm that initially described a little boy or girl with all aspects of child's own physical features, home environment, and so on. After this initial programming, the suspected wrong is then recounted vicariously. For example, "Cherrie, you have such nice blue eyes, and you are such a big four-year-old with nice toys and a little brother. I am going to tell you a story. There once was a girl named Annabelle. She had pretty blue eyes and she was a big four-year-old. Annabelle also had a little brother. One day Annabelle was playing with her little brother, and Annabelle's mother heard the little brother crying. Why do you think Annabelle's brother was crying?"

Evaluate: Cherrie, "Because he took Annabelle's toy, and Annabelle hit him."

Note: This procedure works almost always with young children because children of this age do not have the power to think abstractly. It is often extremely difficult for parents to believe that children do not realize they are describing themselves.

Professional Application

Example 8

Pinpoint: Physical aggression (nursery school, 27 3 to 4-year-old boys)

Record: Physical aggression frequency during observation period totaled 41.2 incidents, verbal aggression 22.8, with total 64.0 incidents (one-week observation).

Consequate: Teachers ignored aggression and rewarded cooperative and peaceful behaviors (interfered only when bodily harm was likely). Approval techniques replaced reprimands.

Evaluate: Total aggressive behaviors decreased—64 incidents to 43.4. (Physical aggression 41.2 to 26.0; verbal aggression 22.8 to 17.4.)

Consequate II: Following initial consequate, researchers told teachers experiment completed. However, observations again recorded three weeks later.

Evaluate II: After experimenters left, teachers not as consistent. Total number aggressive responses increased 43.4 to 51.6. Physical aggression increased 26.0 to 37.8. However, verbal aggression decreased 16.4 to 13.8. Teachers found it harder to ignore fighting than to ignore verbal threats.)

Consequate III: Consequate I reinstated.

Evaluate III: Total aggression decreased 51.6 to 25.6. Physical aggression decreased 37.8 to 21.0; verbal aggression 13.8 to 4.6.

Note: This study substantiates the necessity of *absolute consistency.*

Scientific Application (p. 306)

Example 9

Pinpoint: *Aggressive hitting* (preschool boys, private kindergarten)

Record: Teacher complained boys went "out of control" during outside play periods (five children hurt in one week). ·

Consequate: Large punching bag dummy with red nose installed on playground.

Evaluate: No noticeable decrease in human hitting—six children hurt during week. Dummy punched frequently, especially in nose. (Actually, boys fought each other to take turns at dummy.)

Consequate II: Punching dummy removed. Individual boys isolated for duration of play period when observed hitting another child.

Evaluate II: After five days (seventeen isolations), hitting completely eliminated.

Note: Hitting, like other behavior, is most probably *learned.* The more children are reinforced for hitting, the more they will hit. Some people even develop a curious "self-fulfilling prophecy" in this regard. They sincerely believe that if they could just hit something they would feel much better. Thus, when frustrated, they hit something and, sure enough, they feel better.

Professional Application

Example 10

Pinpoint: Isolate behavior (girl, age 4.3 years)

Record: Varied repertory of well-developed skills pleased adults but did not gain child-child interactions. Observations during entire mornings by trained observers (one week) indicated: 10% child interaction, 40% adult interaction, 50% isolate.

Consequate: Maximum adult attention for child interaction. *No* attention for isolate behavior or adult interaction.

Evaluate: Over six days, child interaction increased to 60%, adult interaction decreased to 20%, time spent alone 20%.

Consequate II: Contingencies withdrawn.

Evaluate II: Child interaction *decreased* to 20%, adult *increased* to 40%, isolate 40%.

Consequate III: Contingencies reestablished. Attention for interaction with children. Child interaction increased to 60%, adult decreased to 25%, 15% isolate.

Note: Follow-up observation showed girl to be maintaining the increased ratio of child interaction.

Scientific Application (p. 306)

Example 11

Pinpoint: *Walking in the street* (1.5 to 4-year-old boys and girls)

Record: Various occurrences (parent's self-report).

Consequate: Children spanked, yelled at for going into street, given approval for verbalizing comments concerning "not going into street"; taken to edge of pavement and taught discrimination if preverbal, that is, child put on grass, given approval taken barely onto pavement spanked, yelled at. Child taught that when they hold parents' hand then and only then may they walk in or across streets, parking lots, and so on.

Evaluate: ?

Note: The strength of reinforcement required for teaching should be in direct proportion to the danger involved. (It seems unwise to put both dirty hands and potential death into the same "no-no" basket.) Sometimes complete supervision or instilling fear is the early alternative to potential danger; sometimes teaching for discrimination is advisable (i.e., concerning knives, hot stoves, scissors, electricity, poisons, water). *The adult must decide what is important.*

Professional Application

Example 12

Pinpoint: Repeated crying (4-year-old boy, preschool)

Record: Eight crying periods each morning following mild frustrations.

Whenever boy cried, teachers comforted him (picked up, talked softly, held on lap, etc.).

Consequate: Boy ignored unless "real grounds" for crying; given approval for self-help attempts.

Evaluate: One crying spell in five days after initial decrease.

Consequate II: Teachers again paid attention to crying (10 days).

Evaluate II: Crying almost reached original level during record phase.

Consequate III: Boy ignored when crying; given approval for self-help (10 days).

Evaluate III: Crying decreased to zero and low level maintained.

Note: The cause-and-effect relationship between adult approval and child behaviors is clearly demonstrated in this case. The reader may be wondering why one would deliberately produce inappropriate behavior in a student. In a research study, the experimenter must determine that a particular reinforcer is really causing a specific effect. In this case the reinforcer was attention—the effect, not crying. When a teacher is "sure"what produces a desired change in the classroom, this may be enough. However, the scientist must be certain. The reversal technique will be noted repeatedly in scientific investigations.

Scientific Application (p. 306)

Example 13

Pinpoint: *Sex-role behavior* (175 boys, 85 girls; ages 5 years, 10 months, to 6 years, 8 months)

Record: Series of experimental studies recorded amount of play with toys that have been traditionally considered as sex-typed, as well as neutral toys. ("Girls'" toys included doll, pearl beads, high-heeled shoes, a mirror, and play make-up materials, cups and dishes, and a baby carriage with a doll; "boys'" toys consisted of boxing gloves, a tank, a racing car, a sword, a gun, a catcher's mitt and a baseball; neutral toys included a pegboard, three old blocks, and three pieces of tinker toys. The neutral toys were deliberately less inviting for purposes of the experiments.)

Consequate: Children observed peer and adult models playing with either "sex-inappropriate" or "sex-appropriate" toys. Some models gave approving or disapproving comments; that is, "I don't want to play with those; they are girls' toys." Some models said nothing while playing with toys and others gave verbal cues as well as playing. (Five separate experimental studies were completed with excellent control groups.)

Evaluate: Even with little total time exposure to models (less than 10 minutes), when children saw peer and adults playing with toys, they increased the time spent with toys. Children who saw models receive approval after playing with certain toys played more with these toys themselves (even when no approval was given to children). Children who observed others receive disapproval for playing with certain toys tended to avoid the same toys themselves. Children who observed someone giving themselves reasons for not playing with certain toys and who did not engage in play themselves were better able to gain similar control over their own behavior.

Note: These studies are extremely important for those who desire to increase or *decrease* the sex-role identity of children. Society has changed very dramatically in the last few years, and it becomes more and more difficult to draw distinctions between masculine and feminine roles. Adults who are concerned should label verbally and reinforce whatever they consider to be appropriate behavior from a very young age to discriminate or not discriminate differentiations that fit within the value system of the adults. These studies clearly demonstrate the cause-and-effect relationship between: (1) supplying a child with the label, (2) modeling appropriate behaviors, and (3) producing same. It appears obvious that in the above study the "boys" and "girls" toys could have been reversed or mixed with similar results.

Scientific Application (p. 306)

Example 14

Pinpoint: *Mistreatment of animals* (5-year-old boy)

Record: Neighborhood adults reported to parents they had seen boy beating their dog with sticks. Child also observed putting cats under water (four occurrences in six weeks).

Consequate: Parents purchased small dog, made son completely responsible for care and feeding, including exercise. Boy paid 25¢ per day when pet was fed and exercised. When boy forgot, he fed dog before he was allowed to eat himself. No payment was made when he forgot.

Evaluate: No incidents of animal abuse during next two weeks.

Note: After the boy had cared for his pet for six weeks he stated that he did not want any money for doing it anymore because now he really "loved Rags." It seems we learn to love by doing—perhaps this helps explain why parents love their children.

Professional Application

Example 15

Pinpoint: *Screaming, yelling, fighting between siblings* (two boys, 3 and 6 years old)

Record: Boys fought whenever alone, damaged toys and furniture, older boy had recently broken neighbor's window. Observers (trained) watched when mother was not present (60 to 90 minutes daily). Inappropriate behaviors (kicking, hitting, pushing, name-calling, throwing objects at each other) and cooperative behaviors (asking for something, requesting help, pleasant talking, playing close), combined, produced a cooperative behavior ratio of 46% (cooperative behavior divided by cooperative behavior plus inappropriate behavior). Six-year-old boy professionally diagnosed as "immature and brain-damaged" as he was hyperactive, aggressive, and destructive. Observations indicated mother paid attention only after high-intensity inappropriate responses.

Consequate: Cooperative responses given approval by placing small candies in mouth and saying "good" every time a cooperative response occurred during *first two days*. Approval (things and words) given every second to fourth cooperative behavior next two days. Mother's helper (professional) told boys they would receive approval if they asked for things saying please and thank you, answered questions, and played nicely together. Instructions repeated each day. On the fifth day a token check mark system plus instructions instituted. Both boys' names written on chalkboard in playroom. Checks earned for cooperative behaviors were removed for inappropriate behaviors. Checks exchanged for candy bars, bubble gum, caps, kites, comic books, puzzles, small toys (total cost $10.67). Boys' "price" paid for goodies was continually increased. Candies discontinued on twelfth day; a check system only for last four days.

Evaluate: Cooperative play averaged 85% (16 consequate days). Gradual rise in cooperative behavior prevailed (last day 100%) even though prices increased throughout program.

Consequate II: Check system removed for five days (observers recorded behavior but did not dispense approval).

Evaluate II: Cooperative behavior declined when no approval given (average 50%).

Consequate III: Check system reinstated with mother taking over management second day. Cooperative behavior increased but since some intense fighting occurred periodically, mother added disapproval contingency. When either child kicked, hit, pushed, name-called, or threw object mother placed boy in bathroom (interesting items removed, closed door, and left him) for five minutes (last three minutes had to be quiet time for boy to rejoin group). Isolation used once per day for each child during first three days, only once overall during last four. Mother also increased amount of checks necessary for approval rewards (raised prices). Children cooperated for three days before purchase possible. Mother also given help in knowing when to use contact and words in approving manner.

Evaluate III: Combination of procedures, administered by mother, resulted in cooperative play ratio of 90%. Experiment in effect for an hour and a half during day, but as study concluded both parents practiced using behavioral principles throughout day. Teacher of older boy reported school behaviors improved.

Note: Authors of this scientific study reported parents had probably extinguished many behaviors of the older boy for lack of attention except for very high-intensity behaviors, which received much verbal and physical attention (many spankings). Following study, parents started to change, that is, they reported using more approval to initiate and maintain appropriate behavior and established token systems for some household chores. Authors reported parents surprised that a "brain-damaged" child could respond. It would appear that placing these kinds of labels on children solves few if any problems and may even generate feelings of futility within the parents rather than determination to do the best job possible. Some parents give the problem away (abdicate responsibility) because child is brain-damaged, retarded, autistic, neurotic, emotionally disturbed, or any number of labels that may lead to resignation rather than a behavioral analysis of what is possible. *Every* child is "normal" in many ways, and *every* child is abnormal in others.

Scientific Application (p. 307)

Example 16

Pinpoint: Temper outbursts. (4-year-old boy—IQ recorded 72 and 80—possible brain damage)

Record: Frequency of objectionable behaviors varied from 18 to 112 during 16 one-hour periods (sticking out tongue, kicking, yelling, threatening to remove clothing, calling people names, throwing objects, biting, and hitting self).

Consequate: Consequences applied by mother in home two to three times per week for six one-hour sessions. Researchers helped mother by giving signals indicating: (1) she should tell her son to stop what he was doing, (2) place him in isolation for five minutes, or (3) given attention, praise, and affection.

Evaluate: Rate of objectionable behavior decreased (range one to eight per session). Isolation used four times; special attention given ten times.

Consequate II: No signals given; mother told to *"act as before."*

Evaluate II: Objectionable behaviors increased, but ranged well below original recordings (two to twenty-four per session). It appeared mother "learned." She reported more self-assurance, increased attention, delivered firm commands, and did not give in after denying a request.

Consequate III: Consequate I reinstated, except special attention for desirable play excluded.

Evaluate III: Objectionable behavior again *decreased* (almost identical to Consequate I, ranging from two to eight per session).

Note: No contact was maintained with the mother for twenty-four days after the experiment. She was given no instructions as to how to act and was given complete freedom to use any technique she desired. Later, three-session postcontact check was made. Even after this long delay, the behaviors considered objectionable were still very low. The mother reported that her child was well behaved and less demanding. Isolation was used on the average of once per week. The mother's attitude toward her son was also considered to be more approving.

Scientific Application (p. 307)

Example 17

Pinpoint: *Determining effective rewards to increase learning* (kindergarten classes, 88 children)

Record: Low-level discrimination on auditory discrimination test.

Consequate: Contingent rewards for meeting daily criterion on auditory tasks. Reward groups consisted of (1) TV music lessons, (2) free play, (3) choice of TV *or* free play, (4) no-contact control group.

Evaluate: All those reward groups improved significantly on tested auditory discrimination.

Note: The children who were assigned to the TV reward improved as much as the group who were assigned the free play contingency. Since the educational television also produced academic learning, it would seem advisable to use educational rewards as much as possible.

Scientific Application (p. 307)

Example 18

Pinpoint: *Breaking household rules* (3- and 4-year-old boys)

Record: From 9 A.M. to 12 noon, mother's recording (six days) indicated an average of 29 rule violations—playing in toilet, pulling dog's tail, climbing in kitchen, breakable items removed from cupboards, toys left out, changing TV and stereo knobs, taking telephone off hook, throwing artificial fruit; that is, "doing the don'ts." Mother "caught the boys" about 22 times daily and (1) told them "why" what they were doing was wrong (reasoning), (2) scolded them, and (3) either slapped their hands or bottoms. Mother remarked, "Why can't they just play and stay out of things until I get the housework done; I play with them in the afternoons.

Consequate: Mother instructed to (1) ignore minor deviations unless someone could be hurt, (2) give great deal of praise for good behavior; that is, "catch each child being good" and verbally praise at least five times per hour each day, at same time pass out chips, let boys "spend" them later on goodies," (3) use approval for one child when the other is inappropriate; for instance, "you're playing nicely, you didn't turn the TV dials," (after brother has turned dials), (4) when disapproval is warranted punish immediately with no talking or warning, generally by complete isolation, for a period of not more than minutes, and (5) go over household rules each morning plus three or four times per day when boys *are following* rules, *not* when they are disobedient.

Evaluate: Mother praised each child on an average of 13 times per morning. She also stated other instructions were followed. Disapproval averaged 34 during first three days with 27 isolations. Mother called consultant to report records and said behavior "hadn't changed" but had increased. Conversation indicated behavior change had indeed taken place (an increase in misbehavior). Mother instructed to maintain the contingencies for 10 days. Next day (fourth) misbehavior decreased (23) with further daily decreases to average of three per day (ninth day).

Note: Disapproval (corporal punishment) was used in this case to stop inappropriate behavior as well as isolation. When removing the child from a positive surrounding, one must be certain that isolation is not more rewarding (e.g., playroom) than the closeness and verbal approval of the mother. Parents should also realize when starting new routines, as in this case, payoffs have been received for a long time by "doing the don'ts."

Professional Application

Example 19

Pinpoint: *Self-help behaviors* (4.5-year-old boy)

Record: Nothing. Boy born blind, severe hearing problem, could not walk, braces on legs, not toilet trained, said no words, could not feed self. (Tested IQ of 22.) Mother waiting to admit boy to large custodial hospital for mentally retarded.

Consequate: Pediatrician assured mother that boy was in good health and that food deprivation would not be harmful for up to 36 hours; mother instructed to not use spoon but to place Rob in high chair, put his fingers in food and lift food to his mouth on his own fingers, three meals daily for two weeks. Following this procedure, his mother prepared Rob's favorite food, sat him in high chair, put his fingers in food, lifted them to within two inches of his mouth, then dropped her hand (this repeated until Rob fed himself or until it had been done 120 times at which time he was taken out of chair and not placed back for period of two hours).

Evaluate: Rob cried when mother dropped her hands, threw his food, and made what mother called "his angry noises." Rob did not eat until deprived of food for 34 hours, and mother left house twice because of his "terrible crying and whimpering."

Note: Most very young children have learned thousands of cause-and-effect relationships regarding consequences of their own behavior, but in this case this young boy had not learned even the very first (i.e., put food in mouth, swallow, pleasant sensation). He had only learned the latter part of the sequence with no causal relationship between his internal behavior and the behavior of the outside environment, that is, getting food into his mouth. Starvation was used to maximize the effect of pleasure derived from the food. This boy, through elaborate series of shaping procedures, learned how to find his own way around the house (rolling to his food from ever greater distances as he couldn't walk), toilet training (using liquid juice as a reward), verbalizations (pairing feel and words starting with body parts), play skills (through the use of contingent music), and then progressed to more normal activities of childhood. These procedures allowed this child first to be placed in a private school for the retarded (behaviorally oriented) and later to enroll in a normal kindergarten. After three years follow-up the child has progressed normally into and through the public schools. Extremely strong contingencies were necessary in this program that started *where the boy was.* It sometimes must be remembered that there is an infinite distance between zero and one.

Professional Application

Example 20

Pinpoint: *"Disobedience" and "aggression"* (4-year, 8 month-old boy)

Record: Trained observers recorded occurrence or nonoccurrence one hour per day (percent of time intervals behavior occurred). Aggression—defined as hitting, pushing, kicking, throwing, biting, and scratching—occurred 7.7% of the time and disobedience—defined as not following instructions by mother, which included name and a command to do or stop doing something specific—occurred 70.0% of the time (average for ten-day observation period). Observers noted that mother gave approval to undesirable behavior and was inconsistent in techniques of reinforcement.

Consequate: Appropriate behavior received praise and "goodies." Whenever mother noted aggressive or disobedient behavior she would tell boy, "You may not stay here (yard or playroom, etc.) if you do not do as you are told," and rapidly take him to time-out (isolation) room and leave him for two minutes. All items of child interest had been removed from the room. Boy remained two minutes *after* he stopped crying, screaming, noise-making.

Evaluate: Aggression decreased to 1.2% and disobedience decreased to 22.0% (average for 10 days of consequences with generally better behavior each day).

Consequate II: Mother returned to original routines, refrained from using "time-out" room.

Evaluate II: Aggression increased to 4.0%, disobedience increased to 57% (average for six days, however, disobedience was 80% on last day).

Consequate III: Mother used "time-out" (isolation) room and comments again as well as praise and "goodies" for appropriate obedience.

Evaluate III: Aggression decreased to 0.3% and disobedience to 22% (four days).

Note: Consistency in following a routine until behavior is changed is demonstrated by the mother applying consequences, removing consequences, and applying them again (reversals). Some children may take an extended period of time to "change wrong associations" and even longer to become "self-motivated." Any new program should have as much consistency as possible for two weeks before something new is attempted.

Scientific Application (p. 307)

Example 21

Pinpoint: Children manipulating parents (three children and mothers trained in Child Development Clinic; a 6-year-old boy attempted to force parents to comply with his wishes; a 4-year-old boy considered excessively dependent at home, aggressive in nursery school; another 4-year-old extremely stubborn in presence of mother but not with other adults)

Record: Each mother observed while interacting with son.

Consequate: Mothers instructed: (1) in delivery of approval techniques, (2) to ignore inappropriate behavior, and (3) to respond with praise and affection for appropriate behavior. Mother A responded positively to child *only* when he did not attempt to force compliance.

Mother B ignored child's dependency, responded approvingly to independent behavior. Mother C ignored oppositional behavior, responded to cooperate behavior. Later, Mother C was instructed to isolate son in empty room for at least five minutes immediately following oppositional responses.

Evaluate: First two boys' behavior improved markedly through mothers' attention to appropriate behavior and ignoring inappropriate responses. The third boy improved only after isolation.

Note: This is a good example of differential treatment. The teacher should always remember that it is necessary to structure for each student. It should be noted that the use of disapproval (isolation) was necessary for one child before improvement took place.

Scientific Application (p. 307)

LOWER PRIMARY EXAMPLES

Example 22

Pinpoint: Show-off (8-year, 8-month-old boy)

Record: Three specific behaviors approved by peers. Out of seat 20 times per day, talking without permission 18 times per day, five incomplete assignments (one week).

Consequate: Program initiated retaining approval from peers. Instead of receiving laughter for getting out of seat and talking, child allowed to tell jokes; instead of receiving attention for misbehaving, child received praise for proper behavior. Boy stayed after school as reward rather than punishment.

Evaluate: First week, talking decreased to two occurrences, left seat only once. Second through fourth week, *no* rules broken. Only one inappropriate behavior in fifth week.

Note: A great deal of "show-off" behavior is maintained by peer attention. If teachers remove one child from the group this often solves the problem.

Scientific Application (p. 307)

Example 23

Pinpoint: Fear of going to school (50 children—ages 4 to 16)

Record: All children frightened of going to school were referred to University Human Development Clinic over eight-year period. They had at least 7 of the following 10 behaviors: (1) first episode of school fear, (2) begun on Monday following an illness previous Thursday or Friday, (3) had begun with no warning, (4) more prevalent in lower grades (40 of 50 children were age 12 or under), (5) mother ill or presumed so by child, (6) child expressed concern about death, (7) parents communicate well, (8) mother and father happy and adjusted in most areas, (9) father shows interest in household management and problems, (10) parents easy to work with (school, church, clinic, etc.).

Consequate: Parents ignored bodily complaints (did not reinforce child's talk about feeling sick), merely made appointment with pediatrician for a time *not* during school hours or, if necessary, a quick examination on way to school. Child was taken to school usually by father, with school personnel instructed to keep child in room when parents left. Parents were told that child's difficulty transient, informed Monday would be difficult, Tuesday better, and by Wednesday, problem generally absent. Parents told not to discuss school attendance over weekend (most referrals late in week). Sunday night parent stated, "Tomorrow you go back to school," and discussion attempts were ignored. Monday morning child was dressed and given a light breakfast (nausea generally existed). No questions were asked about fear (parents therefore did not reinforce fear). Monday evening parents gave approval for going to school *and* staying at school (no matter how many times child cried, vomited, or tried to leave). Child also often seen briefly and explained advantages of going on in face of fear (getting right back on a horse after a fall, etc.).

Evaluate: All 50 cases responded with complete elimination of school fear. All cases followed for at least two years with no recurrences of fear.

Note: Any inappropriate behavior of recent duration with an acute onset is probably best handled immediately. Talking about the problem merely serves to intensify and prolong the behavior by giving a great deal of approval as well as reinforcing procrastination. The time to talk is after something has been done to change. *Talk should not take the place of action.* Of course, where any medical problems may be indicated careful examination is mandatory but should be handled by parents matter-of-factly. Most parents are perfectly capable of handling this type of school fear themselves. Should problems develop that you think extremely severe, then seek professional help immediately.

Scientific Application (p. 307)

Example 24

Pinpoint: Increases in speaking about oneself (third-grade boys, 30; third-grade girls, 28; sixth-grade boys, 21; sixth-grade girls, 20; tenth-grade boys, 20; tenth-grade girls, 30)

Record: Each child verbalized 60 sentences during individual session.

Consequate: Students instructed to begin 60 sentences with pronoun of choice. Researcher commented "good" *only* after sentences starting with the pronoun "I." No comment after any others.

Evaluate: Number of sentences beginning with "I" increased significantly.

Note: This study demonstrated effectiveness of simple approval. However, the study also indicated that the sex of a teacher may also be a factor in effectiveness of approval. *Adolescent* girls responded to praise from the male researcher (first-year medical student) to a greater extent than did adolescent males. With *younger* students, the *boys* began more sentences with "I," indicating a same-sex preference for younger children.

Scientific Application (p. 307)

Example 25

Pinpoint: Talking, standing, blurting out, noisy inattention, turning around (10 children—five different classrooms; ages 6 years, 8 months to 10 years, 6 months; teachers recommended most severe problem children in class)

Record: Trained observers recorded inappropriate social behavior for six weeks. Average inappropriate behavior was 72%.

Consequate: Teachers: (1) made classroom rules explicit; (2) ignored behaviors that interfered with learning or teaching unless dangerous; (3) used withdrawal of approval as punishment; (4) gave praise and attention to behaviors that facilitated learning; and (5) attempted to reinforce prosocial behaviors *incompatible* with inappropriate social behaviors.

Evaluate: Average inappropriate behavior decreased from 72% to 19.5% over an eight-week period.

Note: Participating teachers were given a workshop in behavior modification during the experiment. Opportunities for each teacher to
see daily observation graphs probably helped to increase effectiveness
of the procedures.

Scientific Application (p. 307)

Example 26

Pinpoint: *Child asks about sex* (18 children, 5 to 9 years old)

Record: Children exhibited no factual information—a few "inappropriate" responses when questioned.

Consequate: Program instituted to teach: (1) physiological functions
with appropriate pictures from encyclopedia and other appropriate
sources; (2) appropriate scientific terminology from same; (3) "improper terminology," that is, language used in different settings and by
various subgroups to describe similar processes; (4) value indoctri-
nation, that is, placing all the above within the value orientation of
parents.

Evaluate: Factual information concerning sex verbalized; identification and discrimination concerning use of various words within
proper context (at least four occurrences for each child over two-
week periods).

Professional Application

Example 27

Pinpoint: *"Off-task" during individual seatwork* (six elementary
students, one first grader, two third-grade classmates, three other
classmates)

Record: Observers recorded 40% study time (percentage of on-task
10-second intervals) during 30 minutes of seatwork. (Number of
observations varied from 7 to 15 days.)

Consequate: Observers helped teachers by holding up small colored
papers when children were studying. Teachers would go to the student
and use verbal, facial, and contact approval.

Evaluate: Study behavior increased to average 75% for the six students.
                    What would happen if . . .
Consequate II: Teachers *stopped* giving approval to study behavior.

Evaluate II: Average study behavior dropped to 34%.

Consequate III: Teachers again gave approval when observers signaled.

Evaluate III: Study behavior increased to 73%.

Note: Most teachers' attention to problem children was for nonstudy behavior during Record phase. It was also reported that classrooms were initially well controlled with a few students who did not stay on-task. Teacher approval was made contingent through observers' signals that later proved to be unnecessary, and the cues were eliminated. The cues were initially used to make the teachers aware of the contingencies.

Scientific Application (p. 307)

Example 28

Pinpoint: *Striking children with objects* (9-year-old boy)

Record: Boy hit other children five times during four free-play periods.

Consequate: Adult assigned in vicinity. Boy praised and given donut when playing properly, although when boy hit someone, supervisor instructed to hit him back with same object. During second supervised play period, boy hit another child in head with plastic baseball bat. Immediately, supervisor picked up bat and hit boy. Explanation to child: "When people are hit, it hurts."

Evaluate: Boy never observed hitting another child.

Note: This boy had been characterized as "having no conscience." Perhaps it would be more accurate to say that he did not realize the consequences of his own actions regarding pain. Although this consequate "worked" it easily could have created other problems. Physical punishment should be used seldomly if ever.

Professional Application

Example 29

Pinpoint: *Following instructions* (kindergarten, five students)

Record: Students followed teachers instructions 60% of time during five days recording. Instructions included: pick up the toys; sit down; come and get a paper and pencil; write your name on the paper; fold your paper; bring your paper to my desk; put your chair on the table; get your mat out; lie down; be quiet.

Consequate I: Teacher attended students who followed rules (within 15 seconds) by giving verbal approval. Teacher tried to catch children being good during act of following instructions (six days).

Evaluate I: Instructions followed increased to average of 78%.

Consequate II: Teacher no longer caught students being good, acted as during Record phase (five days).

Evaluate II. Average instructions followed, 68.7%.

Consequate III: Attention given specific children for following rules again as in Consequate I.

Evaluate III: Average percent of instructions followed, 83.7%.

Note: Instructions were followed when the teacher caught the children being good and gave verbal approval for following rules. Whether or not children continued to follow rules is specifically dependent upon the extent that consequences follow desired behavior.

Scientific Application (p. 307)

Example 30

Pinpoint: Inappropriate behaviors (third grade, adjustment class, 17-9-year-olds)

Record: Normal kinds of reinforcers (praise, grades) ineffective. Compliments from teacher resulted in children making faces at each other. Eight most disruptive children observed for one hour and forty minutes three days per week. Daily average of inappropriate behavior during three-week observation was 76% range 61%-91%).

Consequate: Reward program instituted for afternoon hours; activities included stories, records, arithmetic instruction, and group reading. Reward procedures explained to children every day for one week prior to consequate. Small notebooks taped to child's desk. Every 20 minutes teacher gave each child a score from 1 to 10. Points exchanged for playthings at end of 1 hour and 40 minutes during first 3 days; days 4 through 9, points exchanged after 2 days. During next 15 days, delay stretched to 3-day period; for last 24 days, 4-day delay. In addition to individual rewards, *group* points earned and exchanged for popsicle party end of each week.

Evaluate: Average inappropriate behavior decreased from 76% to 10% (range 3%-32%). Decline evident for every child.

Note: The total cost for entire program was $80.67. Teacher's reports and observers records demonstrated profound difference in this classroom. The teacher also indicated that she had more time in which to teach. By pairing verbal praise with dispensing of points, the praise began to have a generalized effect even during the morning hours, when the token system was not in operation.

Scientific Application (p. 307)

Example 31

Pinpoint: *Failure to eat "nourishing" foods* (6-year-old girl)

Record: Mother reported continual nagging, longer periods taken to eat food (finishes last at supper)—four days; refused to eat vegetables—three days in one week.

Consequate: Mother told daughter one morning (during breakfast there were a few problems) that starting at noon the mother would no longer say anything about eating but any food not finished would be saved and that same food would be her next meal. Girl didn't finish noon meal the first day; the mother presented plate directly from the refrigerator after having prepared the child's favorite evening meal. Girl just sat; still refused to eat. Mother re-presented the same meal the next morning; girl ate nothing. That noon girl ate the old food.

Evaluate: Girl has never since refused meals. Mother later put a 20-minute time limit on eating with same contingency. Girl and family are now able to eat peacefully together.

Note: This parent decided that the value of eating the food was important to her and that some negative consequences needed to be employed. Other parents may choose to ignore noneating. Once the value decision has been made as to *what* should be done and contingencies chosen, then consistency is critical. Perhaps a more positive approach could have been developed by *rewarding* eating rather than punishing noneating.

Professional Application

Example 32

Pinpoint: Hyperactivity (9-year-old boy, academic retardation)

Record: Home and classroom observations determined frequency and categories of hyperactive behavior—talking, pushing, hitting, pinching, moving, tapping, squirming, handling objects, that is, did not sit still.

Consequate: A box, 6" × 8" × 5", equipped with counter and light, installed in classroom. Following ten seconds of appropriate behavior, light flashed, counter advanced, and boy received M & M or penny. Accumulated awards divided among classmates. Thus, other children received rewards for ignoring. Training session varied from 5 to 30 minutes; average rewards dispensed 60 to 100.

Evaluate: Significant decrease in activity level (average decrease of 8.4 responses).

Note: The peer group in this study was used to reward the deviant boy. Thus, the group began to have a positive effect on him. Teachers can have an entire class help one or more children. Rewards can be given for both ignoring and paying attention. It is also suggested with *extremely* active children to: (1) use a stopwatch and start with as little as five seconds while counting to the child (verbal cues help the child perform in time); then reward immediately. Make sure the child does not get rewarded if he moves as much as an eyebrow. Gradually build the time sequence so child can remain still for thirty seconds or more; and (2) have the child practice the hyperactivity on purpose for five minutes a day to help the child discriminate between sitting still and moving.

Scientific Application (p. 308)

Example 33

Pinpoint: *Writing vulgar words* (8- and 9-year-old neighborhood boy and girl)

Record: Two letters found by parents within one week; eight vulgar words written by boy, six by girl.

Consequate: Parents talked to parents of boy. Boy's parents said, "You know kids nowadays, what can you do." Parents talked to daughter, explained proper time and place for verbal sexual discussion. Girl received special toys for bringing home notes.

Evaluate: Girl brought home four notes passed to her by same boy during next week. Wrote no more answers.

Note: Parents do not control all possible sources of reinforcement. Following the first week parents discussed notes brought home, indicated girl should ignore any note-passing behavior, and after initial time also spent time role playing how to ignore note-passing behavior.

Professional Application

Example 34

Pinpoint: Standing up, walking around (first grade, 48 students, team-taught)

Record: Average of 2.9 children out of seats during each 10-second interval (291 children were counted [average] during 20-minute period—12 days.) Teachers told specific children to "sit down" an average of six times per 20 minutes. Whenever teacher told a child to sit down, the child did.

Consequate: Teachers instructed to tell children who stood up without good reason to sit down (average once every minute).

Evaluate: Amount of standing up *increased.* Each student sat down when told to sit down, but, overall, *more pupils stood up.* (Pupils standing per 10-second interval averaged 4.14.)

Consequate II: Procedure reversed, that is, children told to sit down only six times per 20 minutes.

Evaluate II: Standing decreased to approximately original level (3.14 pupils standing per 10-second interval).

Consequate III: To demonstrate that teachers' comments "caused" the children to stand up, teachers again told children who were up without good reason to "sit down" (average once every minute).

Evaluate III: Standing up again increased to about same level as the first time teachers "paid attention" (3.94 per 10-second interval).

Consequate IV: *Vicarious approval* introduced. Teachers praised good *sitting.* Whenever one child stood up or walked around, teacher "caught" a sitting student working diligently and praised the "good" child.

Evaluate IV: Standing *decreased* (1.89 average).

Note: Praise delivered to individuals who were *not* standing was very effective in controlling the entire class. (What teacher hasn't noticed that 30 backs straighten when one child is complimented for sitting up straight and paying attention?) In this study the "good child" was used as a model for the group. ("Watch how quietly Susie gets her math counter!" "See how nicely Jim writes," etc.) Vicarious praise, however, was effective only for approximately 30 seconds. Even when first graders "know the rules," it is necessary to deliver praise comments very regularly. It should be remembered that attention is extremely important to most children. Sometimes by paying attention to *inappropriate* behavior, you probably increase the very behavior you wish to eliminate.

Scientific Application (p. 308)

Example 35

Pinpoint: *Using subject matter to reinforce low-level subject matter* (third grade)

Record: Students working on individual prescriptions for math, pretest given covering music skills.

Consequate: Children divided into two groups: Half of the students received no extra instruction, half of the students got to go to the "TV corner" upon meeting criterion for their individual work.

Evaluate: Students who "earned" music instruction via the television increased correct math problems and almost all met their daily criterion. More importantly, those students who earned the TV corner gained significantly in music listening skills. Students who were not allowed to earn the TV corner actually decreased in correct math problems.

Note: Of constant concern to most educators is the development and maintenance of appropriate learning. Yet, after these learning contingencies have been established, one continues to encounter questions not only relating to "extrinsic contingencies" but also regarding the very nature of "behavioral rewards." Perhaps one of the best ways to solve some of these problems is to use "rewards" that not only provide some enjoyment, but teach something of importance as well.

Scientific Application (p. 308)

Example 36

Pinpoint: *Arson* (7-year-old boy)

Record: Boy setting fires for two years in home, always in presence of matches and absence of parents (average one to two times weekly).

Consequate: (1) Father informed son fire-setting would result in loss of highly prized baseball mitt. (2) Matches or match cover brought to parents received 5¢. Matches "planted" around house for boy to find, although told not to expect money *every* time. (3) Boy told he *could* strike full pack of matches under supervision, but for each match left unstruck he would receive 1¢ (first time earned 10¢, second time earned 17¢, third time earned 20¢). (4) Father gave verbal approval throughout program.

Evaluate: Boy brought all matches he could find to parents, stopped striking matches, ceased setting fires (entire instructional program only four weeks long); no fire-setting instances eight months later.

Note: Seeking and bringing matches to adults as well as thinking oneself "responsible" are incompatible with fire-setting. The natural "approval" for setting fires (brightness, excitement, etc.) was made less desirable than the alternate approval from parents (praise and money) and ultimately, self-approval. It is also noted that parents taught boy when he could strike matches. The procedure was helped by the threat of disapproval (loss of glove).

Scientific Application (p. 308)

Example 37

Pinpoint: Rest time disruptions (first grade, 19 children)

Record: Average inappropriate behavior 54% (trained observers, 10 days). Teacher gave praise or reprimands 12 times during 10 to 15-minute rest period.

Consequate: Teacher contingently praised appropriate behavior, ignored disruptive behavior (12 praise comments per day—only two reprimands in eight-day observation).

Evaluate: Disruptive behavior averaged 32%.

Consequate II: Teacher reprimanded so no one except disruptive child could hear (11 per day—no praise seven days).

Evaluate II: Disruptive behavior averaged 39%.

Consequate III: Disapproval comments contingent on inappropriate behavior loud enough for entire class to hear (14 per day; no approval for five days).

Evaluate III: Disruptive behavior increased to an average of 53%.

Consequate IV: Teacher praised appropriate behavior, ignored inappropriate behavior (five days—12 approval comments).

Evaluate IV: Disruptive behavior averaged 35%.

Note: In this scientific study, the teacher controlled disruptive behavior by praising and reprimanding quietly. Loud reprimands (yelling) increased rather than decreased the inappropriate behavior. A combination of approval for appropriate behavior and firm statements to the individual offender often serves to control young children very well. Quiet reprimands eliminate the possibility of the other children paying undue attention to the misbehaving child.

Scientific Application (p. 308)

Example 38

Pinpoint: *Teaching beginning reading* (10 research studies employing 400 children: retarded, slow readers, and unselected kindergarten and first grades.)

Record: Reading scores assessed prior to reading instruction.

Consequate: Programmed reading for periods of up to one semester.

Evaluate: No tutored children failed to read with exception of one "normal" first grader and some (but not all) children with IQ's below 50. One experiment showed relatively rapid acquisition of reading vocabulary by simple pairing of words with pictures. In another study, retarded children taught reading vocabulary to other retarded children with simple tutoring program. In other research, sight-reading vocabulary taught in sentence contexts to slow readers, retarded, and normal children. Two extension studies showed frequent alternation of programmed tutoring and classroom teachings more effective than less frequent alternation. One study indicated reinforcement proportion of approximately 20 percent more effective than higher levels.

Note: It appears that periodic withholding of approval develops a "hope" that is more effective than when the teacher reinforces all the time. The interested teacher can find literally hundreds of experiments in scientific journals concerning the effects of various reinforcement schedules. The central issues related to programmed instructions seem little different from any other teaching-learning sequence. One should begin where the student is. Learning steps should be small, and adequate reinforcement and feedback techniques should be employed. Every teacher can individualize instructions and follow these systematic procedures.

Scientific Application (p. 308)

Example 39

Pinpoint: "Bad attitude" (first-grade boy)

Record: Child continued maladaptive responses just a little past point of instruction. Thus, when teacher said, "Stop talking," he did but continued *almost* to point of being disobedient. When teacher said, "Do not pick the flowers," he picked leaves. When she said, "Come here," he walked very slowly. When she said, "Quiet down," he did—still slightly louder than the group but not so loud as to receive punishment. This child (like so many others) delicately balanced upon the "edge of propriety." Punishment seemed not quite warranted, and reward seemed ridiculous.

Consequate: Teacher set up short lesson using *vicarious modeling*. Three names not duplicated in classroom were written on the board. The class was presented a new word, *attitude*. Teacher paired names with the new word:—"George has a *bad attitude;* Sam has an *all right attitude;* Tommy has a *good attitude.* When their teacher tells these three boys, 'Let's all pick up the mess,' George tries to get out of work or hides his mess in the desk, Sam cleans up his own mess—only his own—, but Tommy cleans up his own mess and then helps other children." The teacher talked through two such specific examples, then let children say what they thought George, Sam, and Tommy would do. (Children are usually very correct in these assessments, especially as they describe their own problems.) Teachers made several praising comments, stating: "I liked Tommy the very, very best." She then asked problem boy whom he would want for a friend. (The teacher now had a word, *attitude,* that she could use to describe this boy's behaviors in specific and general contexts—"That's a good attitude, Cort.") She now began rewarding *good attitudes* instead of being frustrated at not being able to find responses to deal with this child.

Evaluate: Child in question changed "attitude" when rewarded for proper verbal and motoric behavior.

Professional Application

Example 40

Pinpoint: Thumb-sucking (7-year-old girl)

Record: Thumb-sucking occurred 45% of time that the girl watched TV or read (mother's records). Dentist indicated "bite" was getting worse.

Consequate: Mother, after hearing PTA lecture on "A positive approach with record keeping," "caught" girl every time she had thumb in mouth. If thumb removed, girl received praise and special checks on prominently displayed chart in living room. (Checks were to be traded for bicycle—picture of bicycle at end of chart). Mother continued for 14 days.

Evaluate: Thumb-sucking *increased* to 75%. Mother sought professional help from behaviorally oriented counselor stating, "I tried, but bribery just doesn't work."

Note: A cause-and-effect approach rests on record keeping (data). In this case, the consequence did in fact work (changed behavior). Thumb-sucking *increased* 30%. The behavior change, however, was not in the direction desired by the mother (nor the dentist). Regarding the "bribery" issue, some people confuse the use of approval with a notion of "bribery." The girl in this case learned exactly what she was taught—(1) put thumb in mouth, (2) take thumb out of mouth, and (3) get rewarded. The girl was rewarded for what she was not supposed to do. Teachers must be careful not to reinforce the child by making a "deal" *after* the misbehavior has occurred or *after* the time for something to be done has passed. "If you stop dawdling and do your work, I'll give you free time," teaches dawdling. "Stop fighting, and you'll get a reward," teaches fighting. In each instance children are given approval to *stop* inappropriate behavior but actually learn to *begin* the inappropriate behavior so they can make a "deal" to stop so they can get a reward (generally on a partial schedule as we don't give in every time, and, thus, the child also learns persistence in misbehavior). Teachers should either use ignoring or disapproval to stop or extinguish the misbehavior. Teaching for incompatible responses using a positive approach involves setting up the reward beforehand.

Professional Application

Example 41

Pinpoint: Unfinished assignments, bothering neighbors, playing (second grade, two boys referred by teacher)

Record: Trained observers recorded average of 47% inappropriate behavior.

Consequate: Teacher and class formulated rules. Rules repeated six times per day for two weeks.

Evaluate: Little decrease in inappropriate behavior (average 40%).

Note: Apparently just knowing (being able to repeat rules) is not effective.

Consequate II: Teacher attempted to ignore inappropriate behaviors (teacher not entirely successful). Continued to repeat class rules every day.

Evaluate II: Behavior worsened. Average inappropriate behavior for four observations 69%.

Consequate III: Teacher praised prosocial behavior, repeated classroom rules, ignored inappropriate behavior.

Evaluate III: Inappropriate behavior *decreased* (average of 20%). Combination of procedures effective in reducing inappropriate behavior.

Consequate IV: Teacher instructed to act as she had in September. (Observers monitored entire year.)

Evaluate IV: Inappropriate behavior increased same day teacher changed (averaged 38%).

Consequate V: Rules, ignoring, and praise reinstated for remainder of school year.

Evaluate V: Inappropriate behavior again decreased (averaged only 15% for last eight-week period).

Note: Many teachers who believe they use more approval than disapproval do not (monitored by trained observers in classroom). It is necessary to practice delivering responses and to give yourself time cues or cues written on material you are teaching. A mark on every page can remind you to "catch someone being good." It is interesting to note that one boy reported in this study was seen during the entire year by a professional counselor. This boy responded in the same way to consequences as did the other boy who was not seen. It would seem that the teacher is capable of handling many behavioral problems generally referred to counselors, if responses are well developed and applied contingently.

Scientific Application (p. 308)

Example 42

Pinpoint: "On-task" attention, academic accuracy (14 third-grade children, age 10.1 average, IQ average 75, 2.58 arithmetic achievement level)

Record: Each day students worked 100 arithmetic problems drawn randomly from pool of 5,000 items containing equal numbers of addition, subtraction, multiplication, and division. Students worked 20 minutes per session. Average "on-task" behavior 80%, average disruptions 8%, median percent problems correct (number correct divided by number attempted) 55%, median number of correct problems 50% (six sessions).

Consequate I: Teacher circulated through three rows of children once per minute, gave tokens for attending to work task. Each child earned 12–16 tokens per 20-minute session, tokens exchanged for choice of candy, ice cream, inexpensive toys, high interest activities, field trips (14 sessions).

Evaluate I: On-task attending behavior increased during seven days to over 90% last day, disruptions averaged less than one per day, median percent of problems correct remained approximately constant (54%) as did median number of correct problems (50%).

Consequate II: Teacher continued to circulate among three rows once each minute giving tokens *not* for attending but for accuracy and rate of work. Students could now earn one token for seven correct problems, also bonus tokens (21–30% of problems worked correctly one token, 31–40% two tokens up to eight for 91–100% correct and two additional tokens for perfect paper). Students earned 10–18 per day (12 sessions).

Evaluate II: Attending behavior dropped to between 50–70%, disruptions rose to high of 20%. However, median percent of problems correct rose to 76%, median number correct remained approximately constant (50%).

Consequate III: Teachers again gave tokens for attending, *not* for accuracy of work.

Evaluate III: Attending behavior rose slightly from previous phase (average approximately 73%, disruptions approximately 3%, median percent problems correct 72%, median number correct problems 50%.

Consequate IV: Teachers gave tokens both for attending (on-task) and correct work.

Evaluate IV: Attending behavior increased to between 80–85%, disruptions decreased to 1%, median percent problems correct 80%. Median number of correct problems increased to approximately 65%.

Consequate V: Teachers again returned to giving tokens for correct work only, not for attending behavior.

Evaluate V: Attending behavior dropped to approximately 63%, disruptions rose to approximately 10%, median percent of problems correct rose to 83%, median number of correct problems approximately 56% (five sessions).

Consequate VI: Teachers again gave tokens both for attending and correct work.

Evaluate VI: Attending behavior increased steadily to a high of 86%, median percent problems correct 82%, median number of correct problems rose to high of 68% during last two sessions (seven sessions).

Note: The authors in this scientific study and an additional study with the same age children demonstrated that reinforcement contingencies applied to on-task behavior consistently increased attending behavior and decreased disruptions but had little effect on accuracy of math computations. Alternately, contingencies place on correct work produced an increase in accuracy but the number of correct problems remained the same, attending behavior decreased while disruptions increased. Contingencies placed on both attending behavior and accuracy of work increased attending behavior, number of problems correctly completed as well as the percent of problems worked correctly. These two excellent studies indicate the importance of the teacher specifying the precise behaviors to be reinforced. The teacher should not expect automatic improvement in academic achievement if the teacher decreases or increases inappropriate social behavior. Conversely, the students will not magically behave in socially appropriate ways just because they are making accurate academic responses. The teacher must determine what is going to be reinforced in what combinations and structure for both academic and social improvement.

Scientific Application (p. 308)

UPPER PRIMARY EXAMPLES

Example 43

Pinpoint: Bothering teacher at desk (fourth grade)

Record: Students unnecessarily at teacher's desk (28% occurrences— one week)

Consequate: Teacher *ignored* all children who came to desk—made no eye contact, said nothing. Teacher recognized only those children who raised hands at seats.

Evaluate: Occurrences of students at teacher's desk steadily decreased. After two weeks, daily average between zero and one.

Professional Application

Example 44

Pinpoint: Teasing other children (individual student, fourth grade)

Record: Disruptive behavior 83% (teacher's observation—two days)

Consequate: *Isolation.* A coatrack and bookcase rearranged in back of classroom, making small isolation cubicle for child. Child sent to this "time-out place" for 10 minutes every time he disrupted class.

Evaluate: Disruptive behavior steadily *decreased.* After nine isolations (four during first day) disruptive behavior dropped to 10%.

Note: This child's teasing behavior was probably producing "payoff" from class (laughing, complaining, attending).

Professional Application

Example 45

Pinpoint: *Child interfering with older child's play* (3- and 9-year-olds)

Record: Six instances in three days, older child complained to parent. Mother then recorded for five days—average of two to three "blowups" per day.

Consequate: Program developed to teach older child how and when to play with sibling. Older child instructed in techniques of attending younger child's play for short periods while giving approval to *facilitate the complete happiness of younger child.* Rewarded for *complete* attention to young child's happiness with special toys, separate play periods with own age peers after 20 minutes' play with brother. During separate times for older child, younger child kept entirely away; not allowed to interfere.

Evaluate: No instances of annoying interactions over one week.

Note: It is important for adults to realize that unless children are close in age it is difficult for each child to interact with equal benefit.

While it is possible for children to play *independently* side by side (many times this is desirable), great disparity in ages or other abilities usually necessitates that one child must entertain the other if children are to be in close proximity and "get along." Most parents believe that older children should establish these behaviors as well as derive joy from concerning oneself about younger siblings. Thus, parents try to promote children's "loving each other rather than fighting." Perhaps most "sibling rivalry" is caused by the hours, days, weeks, months, and years children actually compete with each other when left to their own resources. Regardless, it is imperative that older child realize who is in control and take responsibility for the interaction.

Professional Application

Example 46

Pinpoint: Overactivity (six boys, 9 to 13 years, low-level intelligence)

Record: Boys observed in playroom for eight days

Consequate: Rewarded following 30 seconds of "quiet time" (tokens exchangable for candy). Procedure continued 30 days; during last 4 days token given after 45 seconds.

Evaluate: Overactivity reduced 67%.

Note: Overactivity was still substantially decreased eight days later when *no rewards* were used.

Scientific Application (p. 308)

Example 47

Pinpoint: Littering (sixth grade)

Record: Materials not put away—25 daily (average one week)

Consequate: Large FRIDAY BOX instituted in classroom. Each student given responsibility for own materials—individuallly labeled. Materials not put away went in Friday Box. Friday Box opened one half-hour weekly—*only then could articles be recovered.*

Evaluate: After second week Friday Box, littering decreased to three incidents weekly.

Note: This procedure seems effective in all situations and at all age levels. An author had to wait four days to recover important research materials placed by his wife in the family Sunday Box. Also, the amount of material not taken from the box that is allowed to remain week after week provides a good indication of its worth to the litterer.

Professional Application

Example 48

Pinpoint: Disruptive classroom behavior (9-year-old boy)

Record: Disruptions recorded by teacher.

Consequate: Disruptive behaviors ignored; appropriate behavior rewarded. Boy kept after school for extreme deviations and sent home on later bus. This put child with students he did not know and withdrew peer attention. Correct behaviors reinforced by teacher praise and peer approval (continuously in beginning, more infrequently later on). Also, job of blackboard monitor followed appropriate behavior.

Evaluate: Disruptive behaviors initially *increased* as payoff withdrawn. After initial rise, maladaptive behaviors progressively *decreased* and were eliminated by end of third week.

Scientific Application (p. 308)

Example 49

Pinpoint: *Positive piano practice* (9-year-old girl)

Record: New behavior.

Consequate: Piano purchased with contingency child would (1) instruct self through two beginner books to earn privilege of taking lessons and (2) pay part of earned allowance to piano teacher every lesson ($.25) for privilege of studying.

Evaluate: "Self-motivation" regarding practice—child practiced daily without admonition—three years.

Note: It was also decided in the above case to contract lessons through six-month periods with some weeks for rests, rather than just begin and act as though lessons might never stop. This obviates the need for children to view themselves as failures when they stop taking lessons. In music study it is curious that children must interpret their learning behavior as "defeat" when they have studied music successfully for from 6 months up to 10 years. It should also be mentioned that six piano teachers were contacted before one was found who immediately realized the importance of accepting the quarter every lesson from the child. Another interesting note concerns the day this child came home and reported to her parents in stark disbelief that "Julie wants to stop taking lessons. And gosh! she doesn't even have to help pay for hers."

Professional Application

Example 50

Pinpoint: Disruptive noise (large class)

Record: Absolute cacophony. *No* recording able to take place.

Consequate: Many children removed from class until class size became manageable. Teacher planned specific assignments and scheduled consequences. After small number of children brought under control, one child at a time added to class. Procedure started with limited number of children during special period while others normally out of room—later extended to entire day.

Evaluate: Teachers indicated procedure very effective.

Note: Teachers also stated that initial control of the *entire* group was absolutely impossible.

Professional Application

Example 51

Pinpoint: *Reading "bad" literature* (10-year-old child)

Record: No instance of child reading "classic child stories" or factual book in two months.

Consequate: Parent paid child 1¢ per page to read any book in family library. Child could take the $1.00 after 100 pages or buy any book of choice for 25¢.

Evaluate: Child read 62 pages of child's encyclopedia first week; thereafter, averaged approximately 50 pages per week from "good" books. Four-month follow-up indicated reading rate also increased. Child "hooked" on scientific book series.

Note: The child in this study kept the records personally. Completion of each 100 pages was countersigned by mother and presented to father for payment on a check-type book that became very important to the child.

Professional Application

Example 52

Pinpoint: High noise level—lunchroom (grade school)

Record: Generalized noise (talking) at high level observed by principal. Other maladaptive behaviors developing, that is, hitting, screaming, not staying at table until finished.

Consequate: Sound-activated switch (inexpensive circuit-breaker device) connected to lights in lunchroom. When noise reached preset level (first day, 90 decibels; second day, 80 decibels, etc.) lights went off. When noise dropped, lights came on.

Evaluate: Selected noise levels maintained without any instruction. Children learned quickly to stay just beneath sound-level setting.

Note: A similar device is available that can be set at any intensity level. This device sounds a shrill pitch until noise stops. Mechanical disciplinarians are absolute and effective. More important, they free a teacher's time for more productive interactions.

Professional Application

Example 53

Pinpoint: *Arithmetic achievement* (sixth grade, 13 boys)

Record: Assignments completed during arithmetic period preceding recess averaged 4.2 (approximately nine incomplete assignments). Recess activity closely observed. All boys played 100% of the time during two-week period.

Consequate: Boys told if assignments not completed, they could not go out to recess.

Evaluate: Only four incidents of recess participation were earned during the next week (three for one child). Arithmetic assignment completion did *not* increase following application of contingency.

If at first you don't succeed

Consequate II: All boys instructed to work through recess and *denied* recess privilege. However, each boy allowed five minutes' play in gym after finishing two arithmetic problems correctly.

Evaluate II: Completed arithmetic assignments increased to nine by end of first week. By Tuesday of second week, all 13 boys turned in assignments every day. After three weeks, accuracy reached an average of 80%.

Note: This application represents a discrimination many teachers fail to make. If the period of work is too long, the child cannot see the immediate rewards for his academic work; thus, behavior does not improve. It was apparent to the teacher that these thirteen boys (all retarded in arithmetic) really enjoyed recess. The teacher used recess contingently, but it did not work. The time span of work without reward for these particular boys was too long. When the rewarding activity was given following a short period of work, they all produced— even though regular recess was denied. To keep the boys coming back from the gym rapidly, the teacher occasionally rewarded them immediately with another period in the gym for prompt return. By the end of the second week, all boys were running back from the gym to work again. When using activities as rewards, it is important to pay very close attention to "structuring activities in time."

Professional Application

Example 54

Pinpoint: Excessive dawdling (fifth grade)

Record: Three to five minutes to get "on-task" in individual study. (Average over eight days.)

Consequate: Teacher instituted multiple divergent token systems. Some children received paper money that bought "surprise gifts" at end of day. Other children received candies on various time interval schedules. Some children accumulated points written in notebooks. Reinforcers changed constantly. Varying token reinforcers "stimulated interest and created mode of excitement in classroom."

Evaluate: Individual dawdling decreased to approximately thirty seconds (average three days).

Note: Expectation level increased general classroom excitement toward goal achievement (receiving tokens), which was later modified by stretching the time interval using only exchange tokens. If students have previously been on a single token system, sometimes it is wise to alter the routine.

Professional Application

Example 55

Pinpoint: Teaching lying behavior (11-year-old boy)

Record: Known misconduct; boy observed stealing $1.00 from sister's bedroom.

Consequate: Father took boy aside and with displeasure said, "Now, I want you to be honest with me, did you do it?"

Evaluate: Lie 1   Child, "No."
                        "Now, be honest!"
            Lie 2   "No, I didn't do it."
                        "Don't lie to me."
            Lie 3   "I'm not, really I didn't do it."
                        "I'm not going to tolerate any lying now."
            Lie 4   "I'm not lying."
                        "Why were you in there?"
            Lie 5   "Where?"
                        "The bedroom."
            Lie 6   "Which bedroom?"
                        "You know which bedroom."
            Lie 7   "No, I don't."
                        "Of course, you do."
            Lie 8   "Dad, I really don't; I didn't do anything."
                        "You took it."
            Lie 9   "What?"
                        "You know."
            Lie 10   "I don't even have any money."
                        "Ah! Who said anything about money?"
            Lie 11   "You did."
                        "No, I didn't."
            Lie 12   "You said that I took Clara's money from her bedroom.
                        "No, I didn't."
            Lie 13   "Dad, I didn't take it."
                        "How did you know it was money I was talking about?"
            Lie 14   "I didn't."
                        "You said, 'I didn't take Clara's money.' "
            Lie 15   "No, I didn't say that."
                        "What did you say?"
            Lie 16   "I said, 'I didn't even know about Clara's money.'"
                        "I'm not going to have you lie to me."
            Lie 17   "I'm not lying, honest."

"Now, once and for all, did you take it?"
Lie 18   "What?"
          "Clara's money."
Lie 19   "What money?"
          "I said I was not going to have any more lying."
Lie 20   "I'm not lying."
          etc., etc., etc., until
Truth 1   "Okay, okay, I did it."

Consequate II: Next morning. "Son, your behavior makes me very ashamed of you. You took your sister's money without her permission. Very few things are as serious as stealing, especially from a loved one. I choose not to give you the privilege of interacting with me or the family until you make retribution to Clara and this family. I know that you will think about this for a long, long time; I also know that you will pay back Clara and apologize to her and to the rest of us. I hope you can also think of a positive project that will demonstrate to us all the kind of person I know you are; right now you make us very, very sad."

Evaluate II: Boy exhibited "guilt" and engaged in project to earn back respect, that is, positive familial interaction.

Note: Obviously consequate II should have been consequate I. Nothing is generally gained by playing detective or cross examiner, except to increase lying. Even though most people can be caught in lies because they do not have good memories and/or are afraid and/or are young, this questioning process does not usually represent a worthwhile pursuit. If one knows for certain that a child has committed an inappropriate act, then the teacher should act on that basis. It does little good to get the child to admit it. If the teacher is not sure, the teacher should think through the possible consequences of the questioning process, that is, to unwittingly teach lying.

Professional Application

Example 56

Pinpoint: *Inappropriate oral hygiene* (12-year-old boy and 10-year-old girl)

Record: Brushing done *only* at parental insistence. (Recording over two-week period.)

Consequate: Two-track program devised:
(1) Children directed (by father—one week) to brush after breakfast

and dinner and "feel your teeth with your tongue and smell your own breath."

(2) During second day of second week father "caught" children after observing tooth-brushing. Father said, "If you've brushed, you may open my hand and have the prize inside" (15 or 20 cents), once daily. During same week father "caught" children when brushing was omitted and said same thing, but when children said, "I haven't" the father said, "open my hand anyway and see what *you might have had.*"

Evaluate: "Brushing" behavior amplified to operational point of acceptability (i.e., four *forgets* each week).

Note: Children can be taught to appreciate the "good" smell of their breath as well as the "feel" of clean teeth.

Professional Application

Example 57

Pinpoint: *Classroom "out of control"* (sixth grade, 30 students, beginning teacher)

Record: Average classroom study rate during first hour 25% (four days).

Consequate: Teacher had two conferences with principal, wrote assignments on board, changed class seating arrangement, watched a helping teacher demonstration (study rate 90% during demonstration).

Evaluate: Average classroom study rate increased to 48% (13 days). Teacher averaged only 1.4 contingent approval comments per day to entire class during the period.

Consequate II: Teacher instructed in principles of contingent approval; contingent approval comments increased to average of 13 per session.

Evaluate II: Average study rate rose to 67% (14 days).

Consequate III: Teacher discontinued contingent approval comments.

Evaluate III: Study behavior decreased steadily to 45% by sixth day.

Consequate IV: Teacher reinstated contingent approval averaging 17 per session; decreased disapproval comments following nonstudy behavior.

Evaluate IV: Study behavior increased average 77% (14 days).

Note: Three postexperimental observations indicated the study rates were being maintained at approximately the same level.

Scientific Application (p. 308).

Example 58

Pinpoint: *Negative comments and high-intensity "screaming" among family members prior to evening meal* (father, mother, children ages 5, 9, 13, and 16)

Record: Thirty-minute observations prior to evening meal (five days). Average 64.3 disapproving comments (38.6 high intensity "screaming" and 8.7 accompanied by parental motor disapproval—"hitting"; 43.1 comments per day by children and 21.2 by parents).

Consequate: Parents decided every time anyone yelled the father would deliver severe reprimand accompanied "when appropriate" by motor disapproval (spanking).

Evaluate: Disapproving comments by children *increased* (58.6) and disapproving comments by parents increased (44.3, mostly by the father).

Consequate II: Timer set on kitchen stove thirty minutes before meal, anyone who engaged in quiet talk during that time received a special treat *prior* to supper. Family role played how to ignore, disapprove, and praise quiet talk using examples from daily records. Father "caught the youngest child in quiet talk" and gave a special treat during the 30-minute period; others waited.

Evaluate II: Disapproval comments by children *decreased* (13.2 average first week and 5.6 second week). Disapproval comments by parents decreased (3.3 average first week and 1.8 second week).

Note: Loud reprimands defined as disapproval by the parents may not be disapproving. Here they served to increase the very behavior the parents were trying to control. "Modeling" also occurs; children observe parents yell and scream and in turn yell and scream. Discrimination was taught using role playing and speaking quietly received approval. Parents presented dessert prior to dinner in small segments. In this case a quiet tranquil house was valued more than a traditional eating sequence.

Professional Application

Example 59

Pinpoint: Volunteering answers (sixth grade, social studies class, four girls)

Record: Number of times girls volunteered during two-week period: zero. Only six questions answered when specifically directed toward them. Sociograms indicated girls isolates.

Consequate: Activities developed with approval from teacher and classmates. Girls recited alone from assigned book, read passages for parents, who praised accomplishment, then read for teacher alone. Girls' voices recorded and positive verbal approval given by teacher for effective talking. Recording later played for entire class, who praised performance. Teacher also praised interaction with other children. Additionally, small groups of girls worked on projects. Each group started with one fearful girl and one girl who modeled appropriate behaviors—number of students gradually increased.

Evaluate: Volunteering in class increased from nothing to an average slightly below rest of class.

Note: These procedures are closely related to many learning situations in which initial fear is gradually reduced by participating in the fear-producing activity (or approaching the feared objects) in small steps, receiving approval for behavior that is *incompatible* with avoidance.

Professional Application

Example 60

Pinpoint: *Bed-wetting (enuresis)* (47 children, ages 8 through 11)

Record: Average of five nights per week including all age groups.

Consequate: Twofold program: (1) To teach child to take responsibility for own bed-wetting behavior and (2) train child to wake up when the bladder pressure is high just prior to urination. Parents purchased a simple battery operated device that consists of a battery case with speaker and two leads that attach to two flexible metal sheets placed on the bed separated by thin porous paper sheets (available fairly inexpensively through Sears, Roebuck and Co.) When the urine passed through the sheet it closed the circuit (no change occurred for electrical shock as the circuit was both low amperage and low voltage) and rang the buzzer, which awakened the child whereupon he went to the bathroom. When accidents occurred the child changed his own bedding, clothing, and helped reset the alarm. (Depending on child's age, the procedures are done alone or with help of parents.) Most parents also placed charts in bedroom with prizes to be given after 2, 6, 9, 15, 18, 21, and 30 dry nights.

Evaluate: Forty-four children eliminated or decreased bed-wetting to one accident within 30 days of starting the procedure.

Note: When using such procedures, many parents make the mistake of limiting the child's liquid intake. This is detrimental in two ways: the acid percentage of the urine will increase and may induce urination, but more importantly the child cannot learn to "get up" with bladder pressure unless bladder pressure is increased. The buzzer procedure is built upon the principle that the child will learn to respond to internal physiological cues (increased bladder pressure) and awakening will occur earlier and earlier in the sequence until the awakening will precede the buzzer whereupon the problem will be solved. Therefore, it is important for the parent to give as much liquid as possible just before bedtime and for most efficient use also to give as much liquid as possible every time the buzzer awakens the child. It is also important for the child to wake up to the buzzer *before* the learning procedure is employed. Put the child to bed and wait until sleep is deep, start the buzzer, leave it sounding and make certain the child is awake (sometimes with "sound" sleepers ice on the stomach is effective), have the child go to the bathroom (do not take hands or lead him), simulate or actually engage in urination, and then let him go back to bed himself, after which the buzzer is turned off and reset. Continue this wake-up routine until you are certain that the buzzer *always* wakes up the child (generally this takes between 3 and 24 experiences). Next give increased liquid, send the child to bed, and wait for the buzzer. (It was found that with seven children increased liquid intake and wake-up procedure alone resulted in termination of bed-wetting.)

We recommend waiting until children are at least three years old or old enough to get themselves to and from the bathroom before this routine is begun.

Should parents not have the monetary resources to purchase the buzzer, another routine built upon the same principles may be employed. The child is given increased liquid and the parents awaken the child after approximately 120 minutes. Should urination occur prior to this time wake the child up on an earlier schedule. The child should go to the bathroom by himself, drink as much liquid as possible, go back to bed, and be awakened in another 120 minutes. This should be repeated every two hours all night for seven days. (The idea is the same as above; that is, insure the bladder is full and awaken the child.) Next the parents should increase the time before waking up the child by 15 minutes (2 hours and 15 minutes) for the next seven days and add 15 more minutes each week until the child gets up by himself. A good physical exam should precede any application of the above routines, but parents should not worry about any special significance concerning bed-wetting. Getting up to go to the bathroom behavior is learned just like any other behavior. If it has not been learned or the learning has been slow, then we should assume the child deserves to be taught.

Professional Application

Example 61

Pinpoint: *Academic underachievement* (25 underachievers, 8 to 12-year-olds, average age, 10.1)

Record: Thirty children originally selected for summer program, five moved. Average educational level of mothers 7.0, fathers 7.2. Average income $3,800. 40% of children from broken homes (separation, divorce, or death). California Achievement Test 1.5 years average below norms. Overall grade point average for preceeding year 1.47 (D grades). Total work time (percent of assigned classroom time engaged in academic activities) averaged 39% (dropped last day to 18%). Rate of work output (number of exercises and problems done divided by number of minutes) averaged 1.40 problems attempted per minute. Accuracy of output (number of problems and exercises done correctly divided by total attempted) averaged 50% (15 days recording of all 25 students). Teachers and aides averaged 13 approvals per hour, 27 disapprovals per hour. Instructional responses (requests, commands, and rules) averaged 55 per hour.

Consequate I: Students given personalized booklets with 50 squares per page (three colors of pages). Points awarded by teacher checking appropriate number of squares in booklet. Academic work reinforced by assigning points for *accuracy* (two-thirds of total) and *speed* of working (one-third of points). Social behavior reinforced by getting to work quickly (20 points), working for 10–20 minutes continuously (20 points), working while fight or noise going on nearby (10 points), raising hand (5 points), obtaining permission to leave desk (5 points). Inappropriate behaviors were given warning first and then 10–50 points fine taken, two fines resulting in "time-out" with contingency to finish one assignment without points to work way back into system. Points redeemable as follows: First 25 points (green) paid for lunch (no child missed lunch entire summer); yellow points earned school store (candy, gum, toys, supplies, goldfish, clothes, jewelry, makeup kits, baseballs, games of many kinds, etc.); red points earned field trips occurring on Friday afternoon (fishing, boating, swimming parties, farm trip, bank, hospital, and pet shop). Teachers passed out store items while giving approval and urging continued success. Teachers and aides paired approvals for academic and social behaviors while giving points in books. Program lasted for 29 days of summer term.

Evaluate I: Total work time increased from 39 to 57% average. Rate of work increased from 1.4 assigned problems attempted per minute to an average of 3.35. (SRA reading workbook .97 to 2.9, SRA spelling .90 to 2.34, SRA Reading Lab .28 to 1.43, Merril Workbook 1.37 to 2.7, spelling workbook .80 to 1.72, math workbook 2.01 to 6.19, math worksheets 2.65 to 4.84); Accuracy increased from 50% correct to 70% correct (SRA Reading workbook 32.4% to 62.2%, SRA reading lab 30.9% to 64.9%, Merril workbook 53.3% to 68.2%, spelling workbook 52.0% to 68%, math workbook 51.6% to 72.9%, math worksheets 58.7% to 75.1%, spelling tests 46.7% to 71.9%). Teachers and aides during Consequate I averaged 47 approvals per hour, 7 disapprovals per hour and 17 requests, commands, and rules per hour.

Consequate II: Teachers eliminated point system but continued approval for appropriate academic and social behavior (children received candy, toys, lunch without contingencies during nine days of program as during Record phase).

Evaluate II: Time at work average dropped to 42%. Problems attempted per minute *increased* to 5.5. Accuracy increased to 73%. Teachers and aides decreased approvals to 27 per hour, disapprovals increased to 9 per hour, and requests, commands, and rules to 16 per hour. CAT scores averaged .42 year higher at end of summer than at beginning.

Note: The normal classroom routines during the record phase were producing less and less work prior to the introduction of the point system. There followed a substantial increase in achievement with the dual introduction of the points and change in teacher verbal approval from an approval ratio of approximately 33% to 87%. Six weeks of contingent points and high verbal approval did not maintain a high work rate after the points were withdrawn. These teachers unfortunately did not maintain the same high approval rate during Consequate II. Perhaps if the teachers had maintained the same rate and ratio of approvals the work time might have remained as high after the points were withdrawn. The rate of work output increased steadily during the six weeks of contingent points and stayed even after the points were withdrawn. It appears that six weeks of contingent reinforcement was able to maintain a high rate of work output even after withdrawing the reinforcers (things and activities) provided that teachers remain predominately positive and use verbal approval. The same is indicated for accurate work. Students reached a high level of accuracy during the point system and maintained the same level with social and academic verbal contingencies. The authors also report that during the record phase teachers were spending much more time in trying to eliminate disruptive inappropriate behaviors but during the consequate phase shifted to teaching behaviors. The students were also able to learn to interact in positive ways with teachers and academic materials. Even though the work time dropped after the point system was withdrawn, students maintained a high work rate and high accuracy rate perhaps indicating that the interaction with academic materials became more reinforcing to the students. It is interesting to note that the students were able to maintain accuracy and rate of problems completed using less time in "on-task" work. Perhaps, as with the teachers, the students were able to spend less time and achieve better results following a precise and well-implemented program of contingent reinforcement.

Scientific Application (p. 309)

Example 62

Pinpoint: *Talking out, standing* (fifth grade, 28 students)

Record: Students averaged 43.3% talk-outs, 5.5% out-of-seat behaviors during English period and 39.2% talk-outs, 10.0% out-of-seat during math period (14 days observation).

Consequate I: Individual contingencies applied only during English period. Reinforcement included free time with choice to participate in desired activities (tutoring, reading, assisting teachers, record listening, viewing filmstrips, etc.).

Evaluate I: Average talk-outs decreased to 2.8%, out-of-seat decreased to .3% during English period. Observations during math indicated talk-outs 24.8%, out-of-seat 4.1%. Individual contingencies during English only, slightly modified the same behaviors during math.

Consequate II: Contingencies removed (five days).

Evaluate II: During English talk-outs increased to 24.8%, average out-of-seat to 6.6%. During math period talk-outs averaged 30.2%, out-of-seat 8.8%.

Consequate III: Group contingency applied to English period only. Five or more rule violations for entire class resulted in entire class losing free-time privileges (five days).

Evaluate III: During English period average talk-outs decreased to 1.8%, out-of-seat to .1%. During math period talk-outs averaged 15.0%, out-of-seat 1.7%.

Consequate IV: Contingencies removed from English class.

Evaluate IV: Talk-outs 3.4%, out-of-seat .4% during English. During math period talk-outs averaged 20.1%, out-of-seat .3%.

Consequate V: Group contingency reapplied to both English period and math period. Five violations for entire class resulted in entire class losing free-time privilege (five days).

Evaluate V: Inappropriate behavior decreased to lowest level during both English and math periods. During English talk-outs averaged .4%, out-of-seat, 0%. During math period talk-outs averaged 1.0%, out-of-seat 0%.

Note: Both the individual and group contingencies had an impressive effect in reducing two bothersome behaviors. When the actual number of talk-outs is counted (rather than percentage of observed intervals) the results are even more impressive. During an average 40-minute English or math period there was a difference of at least 180 fewer talk-outs during the least effective contingency. Results also indicate some carryover to math period when contingencies were applied to English. Group contingencies are easier to apply than individual contingencies (record keeping) and both were equally effective.

Scientific Application (p. 309)

Example 63

Pinpoint: *Tardiness following recess* (fifth grade, 25 students)

Record: Teacher and one student recorded number of students late for noon, morning, and afternoon recesses. Average number of students late for noon recess 7.2 (13 days). Average number late for morning recess 3.7 (21 days). Average number late for afternoon recess 3.9 (27 days).

Consequate I: Students studying patriots and excited about being Today's Patriot. Teacher introduced Today's Patriot Chart. Chart (posted on the board at the end of each day) listed those who got back to classroom on time after noon recess. Chart only for noon recess, did not include morning and afternoon recesses.

Evaluate I: Students late decreased dramatically. Only three students late after noon recess during 19 days chart in effect. However, average number late after morning recess 3.3, after afternoon recess, 3.7.

Consequate II: Patriots Chart expanded to include morning recess. Names appeared on chart only if students on time for both morning and noon recesses.

Evaluate II: No student late during 10 days chart in effect for either morning or noon recesses. Average 3.2 students continued to be late for afternoon recess.

Consequate III: Teacher again raised criterion for inclusion on Patriots Chart to on time for all three recess periods.

Evaluate III: No one late after any recess period during five days criterion.

Consequate IV: Teacher informed class that students had done so well chart no longer needed. Teacher could "count on them" to remain patriots.

Evaluate IV: Noon tardiness averaged 5.0 for five days, tardiness after morning recess, 2.6, and after afternoon recess, 2.6.

Consequate V: Teacher reinstated chart for all three recess periods.

Evaluate V: Not one person late after any recess during five days chart in effect.

Consequate VI: Class voted to post an Un-Patriots Chart (those students who were *late*) instead of Patriots Chart. Teacher posted chart every second day for six days, every third day for six days, and every fifth day for last week of project.

Evaluate VI: One student late after one recess during final 18 days of project.

Note: This study indicated that many teachers can carry out very specific projects without the help of outside observers. Also, if a consequence is used that has some meaning to the student and is consistently applied, the results are predictable. Many teachers have used "good" charts of some kind but they are seldom as precise and consistently applied. The specific name given to the charts is meaningful to the students if they have been studying an area and are allowed to decide the name of the chart as well as criterions for inclusion on the chart in conjunction with the teacher.

Scientific Application (p. 309)

Example 64

Pinpoint: *Remediation of mutually aversive interactions between a problem student and four teachers* (13-year-old girl)

Record: High level of student disapproval, high level of teacher disapproval.

Consequate: *Student* was taught to give approval statements to teachers (cued by a tape recorder and earplug) that earned tokens exchangeable for records, extra gym periods, lunches with the English teacher, and extra credit toward English grade.

Evaluate: Student approval increased for all teachers, disapproval decreased. Teachers approval increased, disapproval decreased.

Consequate II: *Student* reversed procedures. Gave three of four teachers more disapproval than approval.

Evaluate II: Two of the teachers then changed back, giving more disapproval than approval.

Consequate III: *Student* again gave more approval to all four teachers, gave low disapproval.

Evaluate III: All four teachers gave high approval to student, low disapproval.

Note: A postcheck without cues or tokens for the student indicated that for two teachers where the student was still giving high approval, low disapproval, the teachers were reciprocating in kind. The two teachers where the student was equally mixed, were giving the same mixed approval/disapproval back to the student. These interactions were still better than baseline. During the postcheck teachers commented on the student's "remarkable socialization" and new found "maturity."

Scientific Application (p. 309)

MIDDLE SCHOOL/JUNIOR HIGH
SCHOOL EXAMPLES

Example 65

Pinpoint: *Homework study time* (11- and 13-year-olds)

Record: Average 4.5 minutes homework per child per school day after four week's recording according to child's records. Parent's spot checks averaged 3.8 minutes.

Consequate: Television viewing time made contingent on homework time whether or not assigned. Each minute of homework or review time redeemable for six minutes of viewing time. Children kept own time logs. Given extra monetary reward when parent's record within two minutes of child's report.

Evaluate: Homework study time increased to 32 minutes per child per day at which time parents changed the study/viewing ratio to 3-1 with no decrease in study time.

Professional Application

Example 66

Pinpoint: *Low-level skill achievement* (ninth grade, industrial arts class)

Record: No evidence of completed individual project or increased skills after fourth week of term.

Consequate: Teacher continually threatened students with failing final grades for lack of industry and productivity.

Evaluate: Only *one* student of eight finished final project.

Note: Anxiety increased were observed during the last few days of class, as students frantically tried to finish projects. One boy was cut with a bandsaw two days before term ended. Students complained that they tried, but "didn't really know what the teacher wanted." This represents a situation where the teacher "did not start where the student is." Thus, threats of disapproval did not produce constructive behavior; rather, threats produced anxiety and subsequent physical harm.

Professional Application

Example 67

Pinpoint: Noisy transition changing classes (eighth grade)

Record: Length of time after bell rang that students took to be in seats steadily increased to eight minutes.

Consequate: "Record party" contingent on all students being in seats before final bell. One "pop" record (brought by students) played during Friday's class for each day all students in seats before final bell.

Evaluate: Extended record parties by end of third week.

Note: A decrease in other maladaptive responses was observed when one record was *deducted* from "Friday's list" for antisocial behavior from any student.

Professional Application

Example 68

Pinpoint: *Chewing-gum vandalism* (eighth grade, Special Education class)

Record: Five (average) gum wads under each desk. Gum wrappers observed on floor (6 to 10 daily).

Consequate: Gum privilege extended with admonition to "be responsible."

Evaluate: Six (average) gum wads under each desk. Gum wrappers on floor (8 to 11 daily).

If at first you don't succeed

Consequate II: Group gum chewing Monday, Wednesday, Friday contingent upon rules: Rule 1—"If an individual is caught chewing Tuesday or Thursday, individual will lose privileges of chewing gum for one week. He must also clean five wads from under desk." Rule 2—"If more than two wrappers are found on floor Monday, Wednesday, or Friday, *entire class* loses gum chewing privileges for one day."

Evaluate II: After three weeks all gum wads removed from under all desks. Two wrappers Monday, Wednesday, and Friday observed on floor.

Note: If contingency would have stipulated *no* gum wrappers, probably all wrappers would have been put away.

Professional Application

Example 69

Pinpoint: Off-task individual study (seventh grade, Special Education class)

Record: Completion of work taking longer each day and extending into next period. (Average time increase—20 minutes by end of third week.)

Consequate: All water-drinking privileges made contingent on finishing work on time. Water-drinking frequency increased considerably but functioned as a positive reward.

Evaluate: Increase in finished work in allotted time by end of fourth day.

Note: The contingent delivery of other materials previously not associated with proper study (crayons, pencils, colors) was later introduced to reward other academic behaviors.

Professional Application

Example 70

Pinpoint: *Constant talking out and disturbing others during study time* (15-year-old boy, math class)

Record: On-task study behavior ranged from 3 to 45% with an average of approximately 25%.

Consequate: Boy took daily report card for teacher to check. Teacher marked yes or no to such items as acceptable use of class time; assignments completed on time; homework assignments; overall behavior good. When student earned all yesses, he received snacks, TV, and permission to go outdoors. Even one "no" resulted in loss of privileges. (Child lived in a foster home for predelinquent boys.)

Evaluate: Study behavior rose to 95%; it remained high for six days of observation.

Consequate II: Student no longer received teacher's checks; he was told he would be granted privileges anyway.

Evaluate II: Study time dropped to 25% the first day, 10% the second day, and boy also got into one fight.

Consequate III: Privileges again made contingent on card signatures.

Evaluate III: Study time increased to 80% first day, dropped for three days until teacher assigned one "no" whereupon on-task study time increased to 100% and remained high for remainder of term.

Note: This study indicates that home-based rewards can maintain on-task school behavior. Rewards were on a daily basis as it was necessary for the teacher as well as foster parents to "prove" that they would, or could, be consistent.

Scientific Application (p. 309)

Example 71

Pinpoint: Fighting during recess (12-year-old boy)

Record: Teacher watched through window and recorded number of days boy hit other children (four out of six days observed).

Consequate: Every time boy hit another child, he was taken into principal's office and given one hard swat with paddle.

Evaluate: Playground fighting *increased* after consequences.

Consequate II: Procedures changed. Boy allowed talking privileges (five minutes) with principal every day he behaved well on playground.

Evaluate: Fighting behavior decreased to zero over four weeks.

Note: Sometimes severe punishment can be actually rewarding to a child. There are children who associate any attention given by authorities or adults as indications of approval. (This is not as absurd as it seems—remember, we discipline those we care about.) Some children receive only negative attention. The application of approval following *good* behavior changes this wrong association.

Professional Application

Example 72

Pinpoint: Vandalism (seventh grade)

Record: Seven students wrote on or destroyed: (1) desks, (2) walls, and (3) school equipment.

Consequate: (1) Desks—students sanded and revarnished damaged desks, plus two others. (2) Walls—students washed *entire* wall. (3) School equipment—students contributed double financial value. All work strictly supervised and completed to satisfaction of teacher. Thereafter, students responsible for property upkeep, regardless of who caused damage. Parents *not allowed* to contribute to restitution in any manner.

Evaluate: Vandalism eliminated. Students' supervision of school property established.

Note: This is perhaps one of the oldest and most effective discipline procedures.

Professional Application

Example 73

Pinpoint: Disruptive behaviors—talking, fighting, out of seat, throwing objects, noisy (seventh grade, 30 students, beginning teacher)

Record: Class met daily for 40 minutes; had 5-minute break followed by a 45-minute session. Observation during first 30 minutes of session showed study behavior to average 47% (25 days). Teacher gave contingent approval average of 6 times, disapproval for disruptive behaviors over 20 times per session.

Consequate: Teacher increased attention to study behavior, decreased attention to off-task behavior. Contingent approval increased to nine times per session, disapproval to nine per session.

Evaluate: Study behavior increased to average of 65% (six days). Noise level, disruptive behavior remained high.

Consequate II: Teacher placed chalk mark on board when students disturbed class. Each mark reduced class break 10 seconds (24 marks canceled break).

Evaluate II: Study behavior increased to 76% (24 days). Noise dropped.

Consequate III: Teacher eliminated disapproval contingencies (chalk marks). Attention to disruptive behavior was increased.

Evaluate III: Study average dropped immediately; noise level increased.

Consequate IV: All procedures reinstated.

Evaluate IV: Study rate increased to 81% (maintained for remainder of study).

Note: The overall noise level remained high even when there was a large gain in on-task study behavior. It was necessary in this well-controlled scientific study to add a disapproval contingency (deprivation of break time for inappropriate behavior) before the classroom was brought under control. It should be emphasized that approval for good behavior can provide a positive atmosphere for learning even when disapproval procedures are employed.

Scientific Application (p. 309)

Example 74

Pinpoint: *"Joy-riding"* (15-year-old boy)

Record: Picked up by police on first offense.

Consequate: Juvenile judge placed boy on probation in care of parents with charge to supply appropriate disapproval. Parents restricted boy to house except for school but purchased highly desired article to "prove they still loved him in spite of the problem."

Evaluate: Boy continued to get in trouble—three serious instances during the next three months.

Note: Parents inadvertently rewarded boy for getting into trouble with "love present" and boy learned that "when you do bad things, good things happen to you."

Professional Application

Example 75

Pinpoint: Disruptive social talking (junior high school, six girls)

Record: Talking recorded on sheet of paper taped to teacher's desk (77% of time, three days).

Consequate: Teacher explained to class that talking during study time interfered with completion of work assignments (this had been done before). Class discussed importance of rules for study, agreed something must be done, and suggested very extreme alternatives. Teacher then stated: "Anyone caught talking in class during study time must leave the room." Five girls sent out during next two days.

Evaluate: Eightfold *decrease* in talking followed four weeks of contingency.

Note: One caution in using this type of procedure should be mentioned. The technique of removing students from a classroom (isolation) is effective only when the classroom provides many positive consequences (i.e., the student would rather spend his time in the classroom than be isolated). The girls in this classroom were *very concerned* with receiving approval from one another as well as from the teacher; thus isolation was effective.

Professional Application

Example 76

Pinpoint: *Juvenile offender* (14-year-old boy)

Record: Many disruptions at home—came before court on two separate occasions: one theft, one ungovernable charge.

Consequate: Summer vacation: spending money contingent upon no more offenses and finishing summer school.

Evaluate: No arrests, although summer school not finished.

Consequate II: Boy placed in County Detention Center during family's vacation.

Evaluate II: Boy left home, went to live with friend's parents.

Consequate III: Kicked out after four weeks—moved to another friend's parents.

Evaluate III: Kicked out after 13 days—went traveling.

Consequate IV: Called father long distance (collect) for money to come home; received money but did not come home.

Evaluate IV: Unknown.

Note: In this case the juvenile was placed by his counselor in the County Detention Center during the family's two-week vacation. It was only then he began to believe that he could not get his own way and thus wanted to live elsewhere. It should be noted that although this boy had just failed all prescribed contingencies regarding summer school work, his parents still planned to take him on vacation in order to "develop a fresh rapport." The above juvenile court counselor reported many failures because of well-intentioned parents who allow children's friends to live with them after these children have run away or been purposely ostracized by their own parents.

Professional Application

Example 77

Pinpoint: Teaching contractual agreements (ninth grade, civics)

Record: Nothing

Consequate: Beginning of term each student wrote contract including amount of work to be completed for special class project as well as evaluation criteria for determining student's grade. Individual contracts exchanged among students. Entire class then chose a project and wrote one contractual agreement determining individual and collective responsibilities, including penalties for "illegal" behaviors. Teacher assumed role of interested bystander as students pursued class project. Disputes during course of project adjudicated in "class court" (some students did not do their share of work).

Evaluate: Effective learning judged by teacher on basis of *ex post facto* essays written by students.

Note: It is interesting that the predominant theme of most essays concerned "fairness." Written contractual agreements are very effective for this age group and can concern any cause-and-effect relationship between the parties (teacher/student, parent/student). Contracts specify contingencies ("If I do my work you promise to pay me," etc.) and may be used for individuals and/or groups. Exactly the same benefits accrue from such written contracts as from similar, more sophisticated adult agreements.

Professional Application

Example 78

Pinpoint: Academic failure (general—12 students, different classrooms, age range 11–14)

Record: Each student failed at least two academic subjects.

Consequate: Individual work-play routines developed with consent of parents. Students given special after-school assignments (approximately 30 minutes). Work immediately checked by parents and points assigned. Points were totaled each day to "buy" privileges and things (TV watching, outside peer playtime; two children received money;

one child—supper; one student—Saturday hiking plus one television program nightly; one student—time using "ham radio"). Time ratio for work-play approximately 1:4 in most cases. Thus, 30 minutes on-task work carried points worth two hours' activity or other reward.

Evaluate: Eleven of 12 students improved (average increase 1.5 letter grades in four months); one 14-year-old ran way from home—this student entirely on money contingency—parents later admitted they began to pay him before, rather than after, study sessions, that is, he was manipulating them, rather than vice versa.

Note: This program is effective, but demands absolute cooperation from parents. Many parents will respond to such a program when they: (1) admit their child has a problem, (2) have some confidence in the programmer (teacher/counselor), and (3) will be *honest* in dispensing rewards.

Professional Application

Example 79

Pinpoint: *Rebelliousness, disagreements, and refusal to talk to parents* (11.5-year-old boy, large for age)

Record: Summer camp and school behavior in sharp contrast to misbehavior at home. (Young man reported camp and school misbehavior punished immediately; related interesting activities contingent on good behavior; therefore, no problem.) Boy indicated obedience only when father angry as father oblivious to misbehavior except when in a "sour mood."

Consequate: Counselor enlisted boy's aid in "experiments." Boy to be on lookout for situations when he could disagree or disobey, then to stop and imagine to himself that father was so angry he was ready to attack verbally and physically. It was explained that if he could control his behavior by imagining an angry father, probably he would not have to face an actual one. Role-playing practice in imagery produced reactions similar to when he actually faced an angry father. Further treatment focused on the boy accepting authority of his father, even when unreasonable.

Evaluate: Home situation improved. First nine days boy reported using the "little trick" anywhere from 10 to 25 times. The first week father had even taken him to an auto show and spent an enjoyable day. (It was pointed out that present obedience and restriction in freedom would result in more freedom later–delay of gratification.) Following some weeks boy took father more into account (turned down volume on record player so it wouldn't disturb father, etc.). During the fourth week an argument developed that was so violent the boy didn't want to return home. Father stayed away from boy for awhile with improvement in relations continuing. Boy received more freedom; it became unnecessary to use "imagining father angry" technique as father became more reasonable and son less inclined to disagree on every little thing.

Note: A professional behavioral therapist helped this boy over a five-month period. The most significant factor appears to be that the boy, by pretending the father was angry, was able to tell himself that disobedience would lead to disapproval. This method of having children "talk to themselves and imagine potentially good or bad results" is a method of assisting in the development of self-control especially if the thoughts are immediately followed by approval. This technique can be enhanced as parents teach children to "label" many aspects of their behavior and follow the reproduction with approval. The results may not be as dramatic as the present case where the use of a thought "trick" improved a terrible home situation, but with continued communication parents are able to assist children in self-control procedures.

Scientific Application (p. 309)

Example 80

Pinpoint: *Increasing math responses* (middle school, 88 students)

Record: One hour spent on individualized math kit. 33.21 average correct responses.

Consequate: Correct responses during 20-minute work session earned 10 minutes of (1) nothing, (2) math games, (3) earphone music listening, (4) group dance.

Evaluate: Gain scores for correct responses after one week: (1) no reward, −2.86; (2) math games, −.41; (3) earphone music listening, 26.05; (4) group dance, 16.00.

Note: The contingent application of reward (music) served to cut the math period in half and still increase correct responses. It is interesting that individual earphone listening, which can be easily dispensed, was actually superior to the group dance in increasing correct math responses. Also, the teacher had been using math games "to help motivate" but upon analysis math games did not function to increase responses.

Scientific Application (p. 309)

Example 81

Pinpoint: *Low arithmetic achievement* (seventh-grade boy, 13 years old).

Record: Number of completed correct problems per minute .47, attention to assigned work averaged 51% (five days recording). Each days assignment corrected and returned the following day.

Consequate I: Student given immediate praise, correct answers marked for each two problems completed (two days), four problems completed (next two days), eight problems (next two days). Final two days of treatment student completed 16 problems before receiving approval.

Evaluate I: Correct answers per minute increased to 1.36. Average percentage attending behavior increased to 97%.

Consequate II: Teacher returned to original procedure: gave student daily worksheet, corrected assignment, and handed back the following day without immediate approval (five days).

Evaluate II: Rate of correct answers decreased to .98. Percentage of attending behavior *decreased* to 82%.

Consequate III: Teacher again instituted immediate feedback. Five problems prior to approval (first day), 10 (second day), 15 (third day). Student completed all 20 problems before receiving approval (last two days).

Evaluate III: Correct arithmetic answers per minute increased to 1.44. Percentage of average attending behavior increased to 97%.

Note: This study demonstrates that when the teacher starts where the student is and gradually trains the student to delay feedback the student's on-task behaviors may increase at the same time. The teacher in this case used a "fixed-ratio" schedule that was adjusted either every day or every other day.

Scientific Application (p. 309)

Example 82

Pinpoint: *Obesity* (64 individuals, 5 to 57 pounds overweight, where medical examination revealed no medical problem and physician supervised medical aspects of diets)

Record: Many environmental stimuli, as well as some bodily responses (emotions), generally become connected with eating in previous history of overweight person. (Many of us eat when we get angry or perhaps when we are sad or just plain tired, "I always feel better if I have something to eat.") In addition certain activities are generally associated with eating or drinking—TV viewing, fixing meals, "I have to see what it tastes like," in coffee breaks, hard work, "A cold beer sure tastes good after working," cocktail parties, "I really shouldn't but just to be sociable," card parties, and so on. Generally many normal everyday activities are habitually associated with food or liquid intake.

Consequate: Instructions given to obese:

1. *Eating place*

The first step is to designate a place (specific chair at specific table) where eating will occur. This place should be maintained with rare exceptions until your weight is down. Engage only in eating at that particular place (i.e., no reading, studying, working, playing). Henceforth, this is your *eating place*. All meals, snacks, and drinks (other than water or low-calorie liquids) should be consumed in that location.

2. *Eat on purpose*

Most of us have become used to engaging in many other behaviors other than eating during meal or snack time. People talk, work, play, watch, listen, and exercise at the very same time they eat. Weight control under these conditions is very difficult. Therefore, discriminations need to be made. To build discriminations one must *eat on purpose*. Do not be distracted from eating in the "eating place." You should contemplate every spoonful, forked morsel, or swallow. The easiest way is to talk to yourself about eating as it occurs. This is behavior incompatible with many other behaviors during mealtime. As you look at a morsel of food you say, "Now I'm going to cut my meat. I must pick up my knife and fork and cut my meat so I can eat it. Now I'm picking up my knife and fork, and now I am cutting my meat so it can be eaten. I lay down my knife, pick up my meat, and take it to my mouth." Stop just before the food gets to the mouth and say, "This meat is now going to be chewed and swallowed." Place the food in the mouth and think about chewing the food and say, "Now I am chewing my food" (chew 20 times saying how good the food is), next as you swallow say, "Now I have swallowed the food, and I am going to get the benefit from that bit of food." This procedure should be followed every meal for a period of two weeks before any diet is started. This procedure insures that food taken into the mouth will get into the mouth *on purpose*. This also serves to bring eating behavior under control of your intentions and to break learned connections between eating and other behaviors. It also slows the rate of eating.

3. *Obesity chart*

During the two weeks that you eat on purpose in your designated place take your morning nude weight every day at the same time (preferably just after getting up in the morning). Construct a large chart that in large letters at the top reads: OBESITY CHART. Record your weight every day. The best procedure is to have someone watch you weigh who should check the scales and make a comment about how fat you look ("Look at those rolls around your stomach: your hips are not very nice looking when you are so fat," etc.). The two-week chart will give you a baseline from which to measure progress and the person (mother, spouse, sister, etc.) will give added incentive to reduce. Make certain the chart is attached to the wall in a prominent place where you can see it as you get ready for the day's activities. Some people also find it helpful to include a measurement chart (waist, etc.).

4. *Breakfast*

Breakfast should be considered a reward for looking neat and clean. A sloppy appearance is conducive to gaining weight (even though you stay at home). Wear clean clothes and engage in appropriate sprucing. Men should shave and be neat even on days off, and women should put on makeup every morning before breakfast.

5. *Diet sarcasm card*

A small card with sarcastic comments relating to eating should be typed, carried with you, and read before, during, and after every meal; also, whenever you feel hungry during the day. Such a card might contain the following statements:

a. I enjoy eating more than feeling good.
b. It is fun to be overweight—everyone enjoys looking at me.
c. Fat persons are so likeable they receive many invitations for dates from neat people.

d. High blood pressure doesn't bother me because it is better than losing weight.
e. I could never have a heart attack. It only happens to those other fat people.
f. It is so pleasant to wear my dresses that are as large as tents. In fact, I may develop until I can get work in a circus.

6. *Eating Cue*

Use something at the table that is always present when you eat. For example, use a small hourglass or brightly colored napkin or conspicuous charm (any brightly colored object will do). When you sit down to eat take the object, place it in view, and say, "This gives me permission to eat," then read the card, look at the object, and go through the *eating on purpose* routine. This object with the card gives a carryover to other situations, and you may come to feel guilty if it is not being used.

7. *Eat off schedule*

Schedule meals at variable times during the day and stick to your *variable schedule*. If other members of the family are unable to meet your schedule, then it is better to eat by yourself. *This does not mean to snack between your variable schedule.*

8. *Calorie chart*

Every morsel of food should be logged with number of calories as it is eaten on an intake chart that shows your quota for each day.

9. *Additional helps*

a. If you shop, shop by list only, and never allow yourself to buy anything that is not on your list.
b. Prepare the shopping list immediately after dinner.
c. Food should be out of sight when beginning the program except when actually eating or preparing meals.
d. One-half hour before each mealtime take a small 6-ounce glass of juice or appropriate liquid. Thus, you will probably not be as hungry when mealtime arrives.
e. Remember to get your diet from a doctor and stay under his supervision during your program.

Evaluate: All individuals lost weight (average 15 pounds) from following the above procedures. In combination these procedures are extremely effective; some people report weight loss by using just one of the above. Proper body weight is much like most other aspects of life, it usually takes discipline.

Professional Application

Example 83

Pinpoint: *Negative verbalizations* (three youngsters—9, 12, and 14 years old)

Record: One hundred nineteen occurrences in one week counted during afternoons and evening by mother.

Consequate: (Negative modeling.) Bad examples illustrated using TV commercials (e.g., "My wash is whiter than your wash." "Isn't Gladys fat, oh! here she comes . . . tried that old (product) time and time again. Okay, have it your way—you'll see." (later) "See I told you so, you never listen." "Husbands can't do anything—let me do it—*see*," etc.)

Evaluate: Youngsters began to become sensitized to their verbalizations and actually started keeping records to help each other decrease such "nasty" comments. Mother counted only five comments during the fifth week.

Note: Television provides an excellent source for both positive and negative behaviors. TV can be used to sensitize as well as shape both appropriate and inappropriate behaviors. Adults must be present, however, if they want to take part in the definition.

Professional Application

Example 84

Pinpoint: Physical abuse of mother (15-year-old boy)

Record: Boy placed in county juvenile detention center for physical abuse of widowed mother, throwing her out of house, threatening others with a gun. Boy stated that he only wanted to play his guitar and be left entirely alone.

Consequate: (1) Guitar lessons contingent on assigned work tasks. Guitar removed if tasks not completed. (2) Communication sessions developed between mother and son, using boy's music as subject matter. Also, music paired with talk sessions to decrease high emotional responses. (3) Role-playing sessions between counselor and mother to establish correct verbalizations.

Evaluate: Case terminated after four weeks (guitar was removed once); no beatings, arrests, or verbal abuses.

Note: The mother in this case was being unwittingly controlled by her son. In her words, "Every time I try to talk with Fred and explain how I feel, he somehow turns my words against me and then goes into his room to listen to music; I am deeply concerned that he just doesn't understand me." Many adults, as the widow in this case, try to reason and explain their feelings, yet become "used" by young people. Reinforcing this insensitive behavior is certainly unproductive for adults and does little but produce a kind of "sadism." It seems extremely unproductive when adults allow young people to use divorce, adoption, lack of love, peer or sibling comparisons, and so on, to get their way. In this case, the mother had fallen into the trap of "trying even harder to make her son understand her." It should be noted that after the boy's verbal and physical abuse stopped and he was rewarded for *appropriate* behavior (i.e., household duties, clearing the year, not arguing, etc.), he did start to "understand" his mother.

Scientific Application (p. 308)

Example 85

Pinpoint: Off-task, low-achieving students (seventh grade, 12 students)

Record: Students off-task 56.4%, teacher academic approval 44.9, teacher social approval ratio 3.0 (10 days observation).

Consequate I: Eight students taken from room and received daily group counseling (four were given behavioral counseling through role playing, modeling appropriate classroom behaviors, and reinforcement for verbalizing appropriate classroom behavior; four students were given "client-centered" counseling and helped to verbalize and interpret classroom behavior). Four students remained in room as a control group to check effects of group counseling.

Evaluate I: Four students in behavioral counseling increased on-task behavior 6.8%. Four students in client-centered counseling increased on-task behavior 2.2%. Control group decreased on-task behavior 11.3% (average on-task for all 12 was 57%). Teachers' academic approval ratio was 11.7 and social approval ratio was 1.5.

Consequate II: Counseling continued for both groups (four weeks of treatment) instructed in contingent use of approval techniques (one week).

Evaluate II: Behavioral counseling group increased on-task behavior an additional 38.1%, client-centered counseling group increased on-task behavior an additional 27.7%, no-contact control group increased on-task behavior 40.7% (average on-task for all 12 was 21.3%). Teacher academic approval ratio was 62.2%, social approval ratio was 62.4%.

Consequate III: Counseling continued, teacher continued attention for both academic and social behavior, also instituted a token reinforcement system (tokens were given for appropriate social behavior, redeemable on Friday afternoons for donuts and soda pop, 2 weeks).

Evaluate III: Behavioral counseling group increased on-task behavior another 7.8% (2.1% total off-task), client-centered increased on-task behavior another 10.8% (total off-task 18.5%), control group increased on-task another 5.7% (total off-task 19.6%). Average off-task for all twelve 13.4%. Teacher academic approval ratio was 76.3%, social approval ratio was 86.7%.

Consequate IV: Counseling discontinued, teacher instructed to behave as before the study began (one week).

Evaluate IV: All 12 students increased inappropriate behavior (41.2% off-task). No significant difference between three counseling groups.

Consequate V: Teacher reinstituted approving academic and social behavior, also reinstated token system.

Evaluate V: Average on-task behavior for all 12 students averaged 93.2%. Teachers academic approval ratio averaged 42.8%, social approval ratio averaged 91.1%.

Note: This study indicates that the teacher is the major instigator of both appropriate and inappropriate behavior even on the seventh-grade level. It also indicates that counseling outside the classroom for classroom behavioral problems is probably not effective unless the teacher reinforces appropriate classroom behavior. Even though behavioral counseling was more effective than client-centered counseling, behavioral counseling had little effect until the teacher used contingent approval. The study also indicated that the teacher is better able to change behavior where the problem occurs (in the classroom).

Scientific Application (p. 310)

HIGH SCHOOL/ADULT EXAMPLES

Example 86

Pinpoint: School failure (16-year-old boy)

Record: Failed all academic subjects first half of year. Parents and teachers unable to "motivate studying."

Consequate: School counselor developed system with parents' co-operation. Every teacher signed individual *daily progress report* (one small sheet) after each class. Decision of signing for appropriate social and academic behaviors based on teacher's criteria. Allowance, social engagements, car privileges contingent on number of signatures earned each day.

Evaluate: Better grades. C+ average attained for last six-week period of same year.

Note: Many parents offer rewards for good grades but cannot find a way to cut down the time interval so that rewards are meaningful in motivating the student. A complete academic term is very long for a student who cannot exhibit correct study patterns throughout one day.

Professional Application

Example 87

Pinpoint: *"Love note" passing—boy-girl talking* (eleventh grade, biology class)

Record: Five intercepted notes in one week (three innocuous—two vulgar). Twenty incidents of talking during one class period.

Consequate: Friday field trip privilege contingent upon "no more talking or letter writing."

Evaluate: Friday field trip *denied* two consecutive weeks—given third week after talking and letter writing stopped.

Note: Field trips were continued throughout year. However, trips were subsequently denied four times for talking—sometimes students forget.

Professional Application

Example 88

Pinpoint: Homework study (high school, 17-year-old girl)

Record: Grades monitored for one semester. Average grade D—with frequent failures.

Consequate: Flash cards developed by student to assist study in history, civics, Latin. Meals contingent (except breakfast) on success in responses to cards.

Evaluate: Within eight weeks grades rose from D to a B—average.

Note: Researchers noted the /flash cards may have been reinforcing instead of the food. However, a follow-up at a later semester indicated grades had returned to a D average. Obviously, cards or grades alone were not sufficient rewards for this girl. Motivation must come from without before it gets "in." The question of how long it takes for motivation to "get in" for each individual is not known. However, it would appear that even constant rewarding is better than constant failure.

Scientific Application (p. 310)

Example 89

Pinpoint: Boredom (tenth grade, Spanish)

Record: Lack of enthusiasm for subject-matter acquisition—only 2 of 23 assignments completed in two-week period

Consequate: Friday football game instituted: teams chosen, rules established, points, yards, substitutions, and so on, developed for correct *academic* responses. Game played on chalkboard with losing team providing "treat" for winners.

Evaluate: "Enthusiasm replaced boredom"—all assignments completed by second Friday.

Note: Any game can be used for any subject matter. It is best to choose a game specifically appropriate to the general outside interests of the student age group.

Professional Application

Example 90

Pinpoint: *Guffaw laughing* (tenth grade, six boys)

Record: Girl's recitations elicited loud laughing from boys.

Consequate: Boys collectively taken out of room—brought back individually in front of class as girls applauded. Seating arrangements also changed to place each boy among group of girls.

Evaluate: Guffaw laughing ended.

Note: The same procedure of boy-girl seating was employed for the student body during general assemblies, resulting in considerable decrease in catcalls and noise. It also helped boy-girl socialization.

Professional Application

Example 91

Pinpoint: *Positive verbalizations about oneself and positive social interactions* (16-year-old boy)

Record: Boy avoided peer interaction; stated he did not like himself because his parents couldn't stand him; stated he was no good and no one could possibly like him (self-records indicated over 20 times per day debased self and no positive peer or adult contact—two weeks' records).

Consequate: To teach good "self-concept" (appropriate self-labeling), boy was instructed to: (1) record positive verbalizations, (2) list hierarchy of interests and good points (himself and parents), (3) carry list in pocket and read list whenever he caught himself in self-abasement (incompatible response), (4) initiate peer contact (one per day) based on similar peer interests, (5) interact verbally with parents 10 minutes per day in positive way.

Evaluate: One close friendship within six weeks (average three to four positive contacts daily); joined boy's science club. After three weeks, he talked positively regarding parents.

Note: "Self-concept" usually relates to cognitive behavior and to a phenomenon called *labeling*, that is, "I am a good person" as opposed to "I am no good" or "My student is a good person" versus "He is just a bad boy." Research regarding "labeling" seems quite conclusive in its implications regarding cause-and-effect relationships between labels and behavior. If a student gets the idea that he (she) is a "bad person," this will probably influence his (her) behavior. That is, the student will behave in accordance with this "self-concept."

Professional Application

Example 92

Pinpoint: *Noncooperation* (eleventh grade, English, five boys)

Record: No English assignments completed during two-week period. Students also refused to recite orally. Boys caught "shooting craps" in back of room.

Consequate: All boys sent to principal's office and given a "good talking to" concerning classroom responsibilities and advantages of learning English.

Evaluate: No change occurred in behavior. Boys became more non-cooperative and began to mimic female teacher. Caught shooting craps twice during following week.

If at first you don't succeed

Consequate II: Teacher began to praise every class member who cooperated in giving oral recitations from selected literature.

Evaluate II: No change noted. Not one boy volunteered to participate in oral recitations. Teacher saw dice once but didn't catch boys in any games.

Consequate III: Everyone who participated in oral recitations allowed to bring any book or magazine to class for 30 minutes of private reading.

Evaluate III: One noncooperative boy brought a *Playboy* magazine to teacher after class and asked sarcastically: "If I read aloud from your book, can I read mine?" Teacher agreed. Next session he did. Within four weeks all boys recited.

Note: The teacher was also able to shift these boys' interest from *Playboy* to *Hot Rod,* and after four months to sophisticated sports magazines found in the school library. This case demonstrates effective use of peer contingencies and approximations toward better literature through lack of censorship.

Professional Application

Example 93

Pinpoint: *Use of illegal drugs* (17-year-old boy)

Record: "Pot," three to four times weekly; LSD, two occurrences.

Consequate: Boy began research on effects of drugs and was paid $8.00 for each two-page paper written.

Evaluate: LSD discontinued.

Note: This boy stated he found what he considered good evidence for discontinuing LSD but found conflicting evidence on the dangers of marijuana, so he decided not to stop. Many others with same contingencies have decided to give up all drugs because of legal, occupational, religious, and/or societal consequences. The use of drugs is becoming more and more widespread and the age of users progressively younger. New drugs are being used indiscriminately and many times there is not scientific data available as in the above case. PCP "angel dust," cocaine "coke," as well as other drugs are becoming more and more prevalent. While newspaper stories attest to the dangers of drugs, almost all users know or think they know the many differentiations of what will hurt or not. Most often this information is gotten from other participants. As has been repeatedly stated the effects of "modeling" are tremendously powerful and this is especially true from peers. Regardless, solid information concerning drugs when available (e.g., differentiating among drugs) and early *preventative* measures seem most effective.

Professional Application

Example 94

Pinpoint: Fear of failure, worrying (17-year-old girl)

Record: Girl reported "worrying constantly." Mother recorded average of 12 times per day daughter talked about upcoming "problems."

Consequate: (1) Time set for 15 minutes of daily worry. Must worry "hard" during this time, imagining all the bad things that might happen. (2) Rank ordered all possible outcomes of failure in upcoming events. (3) Instructed to say "stop," subvocally, every time worrying started during other times of day and change to organized study routine immediately after recording one instance of worrying on worry card carried by girl.

Evaluate: Worrying increased to "constantly" (daughter's own statement, no actual record). Worrying during prescribed time seemed "silly."

Consequate II: Girl told worrying had probably actually decreased from "constantly," had actual record been made, to point that she could discriminate between when she was or was not worrying; therefore, worry could be counted.

Evaluate II: Worrying decreased to twice daily; 15-minute worrying period decreased to 5 minutes (worry time became negative).

Note: Eventually the worrying time became extremely silly as girl learned to plan constructive activities, and worry time was discontinued.

Professional Application

Example 95

Pinpoint: Rehearsal effectiveness (high school band)

Record: *All* stops by conductor constituted disapproval responses (traditional rehearsing procedure).

Consequate: Band director marked two notated musical scores (equal difficulty and unfamiliar to band) with periodic pencil checks that divided musical phrases. During first score, director stopped at each checkpoint, delivered *disapproval* responses regardless of performance quality. During second score, director stopped at checks and delivered specific compliments to performers.

Evaluate: Compliments produced "a better performance and rehearsal attitude." Rehearsal time judged for equal performance level: disapproval 33 minutes; approval 19 minutes.

Professional Application

Example 96

Pinpoint: Using adoption to control adults (16-year-old girl)

Record: Girl used statements concerning her adoption to "get her way." Engaged parents in "proving their love" and providing "payoff" (seven instances in one month).

Consequate: Parents instructed to ignore all talk concerning adoption, to leave girl's presence when subject brought up unless girl verbalized approval statements, and to prepare for extreme test.

Evaluate: Girl ran away; she returned the following weekend.

Consequate II: Girl instructed by parents that parental approval would continue to be contingent on good behavior, not on genetic involvement.

Evaluate II: The use of "adoption" to control parents ceased.

Note: Many children (at all ages) use adult concern, worry, or guilt to change the adults behavior. The child learns one of several perverted associations. "When I get punished and act hurt long enough, someone will give in," that is, good things happen after I suffer. "They love me, so if I act nasty long enough they'll give up," that is, to stop the negative behavior adults provide payoff. This reinforces the adults as obnoxious behavior stops, but children are reinforced for persisting in negative behavior for longer and longer periods. "When I get their goat anything is likely to happen," i.e., child's payoff *is* the anger of the adults (parents or teachers).

Professional Application

Example 97

Pinpoint: *Garbage removal from kitchen* (15-year-old boy)

Record: Mother recorded reminding boy to take out garbage an average of five times prior to any action.

Consequate: If garbage not removed prior to supper, garbage can was placed on boy's chair at evening meal.

Evaluate: Entire family laughed the first time son discovered the can. Boy promptly took the can outside and returned to the kitchen. Three days later the same procedure was employed. Following six instances (during three-week period), boy decided to give himself reminder cues, constructed a sign in bedroom "empty the trash." Job completed with no relapses.

Note: In this case parents were able to remove themselves from an unpleasant disapproval and interact in joking fashion while still making it very clear the job should be completed. Similar techniques have been used for other household chores. One father put his 16-year-old's dinner on a tray and placed it under her bed behind some dirty clothes. The clothes had to be removed before the dinner was obtained. With older children these consequences primarily serve as reminders.

Professional Application

Example 98

Pinpoint: Embarrassment (tenth-grade music, three girls)

Record: Self-evaluation indicated students possessed "no musical talent." Students refrained from individual singing, stating "My voice sounds funny," or "I cannot carry a tune."

Consequate: Twofold program to: (1) teach all students discrimination between (a) possessing ability and (b) performing before class, and (2) teach entire class role playing to deliver approval feedback to "insecure students."

Evaluate: Students learned to participate in activities, even though they did not possess even moderate "talents." Class also taught to smile, nod heads, keep eye contact, and approvingly reinforce a terrible performance. Teacher played role of extremely poor singer while class learned to "put a performer at ease" by *not* responding to performer's fear and avoidance with fear and avoidance, but with approving reinforcement. Shy performers began participating regularly. One girl stated: "I have always known I've had a lousy voice, but now I love to sing."

Note: Students in upper grades who have a problem with embarrassment in relation to any activity have *learned* this embarrassment from someone. It is usually learned traumatically. For example, the young child sings and enjoys himself until one day he shockingly learns his voice sounds terrible, whereupon he stops singing.

Unfortunately, some teachers do not understand the importance of teaching discriminations, and therefore continuously prepare many youngsters for disillusionment—some for catastrophe. Dedicated to well-intended censorship, many teachers pretend that no one is different from anyone. "Celia has only one arm, but in my classroom she has two, just like everyone else." "Fred has a lisp, but in my classroom we ignored his impediment." "Spencer is a Negro, but in my classroom everyone's skin is the same." It is unfortunate that these children must get out on the playground where other children do not censor: "Hey, Celia, what happened to your arm?" "Gosh, Fred, you talk funny." "Why are your hands white, Spencer?" Some children even make fun of these differences. Yet where can children learn to accept differences proudly and not make fun?—certainly not in a classroom in which differences *do not exist*. Children can easily be taught discrimination of differences. Much more important, they can be taught *acceptance* and *respect* for differences. This learning, however, will not come from censorship.

Professional Application

Example 99

Pinpoint: *"Inappropriate" sexual advances* (16-year-old girl)

Record: Six cases of boys responding on dates with sexually aggressive behavior opposite to that desired by girl (last school term, following recent move to new school).

Consequate: Girl instructed (practiced role playing) in delivering verbal response and changing bodily responses in order to elicit more "appropriate," fewer "inappropriate," responses from male peers. Girl instructed to dress differently.

Evaluate: "Inappropriate" sexual behavior decreased to zero after four weeks. Dating also decreased by one-half.

Note: Effective social behavior is made up of correctly interpreting and giving cues. Sometimes even when *NO* cues are given people are subjected to sexually aggressive behavior. Regardless, people should not be naive in assessing the effects of their own actions.

Professional Application

Example 100

Pinpoint: Lawbreaking (40 delinquent boys, average age 17.8, lower socioeconomic)

Record: Average age at first arrest 13.5; average number arrests 8.2; total time incarceration 15.1 months. All boys arrested approximately same age, same nationality, equal number of months in jail, similar residence and religious preferences.

Consequate: One group participated in consequences, one "control" group did not. Boys were not in school (most of them should have been) and met on street corners or other places of frequent occupancy. Each boy was offered job and told that the researcher wanted to know "how teenagers felt about things." Boys who participated were rewarded with food, cokes, money, or tokens, depending on each individual case. No punishment was employed. Occasionally, bonus rewards given for prompt arrival, proper verbalizations, and spontaneous interest.

Evaluate: Groups were compared three years later. Consequate group averaged 2.4 arrests, other group 4.7; average number of months in jail 3.5 for consequate group, 6.9 for other group. Illegal acts committed by consequate group less frequent and much less severe.

Note: In this particular study, consequences were *not* directed toward criminal behavior itself but represented an attempt to teach prosocial behavioral patterns. When a boy did not appear, the researcher would meet him out on the street and bring him to the lab. It is sometimes important for the teacher to go after a child and bring him where he should be. Any peer group such as the above juvenile group can exercise tremendous pressure toward group conformity. Often peer rewards must be broken down or changed if the teacher is to succeed.

Scientific Application (p. 310)

Example 101

Pinpoint: *Excessive local directory-assistance telephone calls* (over one million persons in a large city area)

Record: Telephone directory-assistance calls monitored from 1962–1976.

Consequate: Telephone subscribers allowed three local directory-assistance calls per month. Subscribers were then charged 20¢ for each additional local directory-assistance call. No change was placed on long-distance directory-assistance calls.

Evaluate: Frequency of local calls dropped markedly (60,000 per day). Frequency of long-distance directory-assistance calls remained the same.

Note: The use of the 20¢ charge fits the description of a *response cost procedure.* That is, the charge is contingent on the response of making a directory-assistance call. Many similar response cost procedures have been used in educational token systems. Often the response cost represents the most viable alternative to punishment (e.g., taking away tokens for cheating or breaking rules).

Scientific Application (p. 310)

Example 102

Pinpoint: *Low-level English achievement* (high school dropouts, 17 students)

Record: No academic performance, all students out of school during summer.

Consequate I: Students contacted on city streets during summer induced to "try coming to school a few days for rewards." Local merchants donated (1) food—hamburgers, cokes, malts, sandwiches, etc.; (2) music—records and passes; (3) free time; (4) teacher attention; (5) grades. Students assigned a different consequence each day.

Evaluate I: Fourteen boys completed English requirements during regular year, decided to return to high school in fall.

Note: Of special interest in this study was the disparity between stated preferences and actual behavior. At first of summer all boys were presented paired items from reinforcement menu and asked which they would work for (e.g., would you work harder for a McDonald's hamburger or 10 minutes of free time). All classes of items were paired with all other classes. The order of preference at the beginning of the summer was (1) food, (2) music records and passes, (3) free time, (4) grades, (5) teacher attention. At the end of the summer the same questionnaire was given all boys. The order of preference as stated by the boys was exactly the same at the beginning of the summer as at the end. However, accurate records kept on the actual work output of each boy indicated that during the first week of summer school they did indeed work harder for material rewards and food but during the last week of summer school, while the stated preference had not changed, the most work was actually produced when followed by *teacher attention.*

Professional Application

Example 103

Pinpoint: Academic "apathy" (eleventh grade, history, poverty-level backgrounds)

Record: *No* evidence of *any* study behavior. Five days constant harassment.

Consequate: Teacher left *all* books and teaching materials home, sat at the desk, looked at students, and said nothing. Teacher continued procedure day after day throughout *one entire week.* Did not attempt to teach, control class, or respond in any way.

Evaluate: During the second week, two students timidly brought books to class and asked what to do. Teacher brought the two students to front of room and began teaching. As days passed, other students joined the small learning group. By end of six weeks, every student was involved. Last seven students came into learning group on same day.

Note: Much is said in education about students establishing their own goals. This study is an excellent example of this concept at its most basic level—for there is an infinite distance between zero and one. Most students do not know what their goals are. If they can engage a teacher in battle, this often becomes their goal. In the above case, students were left with nothing. In time, they began to want something, anything, even school work. Ignoring takes a temporal patience many teachers could well develop. Concerning these students, it should be noted that children who live in extreme deprivation meet boredom and apathy as an old friend. Perhaps more sophisticated students would have developed goals during this long period that excluded the teacher entirely.

When a teacher decides to accept the contingencies (goals) of the student peer group, he should do so in full knowledge of possible results. When speaking of "children establishing their own goals," it would seem wise for teachers to think this concept through. Most often this cliché indicates that the teacher *decides* to let children *decide* certain innocuous things. "You may choose any color you wish—you may not color on the wall." If, from the beginning, goals were left *entirely* to children, formal education would cease to exist. Knowledge and/or decisions cannot exist in a vacuum—"Tell me something you *do not know.*"

Professional Application

Example 104

Pinpoint: *On-task versus cluttered communication* (13-, 15-, and 17-year-old teenagers, adults)

Record: "Lack of communication" reported by teenagers and parents after initial misunderstandings regarding use of car, hour of return from dates, work responsibilities at home, school work. Discussions characterized by noise, interruptions, TV, telephone, loud talking, etc. (80 occurrences in three two-hour periods).

Consequate: Family communication sessions instituted with rules: (1) we speak softly, (2) we speak one at a time, (3) we listen carefully, (4) we do not contradict, (5) we might have to *agree to disagree* on some issues, and (6) we will verbalize opposite viewpoint to satisfaction of other person to prove we understand. Sessions free from any extrinsic interruptions, set up daily after dinner beginning with 5 minutes (oven timer set) and gradually increasing to 25 minutes.

Evaluate: "On-task" communication. No interruptions during communication times—other problems decreased.

Note: As adults, it is important to help children (perhaps even ourselves) to make some basic discriminations. On-task communication, for example, does not automatically occur just because two people are in proximity to one another. Time must be scheduled that ideally has no interruptions. On-task communication does not occur in movie houses, while watching television, or necessarily even when the families take some time off and spend a weekend or longer vacation together.

Although worthwhile activities should be given the time and attention deserved, on-task communication should not be confused with other activities. The classic example is the father who wondered why he couldn't communicate with his son after eight years of weekend fishing together. Many parents, as well as older children, actually believe that going to the movies together, camping together, attending school functions, going to church together, and so on, are prerequisites for, or somehow take the place of, communication and other important interactions. The boy in the above example could fish very well.

Certainly activities may give an impetus to start communication, but human beings are not able to be on-task to two things at precisely the same time and do justice to both. When people enjoy activities, they should not confuse the emotional involvement of "feeling good" while engaged in the activity with other important behaviors (communication). There are individuals who appear to never engage in any family activities, yet are on-task in time spent communicating, teaching kindness, and maintaining extremely satisfying lives with significant others.

Professional Application

Example 105

Pinpoint: Developing a study routine (36 teenage students, girls and boys)

Record: Average grade level considered by both teachers and parents to be at least one letter grade below potential (average grades C−).

Consequate: Students were asked to indicate amount of time each felt appropriate to achieve goal (raising grades). Total time indicated was cut by 40%, after which a contract signed by pupil, teacher, and parent. Specific routines developed to aid in concentration:

1. *Underlining*

First it was explained that learning to underline or to outline were *not* the same as learning assigned material (many students have developed negative reactions particularly to these two activities). If students want to learn to draw lines it should be done with many colored pencils, a ruler, and blank paper. If students want to outline, the daily paper will do just as well as school material.

2. *Concentration*

The important aspects of study are *on-task* concentration and repetition of materials not fully learned (asking oneself questions and answering as the material is studied—talking to oneself). On-task study time determined by each student before beginning to study material. Students also noted the number of their distracting thoughts (no student was able to complete *six* minutes of study time with fewer than eight distraction marks). On-task study time was increased in following manner: Each student purchased a timer (kitchen timer, $4.00 to $7.00) with his own money and set aside only weekday study times that fit individual schedule (weekends free from nagging parents appealed to all students).

3. *Study place*

Students chose a "study place" where only study would take place. If necessary, other members of family used the same spot, but the student with the problem could study only there and nowhere else in the house. A straight-backed chair was chosen, with attempts made to place chair facing a corner or blank wall. Prominent signs were constructed warning family members (including parents) to stay away during study time. Distractions such as music (radios, "hi fi") were eliminated (these do *not* increase studying effectiveness). Only one book or one set of materials was taken to study place for each study session.

4. *Distraction cards*

Students used 5 X 8 inch cards labeled as to date, time started, time finished, session number, as well as open space for distractions (distracting thoughts or interruptions). Students chose a pleasant activity to engage in during break times (reading, eating, listening to radio, talking with friends, telephone calls, etc.), got materials ready, removed watches and other indicators of time, filled in the card, set kitchen timer for six minutes, and began to study. Whenever the student was distracted in any way (defined by student to help teach discrimination between on-task and off-task behavior), the student marked in space provided for distractions and also wrote in longhand at the bottom of card, "Get back to work." After having first noticed a distraction (competing sound, daydreaming, thinking of opposite sex, etc.), initial inclination is to go back to work; writing little note "Get back to work" prevents this for a moment and serves to make concentration more desirable, discriminations more complete.

5. *Timer* (positioned so students couldn't see face)

When the timer rang, the students stood up immediately, took the timer, and moved away from study area. Reset timer for two minutes, then engaged in "fun" activity until timer again sounded; whereupon students went through same routine filling in new card. This procedure was repeated until the total time period allotted for study passed. Students changed from six-minute study session to nine-minute study session when number of distraction marks (and corresponding self-written work instructions) numbered two or fewer.

6. *Study schedules*

Students were permitted 3-minute break for 9-minute study period. Each time distractors had been reduced to 2 or below, students moved up scale (study 6, break 2; study 9, break 3; study 12, break 4; study 15, break 5; study 18, break 6; study 21, break 7; study 24, break 8; study 27, break 9; study 30, break 10; study 33, break 11; study 36, break 12; study 39, break 13; study 42, break 14; study 45, break 15) until reaching maximum. Students were strongly encouraged to never study longer than 45 minutes while using a 15-minute break for pleasant activities. This routine builds strong study skills as well as gives approval rewards following each small study session.

7. *External rewards*

Some parents/students used extra incentives (movies, car privileges, staying out time, money, family outings) for moving up study scale *while maintaining absolute honesty*. Of course, many students were delighted with a routine that didn't start with amount of homework to be finished but with amount of time to be studied (when no homework was available or required, student reviewed materials for test).

Evaluate: Average grades (31 students) increased to B within three school terms. Follow-up indicated 24 students maintained this level or above during entire following school year. Five students who did *not* improve admitted to never getting with the program. Seven students who did not *maintain* grade level did not consistently adhere to program primarily as results of *parents* who did not change their normally punitive, nagging reaction—who expressed doubts as to mental capabilities of their children or effectiveness of program; and who did not encourage positively through words and extra incentives. Five students with parents falling into above category succeeded in spite of parental negativism and lack of support. (All later confided to school personnel they were going to prove to their parents that they were not "stupid" and continued the program in spite of lack of support. Three of these finally set up study places in friend's or relative's homes away from "distracting" influence of negative parents.)

Note: This routine has been used successfully with junior high students, upper-level grade school students, college students, and professionals who need to learn discrimination between on-task study as opposed to clutter. Most students do not enjoy their rest or fun times because they begin to feel "guilty" about not doing work. Alternately, when they attempt to study, they begin to feel sorry for themselves because they are not out having a good time!

Professional Application

Example 106

Pinpoint: Dishonesty (any classroom, anywhere)

Record: Three students caught cheating on first exam of term.

Consequate: F grades assigned without explanation.

Evaluate: Same three students caught stealing "ditto master" of second exam from typist's wastebasket.

Consequate II: Each student asked to write short theme stating reasons for cheating.

Evaluate II: Same three students caught cheating in falsifying laboratory manual.

Consequate III: Students asked to prepare confessional speech to be delivered before entire class. Parents of two students strongly objected, stating such treatment "would not only be a terrible experience, but damage children's reputations." Principal received call from school board member, after which students, parents, and teachers instructed to meet in principal's office. At meeting, all students denied any cheating whatsoever. Teacher presented first themes of confession. Parents of one student immediately placed her in private school. Parents of second student persuaded principal to allow daughter to withdraw from course. Parents of third student did not come to meeting. Teacher required this girl to make confessional statement before class. She did, but broke down crying before finishing. She later told teacher it was the worst thing she ever did in her life. Much later, she told the teacher that it was the *second* worst thing she ever did in her life.

Evaluate III, IV, V, VI, etc.: *The science of behavior is predictable.* You know all three of these students, regardless of age, sex, or position.

Fictional Application

STUDY GUIDE FOR CHAPTER 6

Questions:

Answer all questions and then check your answers by locating the appropriate pinpoint in Part II.

Correct every false answer and rewrite so that the statement becomes true or write 30 additional true-false statements using pinpoints (Examples) not previously used in this activity.

True-False

1. Overt behaviors, such as teasing, probably elicit payoffs from classmates.
2. Behaviors that have been diminished (such as reducing activity to a more appropriate level) may be internalized to the point that they are self-reinforcing.
3. Students learn more effectively if initially taught abstract concepts rather than specifics.
4. Long-term observational feedback increases teacher effectiveness more than daily observational feedback.
5. Student repair of damaged equipment and/or financial restitution rarely stops vandalism.
6. Special activities, such as field trips, may be made contingent on appropriate classroom behavior.
7. Research indicates that teacher approval is always the best reinforcer for controlling classroom behavior.
8. Inconsistent rules are more likely to be manipulated by students.
9. Specific situational rules are made to be broken.
10. Loud reprimands often tend to increase, rather than decrease, disruptive classroom behavior.

11. The technique of removing students from a classroom as punishment is effective only when the classroom provides positive consequences for the student.

12. Some content areas do not lend themselves to making a game out of learning.

13. Academically related materials (pencils, crayons, paper, books, experiments) may be used as reinforcers for appropriate academic behaviors.

14. Rewards following student behavior are more meaningful when given at appropriate time intervals.

15. Children do not learn specific behavioral discrimination through negative practice.

16. Most teachers mistakenly feel that they use more approval than disapproval in the classroom.

17. Practice and/or role playing in delivery of approval or disapproval responses is not necessary for the experienced teacher who can apply these responses intuitively.

18. If students are to learn appropriate discriminations, they must be taught to discern differences.

19. Young students, if given no instruction, are capable of establishing all of their own goals.

20. Once the behavior to be changed is pinpointed and rewards gathered, treatment must be consistent and persistent to be effective.

21. Behavior that has been reinforced in the past may persist even when the specific reinforcers used to establish the behavior are no longer given.

22. Many rewards offered by teachers and parents for appropriate behavior are ineffective because the time interval between the behavior and the reward is too long.

23. Some scientific studies apply contingencies to classroom behavior and then take them out again in an attempt to hide research results from the classroom teacher.

24. Hitting and other aggressive behaviors are to be expected from young children as these behaviors are innate.

25. Attitudes are probably learned through behavioral principles much as other behaviors.

26. The ability to choose specific reinforcers is very important when interacting with older students.

27. Attention to inappropriate behavior may increase rather than decrease behavior the teacher desires to reduce.

28. Withdrawal of approval may be ineffective if the teacher uses predominantly disapproval to control inappropriate behavior.

29. Children may be taught to ignore inappropriate behavior from each other.

30. Many times, it is necessary for the teacher to remediate social behavior before the subject material can be learned.

LEARNING ACTIVITY 11—PINPOINT RANKING EXERCISE

A behavior is anything a person does that can be observed and measured. Ideas (values) are generally made more and more behavioral as behaviors are specified in observable and measurable terms; consider for example the following Values (Ideas)—Behaviors—Values (Goals) Chart.

Definitions lead from inferential nonbehavioral ideas (C) toward very specific observable and measurable behaviors (A).

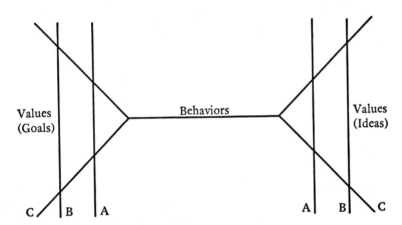

A—Pinpoint defined in terms of specific behaviors. Behavior is both observable and measurable and therefore overtly demonstrable. It can be observed without further definition (nonambiguous).

B—Pinpoint somewhat inferential, some ambiguity involved. Additional definition or more specific delineation necessary before precise observation and recording can take place.

C—Pinpoint definitely an inference, is nonobservable, and nonmeasurable as stated.

Task 1: Assign a definitional category to the pinpoints for the 106 examples in Part II, pages 89–173, using the A, B, and C code given above, adding pluses and minuses as needed (A–, B+, B–, C+, C–). Use only the information given in each Pinpoint section of the Examples.

Task 2: After all pinpoints have been ranked using the A, B, and C code, check each pinpoint ranked lower than an A–. Go back to the appropriate page in Part II and reread any information given in the Record section. When the new information serves to further specify the behavior involved, the rerank the pinpoint. For Example 43, Bothering Teacher at Desk, the first ranking might be B; reranking after reading the Record could give it a B+.

First Ranking Totals	Re-Ranking Totals
106 = % A pinpoints	106 = % A pinpoints
106 = % B pinpoints	106 = % B pinpoints
106 = % C pinpoints	106 = % C pinpoints

Additional practice in specifying overt behaviors in observable and measurable pinpoints may be acquired by referring to the behaviors you have written in completing Learning Activity 5 and rewriting each pinpointed behavior that does not qualify as an A so that it can be readily observed and counted.

LEARNING ACTIVITY 12–CONCEPTUAL BEHAVIORAL ANALYSIS

Instructions:

1. Experienced teachers

   a) Choose from your experience a personal example that you consider an unqualified success. Pinpoint the behaviors involved and analyze your solution in terms of consequences applied. Include some indication of the frequency of the behavior prior to your intervention (Record) and also following (Evaluate).

   b) Choose an example from your prior teaching experience which you consider a failure. Pinpoint the behaviors which were part of the problem, indicate the frequency of the behavior (Record), analyze your consequence(s) in behavioral terms, and discuss the reasons for the failure and what procedures you would now apply to the same case.

2. Prospective teachers
   a) Pinpoint the following problems in behavioral terms.
   b) Indicate potential strategies for short-term and long-term intervention (Consequates).

   (1) Shy, withdrawn girl, noncommunicative, dresses in a manner considered weird by her peers
   (2) Twelve-year-old boy recently returned from a state detention center for delinquent youths, fights with others, has chip on shoulder, lives with foster parents who say they don't care
   (3) Six-year-old who dominates entire house by screaming, yelling, throwing severe tantrums; parents are at wits end
   (4) Sixteen-year-old, tenth-grade boy who states he wants to get out of school, failed all classes preceding term
   (5) Active "hyperactive" student who is continually engaged in minor and major motor behavior as well as humming, whistling, cracking joints, tapping feet.
   (6) Student who tests high on achievement scores but fails to complete any assignments to be turned in within the class

A POSITIVE
APPROACH

CHAPTER 7

Developing
Responses

The teacher has many reinforcers that can be used contingently across time to teach desired behaviors. However, merely reading, talking, and thinking about consequential responses does not produce optimum results. The development of effective responses takes *practice*. Consider for a moment the tremendous practice it takes for a poet to choose the precise word, for a musician to turn a beautiful phrase, for an actor to deliver a line effectively. Practice in developing responses cannot be overemphasized. Just talking to yourself while looking into a mirror is very effective. A tape recorder can also be valuable in developing response skills. At first you will notice some tension—you will feel awkward and perhaps a little childish. Nevertheless, practice. A good place to start is with the words "thank you." Practice saying "thank you" with as many inflections as possible— from extreme sarcasm to sincere appreciation.

If one desires to express a sincere feeling, one must make sure the real intent will be expressed. Those people whom we consider warm and sensitive are people who have developed great skill in expression. Most often, expressions are not overtly practiced; yet all teachers (having been often misunderstood) should be sure to communicate their thoughts and feelings most effectively. Considering all the time we spend in front of the mirror on physical appearances, is it not incongruous we do not use some of this time to develop effective personal responses? After patient practice in role playing, the teacher will begin to notice exciting new skill in the development of responses. Sometimes a teacher may choose to practice with another person who desires to be helpful in giving the teacher appropriate feedback.

Other than subject matter itself, responses available to the teacher can be classified in five categories: (1) words (spoken-written), (2) physical expressions (facial-bodily), (3) closeness (nearness-touching), (4) activities (social-individual), and (5) things (materials, food, playthings, awards). The following lists have been developed as possible *approval* models for the teacher. The teacher should select and develop those reinforcers deemed usable as specific behavioral contingencies for the age and grade level of students involved. Start with one or two responses, develop thoroughly, and evaluate in the classroom before developing others.

APPROVAL RESPONSES

Words Spoken:Approval

Words

Yes
Good
Neat
Nice
O.K.
Great
Fascinating
Charming
Commendable
Delightful
Brilliant
Fine answer
Uh-huh
Positively!
Go ahead
Yeah!
All right
Nifty
Exactly
Of course
Cool
Likeable
Wonderful
Outstanding work
Of course!

Correct
Excellent
That's right
Perfect
Satisfactory
How true
Absolutely right
Keep going
Good responses
How beautiful!
Wonderful job!
Fantastic!
Terrific!
Swell
Beautiful work
Tasty
Marvelous!
Exciting!
Pleasant
Delicious
Fabulous!
Splendid
Well-mannered
Thinking

Sentences

That's clever.
I'm pleased.

Thank you.
I'm glad you're here.
That's a *prize* of a job.
You make us happy.
That shows thought.
We think a lot of you.
You're tops on our list.
That's good work.
Remarkably well done.
You're very pleasant.
That shows a great deal of work.
Yes, I think you should continue.
A good way of putting it.
I like the way ___(name)___ explained it.
That is a feather in your cap.
You are very friendly.
That's an excellent goal.
Nice speaking voice.
That's a nice expression.
It is a pleasure having you as a student.
That's interesting.
You make being a teacher very worthwhile.
That's sweet of you.
Well thought out.
Show us how.
You're doing better.
You are improving.
You're doing fine.
You perform very well, ___(name)___.
That's very good, ___(name)___.
I'm so proud of you.
I like that.
This is the best yet.
That's the correct way.
That's very choice.
You do so well.
You're polite.
Thinking!

Relationships

Nice things happen to nice children.
That is very imaginative.
You are worthy of my love.
That will be of great benefit to the class.
I admire it when you work like that.

That is original work.
I appreciate your attention.
You've been a fine credit to your class.
I commend your outstanding work.
We are proud to honor your achievement.
That was very kind of you.
You catch on very quickly.
Obedience makes me happy.
That deserves my respect.
You demonstrate fine ability.
That is clear thinking.
You should be very proud of this.
That was nice of you to loan her your _____ .
I wish you would show me and the class how you got such an interesting effect.
I like that—I didn't know it could be done that way.
Permission granted.
That's a good job—other children can look up to you.
Let's watch him do it.
He accepts responsibility.
That *was* a good choice.
Show this to your parents.
I know how you feel—should we continue?
I'm happy your desk is in order.
Why don't you show the class how you got the answer?
That's a good point to bring up, __(name)__ .
I agree.
Let's put this somewhere special.
I'd like this in my own house.
My, you have a nice attitude.
Now you're really trying.
Keep working hard, __(name)__ .
You've improved.
Your work appears so neat.
You're a good person.
If at first you don't succeed, try, try again.
Thinking!

Words and Symbols Written: Approval

Bravo!	Good work
Improvement	☆
Fine	Correct
Good	+

Neato
Very good
O.K.
Passing
*
X
✔
Thoughtful
100%
Good paper
Very colorful
☺
Well done
Great!
Wow!
A-1
Perceptive

Satisfactory
Nicely done
Very concise
Complete
A, B, C, D
Enjoyable
Excellent
Outstanding
☞
[Colored pencil markings]
Superior
Congratulations
Yeh
Show this to your parents.
[Honor rolls]
For display
[Rubber stamps]

Rules

In formulating rules, remember to:

1. Involve the class in making up the rules.
2. Keep the rules short and to the point.
3. Phrase rules, where possible, in a positive way. ("Sit quietly while working" instead of "Don't talk to your neighbors.")
4. Remind the class of the rules at times *other* than when someone has misbehaved.
5. Make different sets of rules for varied activities.
6. Let children know when different rules apply (work-play).
7. Post rules in a conspicuous place and review regularly.
8. Keep a sheet on your desk and record the number of times you review rules with class.

Expressions: Approval

Facial

Looking
Smiling
Winking
Nodding
Grinning
Raising eyebrows
Forming kiss
Opening eyes

Widening eyes
Wrinkling nose
Blinking rapidly
Giggling
Whistling
Cheering
Licking lips
Smacking lips

Slowly closing eyes
Laughing (happy)
Chuckling

Pressing lips affirmatively
Rolling eyes enthusiastically

Bodily

Clapping hands
Raising arms
Shaking fist
Signaling O.K.
Cocking head
Skipping
Rubbing stomach
Thumbs up
Shaking head
Jumping up and down
Shrugging shoulders
Circling hand through air (encouragement to continue)

Hand/finger to face, eyebrows, eyes, nose, ears, mouth, cheek, lips, hair, forehead
Grabbing
Bouncing
Dancing
Stroking motions
Opening hands
Flipping head
Taking a fast breath
Expansive movements of hands
Hugging self

Closeness: Approval

Nearness

Nearness concerns physical proximity and ranges from geographical separation—through noticeable contact—to embracing.
Interacting with class at recess
Eating with children
Sitting on desk near students
Sitting within the student group
Standing alongside
Walking among students
Gently guiding
Pausing—while transferring objects

Touching

Hand on hand
Ruffling hair
Touching head
Patting head
Pinching chin
Touching nose
Patting back
Patting shoulder
Touching arm
Straightening clothes

Walking alongside
Combing hair
Tying shoes
Quick squeeze
Dancing
Rubbing back of neck
Gently raising chin
Leaning over
Touching hurt
Kissing a hurt

Hugging
Touching hand
Shaking hands
Squeezing hand
Patting cheek
Nudging
Helping put on coats
Retying sashes

Putting face next to child
Tweaking nose
Tickling
Cupping face in hands
Gentle pull at hair
Running finger down person's
   nose
Guiding with hand

Activities and Privileges: Approval

Individual

Leading student groups
Representing group in school activities
Displaying student's work (any subject matter)
Straightening up for teacher
Putting away materials
Running errands
Caring for class pets, flowers, etc.
Collecting materials (papers, workbooks, assignments, etc.)
Choosing activities
Show and tell (any level)
Constructing school materials
Dusting, erasing, cleaning, arranging chairs, etc.
Helping other children (drinking, lavatory, cleaning, etc.)
Reading a story
Exempting a test
Working problems on the board
Answering questions
Outside supervising (patrols, directing parking, ushering, etc.)
Classroom supervision
Omitting specific assignments
First in line
Assisting teacher teach
Leading discussions
Making gifts
Recognizing birthdays
Grading papers
Special seating arrangements
Responsibility for ongoing activities during school holidays (pets, plants, assignments)
Decorating room
Presenting hobby to class
"Citizen of the Week" or "Best Kid of the Day"

Social

Movies
Decorating classroom
Presenting skits
Playing records
Puppet shows
Preparing for holidays (Christmas, Thanksgiving, Valentine's Day)
Making a game of subject matter
Outdoor lessons
Visiting another class
Field trips (subject matter)
Planning daily schedules
Musical chairs
Competing with other classes
Performing for PTA
Dancing
Going to museums, fire stations, courthouses, picnics, etc.
"Senior Sluff Day"
Participating in group organizations (music, speech, athletics, social
   clubs)
Talking periods
Recess or play periods
Early dismissal
Parties
Talent shows (jokes, readings, music, etc.)

Things: Approval

Materials

Books—appropriate level	Beads
Pets	Gum ball machine
Bookcovers	Balls
Book markers	Sand toys (bucket, shovel, etc.)
Coloring books	Play money
Crayons	Banks
Paints	Peg board and peg towns
Pencils with names	Telephones
Chalk	Silly Sand
Flowers	Silly Putty
Buttons	Play Dough
Pins	Pick-up sticks
Pictures	Blocks
Colored paper	Jack 'n box

Iguana
Counting beads
Games
Stuffed animals
Cards
Stars
Chips
Kites
Balloons
Jacks
Striped straws
Windmills
Miniature animals
Farm set and farm animals
Plastic toys (Indians, animals,
   soldiers, etc.)
Jump ropes
Musical toys
Wind-up toys
Hand puppets
Marbles
Building blocks
Lego
See N' Say toys
Lincoln Logs
Flashlight
Strollers
Kitchen equipment (play stove,
   sink, refrigerator)
Comic books
Food mixes
Utensil sets
Household items (pots, coffee
   can, paper rolls, cardboard
   boxes, etc.)
Dishes
Money (exchangeable, token)
Stamps
Cleaning sets (carpet sweepers,
   brooms, etc.)
Play furniture (table, chairs, etc.)
Purses
Umbrellas

Bath toys (boats, rubber ducks,
   etc.)
Pounding blocks
Doctor kits
Nurse kits
Tops
Tool bench and tools
Tinker toys
Fire engine
Yo-yo
Boats
Trains and equipment
Bean bags
Cars and gas stations
Racing cars
Trucks
Tractors
Steam shovels
Dolls and equipment (bottles,
   clothes, etc.)
Doll houses
Doll furniture
Talking dolls
Buggies
Kaleidoscopes
Typewriters
Playing cards
Record player
Walkie-talkie
Records
Stationery
Calendars
Musical instruments
Bulletin boards
Desk organizers (notes, books,
   pencils, etc.)
Cameras and equipment
Photo album
Label maker
Pencil sharpener
Stapler
Autograph book
Date book

Costumes
Jumping beans
Ice cream maker
Popcorn maker
Cotton candy maker
Cash register
Switch board
Electric football, baseball, basket-
    ball, hockey
Cowboy dolls and equipment
Knights, castles, and equipment
Model kits (cars, planes, ships,
    etc.)
Pinball machine
Bicycle
Tricycle
Music boxes
Rocking horse
Bird houses
Ant houses
Bug houses
Suit cases
Wall decorations
Knickknacks
Sewing machine
Sewing boxes
World globe
View master
Telescope
Microscope
Erector set
Trains
Science kits
    Frog dissecting kit
    Chemistry set
    Slide preparing kit
    Geologist's kit
    Biological kit
    Radio kit
    Computer kit
    Electric builder kit
    Rock identification kit
    Magnetic kits

Address books
Pencils
Pens
Radios
Tape recorders
Watches
Vanity sets
Jewelry
Masks and wax disguises
Perfume
Bath powder
Bath oil
Hats and clothes
Make up
Hair ribbons
Hair bands
Hair barrels
Hairdryers
Belts
Jewelry boxes
Puzzles (jigsaw, trauma tower,
    dice cube, wooden cube, soli-
    taire, pyramid, mad maze, three
    dimensional, etc.)
Collections (coins, rocks, glass,
    leaves, stamps, etc.)
Art sets
    Oils
    Watercolors
    Pastels
    Chalk
    Colored pencils
Bowling equipment (ball, shoes,
    etc.)
Swimming equipment (fins, face
    mask, etc.)
Kickball
Golf equipment (clubs, balls,
    etc.)
Ping pong equipment
Pool table
Football equipment
Baseball equipment

Body kits (man, woman, heart,
    head, skeleton, eye, ear, etc.)
Creative craft kits
    Origami (paperfolding)
    Wood burning
    Hand bag decorating
    Embroidery
    Découpage
    Wall decorations
    Marquetry
    Mosaics
    Pillow
    Clay
    Yarn
    Ceramics
    Beads
    Leather
    Colored pipe cleaners
    Cloth
    Rock polishing
    Papier mâché
    Wood
    Felt
    Tile
    Glass
    Paper

Tennis equipment
Skiing equipment
Ice skates
Roller skates
Scuba diving equipment
Sleigh
Toboggan
Class pictures
Swing
Swing sets
Slide
Boxing gloves
Striking bag
Body building equipment
Horse shoe set
Croquet set
Badminton set
Tackraw
Darts
Tether ball
Camping equipment (sleeping
    bag, lantern, stove, etc.)
Fishing equipment (rod, reel, etc.)
Aquariums
Money
Juke box

Food

Jaw breakers
Chocolate creams
Cake
Lemonade
Popcorn
Peanuts
Ice cream
Cookies
Sugar-coated cereals
Apples
Crackers
Raisins
Candy kisses
Fruit
Life savers

Lemon drops
Sugar cane
Candied apples
Candy canes
Candy corn
Animal crackers
Soft drinks
Milk
Marshmallows
Gum
Juices
Lollipops
Popsicles
Candy bars
Potato chips

Awards

Citations	Medals
Athletic letters	Cups
Plaques	Report cards
Pens	"Good-Deed" charts
Subject-matter prizes (books, science hardware, subscriptions, etc.)	

DISAPPROVAL RESPONSES

The following lists gleaned from actual classroom observations contain *disapproval* responses. The teacher should study these lists carefully in order to achieve two important discriminations: (1) to recognize responses that one may be unwittingly using and wish to eliminate or replace with incompatible approval responses, and (2) to plan carefully, responsibly, and cautiously the application of disapproval. The authors believe most of the following should *never* be used. *The teacher must discriminate.* Even a pleasant "hello" can be a scathing indictment if the tone and intensity of the voice cause that effect.

Words Spoken: Disapproval

This list includes naggings, sarcasms, bitternesses, dishonesties, and other ineffectual teacher responses whose angry delivery generally demonstrates that the *teacher,* not the student, has the problem.

Impractical
Be prompt
Work faster
Try to understand
Do your homework
Do your best
Unclear explanation
Don't you want to do things right?
It can't be that difficult
You're too slow
Stop talking
Behave
Pay attention
Don't
Wrong
Stupid
Be still
Follow directions

Think for a change
Use some thought
No, that's not what I said
Would you like to get paddled?
You don't understand because you don't listen!
If I find you chewing gum once more, you'll wear it on your nose
Be quiet and sit down
You're gutless
That's ridiculous
Meaningless
Absurd
Bad
Nonsense
Too vague
Try harder
Unacceptable
That's not right
Incorrect
Needs improving
Unsatisfactory
Poor
Undesirable
You should be ashamed
Useless
That's not clear
I dislike that
Don't be silly
That's terrible
What is this?
Is this something?
Quit making messes
Let's throw this away
That's not mature
I can't read anything you write
Haven't you learned how to spell?
Grow up
You're not doing as well as you used to
Horrible
Absolutely not!
Shh!
Stop
Listen to me
Maddening

Be quiet
Raise your hand
Stop that laughing
I'll have no more talking
Apologize now
Sloppy
Shut up!
I'll show you who's boss
One more time and you'll get it from me
Finish it now
No talking
I'll slap you silly
Look for the answer
Leave her alone
You march straight to the office
Keep your eyes on your own paper
You lack interest
I'll give you something to cry about
You *couldn't* have done worse
I do not like this
It's not up to requirements
I will not repeat it
I'm not telling you again
You're dull
That's ugly
You idiot
You're a laughingstock
It's hopeless for you
Why are you a fraidycat?
You're cheap
Snob
You're worthless
You're rude
Don't be crabby
You're disgusting
You little monster
Don't laugh at me
Cut it out
You're dumb
You're filthy
You naughty boy
Mock me and you won't hear the end of it
You're narrow-minded

That's childish
Simple Simon
No! No!! No!!!
You haven't applied yourself
Your work isn't acceptable
Get your parent to sign this bad paper
Wat do you mean you're not finished?
Stand up straight
Just try that once more
Anyone else!
Learn that!
You'd better get on the stick
So you're tardy again!
Speak when you're spoken to
Smart alec
You *must* be confused
I don't see your point
You know what happened the last time you did that
You do this over
You know better than that
Play fair
Don't cause problems
You're never dependable
That wasn't the right thing to do
Well, we'll never do this again
If you had a brain in your head, you wouldn't say that
Do it!
You think you're the only one here?
You're bad
Poor stupid oaf
Wrong again
You're doomed to failure
You're wrong all the time
You don't know anything
You make me sick
You're just an inadequate person
Impertinent
You're not thinking
You haven't been paying attention
Wipe that silly grin off your face
I guess I shouldn't expect any more from *you*
You're just plain boring
You have a dirty mind

Terrible! Terrible!
This isn't what *I* had in mind
You know that's wrong
Stupid nonsense
You'd *better* try harder
People never change

Expressions: Disapproval

Frowning
Curling lip
Lifting eyebrows
Looking at ceiling
Furrowing brows
Smirking
Lowering eyebrows
Shaking finger or fist
Wrinkling mouth
Squinting eyes
Staring
Wrinkling forehead
Nose in air
Pointing finger
Putting hand behind ear
Grimacing
Sniffing
Tightening jaw
Sticking out tongue
Twisting side of mouth
Cackling
Snickering

Puckering lips
Wrinkling nose
Pounding fists on table
Laughing
Shaking head
Turning away
Gritting teeth
Biting lips
Squinting eyebrows
Looking sideways
Closing eyes
Clicking tongue
Pushing mouth to one side
Turning head away
Letting out breath
Raising lips
Hissing
Fingers in front of lips
Nodding head (no)
Showing teeth
Pulling in bottom lip

Closeness: Disapproval

Closeness disapproval concerns corporal punishment and ranges from threatening approaches—through spankings—to severe physical beatings.

Activities and Privileges: Disapproval

Disapproval concerning activities and privileges constitutes various degrees of *deprivation*. Deprivation ranges from withholding of privileges—through isolation—to social incarceration.

Isolation
Ostracism

Silence periods
Sitting in corner
Staying after class
Writing misbehaviors
Standing in front of class
Leaving room
Extra work
Staying in from play
Being last to leave
Sitting in hall
Being sent to principal
Eating alone in lunchroom
Away from friends
Pointing out bad examples
Apologizing to class
Writing letters of apology
Bringing parents to school

Things: Disapproval

Concerning things, disapproval refers to inanimate materials that are damaging to the body: (1) intense noises (ear damage), (2) heat (fires and stoves), (3) chemicals (poisons), and (4) objects in motion (knives, cars, bullets, radiation). Obviously *none* of these should ever be used by the teacher (even washing a child's mouth out with soap can sometimes cause tissue damage).

CONCLUSION

Teaching and learning should be exciting and satisfying for both teacher and student. The innovative teacher has too many positive and effective resources available to resort to shoddy and punitive measures. Many experienced teachers state that almost all of their earlier punitive consequences could have been handled in a more positive manner. A teacher who truly cares will practice developing *positive* responses.

STUDY GUIDE FOR CHAPTER 7

Questions:

1. What do you think would be the long-term effect(s) of strong approval?

2. What do you think would be the effect(s) of strong disapproval?

3. Do you believe in corporal punishment? Why? Why not?

4. Is corporal punishment legal in your state? Should it be? Why?

5. List several positive reinforcers that would be appropriate for a high school senior of your same sex. List five for the opposite sex.

6. Why will one type of approval "work" for one student and not for another?

7. If a child has been physically abused, what ought to be the teacher's responses to get this student to do the difficult tasks?

8. Why is it that some of the preceding lists of approval applications seem so "mushy?"

9. What type of disapproval are you used to giving when you are frustrated? When you are trying to get someone to correct an injustice or rectify a mistake what do you use?

10. Do you believe that people who are "naturally" negative should go into teaching? What should one do if one is "naturally" negative?

LEARNING ACTIVITY 13—
CHOICE OF REINFORCERS

1. For all of the following pinpoints (actual classroom incidents), determine three different procedures (logical consequences) that could be tried by the classroom teacher for increasing or decreasing the pinpointed behavior. Be as specific as possible and use at least one approval and one disapproval technique for each pinpoint. (Instructors and/or students may choose to make up their own pinpoints.)

2. State one good reason for the selection of each consequence. Indicate whether the consequence is (a) approval, (b) withdrawal of approval, (c) disapproval, (d) threat of disapproval or (e) ignoring.

3. When all pinpoints have been consequated and designations as to approval/disapproval completed, next categorize the specific reinforcers used for each separate consequate using the following categories:

a) Words
b) Closeness
c) Bodily expressions
d) Activities
e) Things

1. Pinpoint: Refusal to go outdoors for recess (seven-year-old girl)

   Record: Child refuses to go outside during morning or afternoon recess.

   Consequate: 1.

   2.

   3.

2. Pinpoint: School phobia (seven-year-old boy)

   Record: Child refuses to go to school; protests with disruptive behavior (crying, screaming).

   Consequate: 1.

   2.

   3.

3. Pinpoint: Blanket bringing behavior (six-year-old)

   Record: Child insists on bringing "security" blanket to school at the beginning of the second school year. The behavior was not observed during the first year of school.

   Consequate: 1.

   2.

   3.

4. Pinpoint: Headaches (second-grade girl)

   Record: Girl complains of headaches during language arts period a total of twelve times in five sessions.

   Consequate: 1.

   2.

   3.

5. Pinpoint: Teasing handicapped child (third and fourth graders)

Record: Several boys and girls make fun of handicapped younger child every recess period.

Consequate: 1.

2.

3.

6. Pinpoint: Pants wetting (kindergarten)

Record: Teacher noticed wet dress of child seven times during one week.

Consequate: 1.

2.

3.

7. Pinpoint: Tattling (elementary grades)

Record: Child observed to "tell" on others in class 23 times in one week.

Consequate: 1.

2.

3.

8. Pinpoint: Book stealing from library.

Record: Ten books missing during the first week of school.

Consequate: 1.

2.

3.

9. Pinpoint: Damaged musical instruments.

Record: Fourteen instruments damaged in one week.

Consequate: 1.

2.

3.

10. Pinpoint: Damage to teachers' automobiles.

Record: Eight tires slashed, 4 radio antennas bent, and 18 windows broken during one week of school.

Consequate: 1.

2.

3.

11. Pinpoint: Book slamming (ninth-grade boys, English class)

Record: Six boys slam books down on desk upon entering English class, a total of 32 times in one week.

Consequate: 1.

2.

3.

12. Pinpoint: Lunch stealing (seventh-grade boys)

Record: Three seventh-grade boys are observed stealing fifth graders' lunches every day for one week.

Consequate: 1.

2.

3.

13. Pinpoint: Kissing in halls

Record: Seven couples observed kissing in the hall during lunch period two consecutive days.

Consequate: 1.

2.

3.

14. Pinpoint: Turning in assignments late

Record: Teacher notes student delinquent in turning in math homework nine times in one month.

Consequate: 1.

2.

3.

15. Pinpoint: Graffiti

Record: Writing noted on the boys' restroom walls after each cleaning.

Consequate: 1.

2.

3.

16. Pinpoint: Teacher mimicry (16-year-old boy, math class)

Record: Student mimics 15 sentences of female math teacher during three math classes.

Consequate: 1.

2.

3.

17. Pinpoint: Teacher threats (18-year-old male student, English class)

Record: Student threatens to "get even" with teacher if she fails him.

Consequate: 1.

2.

3.

18. Pinpoint: Book tearing

Record: Four male students have 10 page tearing "accidents" in literature class during one week.

Consequate: 1.

2.

3.

19. Pinpoint: Glue sniffing

Record: Four high school seniors caught sniffing glue in the boys' restroom.

Consequate: 1.

         2.

         3.

20. Pinpoint: Profane language

Record: Female social studies teacher records 45 outbursts of profanity during her lectures in a two-week period.

Consequate: 1.

         2.

         3.

21. Pinpoint: Abuse of privileges

Record: Two girls use Honor Society work as an excuse to leave chemistry class six times in one month.

Consequate: 1.

         2.

         3.

LEARNING ACTIVITY 14—TEST ON TEACHING/DISCIPLINE (CHAPTERS 1–7)

Please circle the answer that *best* completes the statement.

1. The foremost question regarding discipline in the classroom is one pertaining to
   a) strict relationships.
   b) strict and permissive relationships.
   c) cause-and-effect relationships.
   d) interpersonal relationships.
   e) strict versus permissive control.

2. The teacher's personal approval is a most effective reward for most children and should be given

   a) discriminately.
   b) noncontingently.
   c) approvingly.
   d) partially.
   e) all of the above.

3. To solve a student's inappropriate behavior, the teacher should

   a) know the reinforcement history of the student.
   b) do something to change the student's behavior.
   c) try to understand the behavior on the basis of previous test results.
   d) seek evaluation of the student's personality.
   e) none of the above.

4. A very simple behavioral principle used to teach children to respond appropriately is

   a) "when you do bad things, bad things happen to you."
   b) "no matter what you do, nice things happen to you."
   c) "when you do nice things, nice things happen to you."
   d) "no matter what you do, bad things happen to you."
   e) both a and c.

5. Why is the principle of specificity important in behavior modification?

   a) The teacher can only deal with specified traits.
   b) Only specified overt behaviors can be dealt with.
   c) The word discipline is a specific category.
   d) Generalized behavior is amenable to modification.
   e) After the behavior is specified, the student will improve.

6. Human behavior can be measured

   a) in time intervals.
   b) within discrete pinpointed categories.
   c) for specific academic responses.
   d) following appropriate student behavior.
   e) all of the above.

7. Partial reinforcement

   a) may refer to inconsistency in responding.
   b) often prolongs inappropriate behavior.
   c) often prolongs appropriate behavior.
   d) may refer to consistency in responding.
   e) all of the above.

8. If a teacher inadvertently gives approval to a student following an inappropriate response

   a) new contingencies may be structured immediately.
   b) it will not function as an error because it was unwitting.
   c) the student will likely repeat the response.
   d) the teacher should disapprove the next time.
   e) both a and c.

9. Disapproval may be used effectively in modifying inappropriate behavior except when

   a) its magnitude is too great.
   b) it functions as a payoff for the inappropriate response.
   c) it is given on a partial schedule.
   d) it is used as a follow-through after a threat.
   e) none of the above.

10. An issue that teachers should consider carefully is that it seems easier for one to _____ his way into a new way of _____ than to _____ his way into a new way of _____ .

    a) think/acting/act/thinking
    b) talk/feeling/feel/talking
    c) work/studying/study/working
    d) act/thinking/think/acting
    e) both c and d.

11. If contingent rewards/punishments are to be effective, they should generally take place

    a) immediately.
    b) with a reward hierarchy in mind.
    c) consistently.
    d) without verbal explanation.
    e) all of the above.

12. _____ is anything a person does, says, or thinks that can be observed directly and/or indirectly.

    a) Data
    b) Reality
    c) Behavior
    d) Behavior modification
    e) Association

13. _____ is defined as a change or modification of behavior.

    a) Contingency management
    b) Reinforcement
    c) Learning

d) Teaching
e) None of the above.

14. Some students may become upset if a teacher makes a class privilege contingent upon the behavior of a few students. Students who become upset are probably concerned with

a) strictness of control.
b) peer approval.
c) group discipline.
d) fairness.
e) threat of disapproval.

15. "Making a game out of learning" may involve

a) structuring learning material.
b) establishing rewards.
c) manipulating the environment.
d) maintaining contingencies
e) all of the above.

16. When a teacher says, "I don't like all that structure and those behavioral techniques. I don't want my students to have to sit quietly all day," he/she is confusing

a) facts with values.
b) techniques with values.
c) social with academic behavior.
d) rules with how to enforce them.
e) both b and d.

17. If creativity can be taught and learned, then the educator needs to be concerned with

a) at what point further teaching might inhibit creativity.
b) whether students can create from nothing.
c) what information and materials students need to get started.
d) the situation in which learning occurs.
e) all of the above.

18. If a teacher noncontingently reinforces all of the student's creative products because the teacher feels the child needs it, the child will probably learn

a) to love himself contingently.
b) to discriminate the quality of his classmates' products.
c) lack of social discrimination.
d) lack of discrimination concerning his work.
e) none of the above.

19. Many teachers quit the teaching profession because of

    a) anxiety relating to teaching pressures.
    b) lack of education in coping with special problems.
    c) inability to discipline.
    d) loss of motivation after initial teaching experience.
    e) personality problems.

20. Motivation is

    a) shaped by strict discipline.
    b) taught by manipulating the external environment.
    c) based on personality factors.
    d) based upon student interest and background variables.
    e) innate within every student.

21. Within the classroom, "being approved of" is probably controlled by

    a) the teacher.
    b) partial reinforcement.
    c) both teacher and students.
    d) self-concept.
    e) the student.

22. Desire to learn is

    a) innate except for special problems.
    b) universal if students are left alone.
    c) taught but not learned.
    d) necessary in all situations.
    e) none of the above.

23. While handwriting is an appropriate learned behavior, yelling out the answer is often a(n) ——————— behavior.

    a) cued
    b) more desirable
    c) innate
    d) more spontaneous
    e) inappropriate

24. Three things are necessary for learning to take place—

    a) motivation, assimilation, and reinforcement.
    b) experience, discrimination, and association.
    c) proper set, attention, and deduction.
    d) accommodation, reward, and adaption.
    e) attention, reinforcement, and discipline.

25. A behavior that results in pleasant consequences will likely be

   a) forgotten.
   b) appropriate.
   c) repeated.
   d) reinforced.
   e) assimilated.

Below are listed five examples of classroom contingencies. In the blank space after each statement indicate, by letter, the particular contingency situation.

   a) approval following appropriate behavior
   b) withholding approval
   c) disapproval following inappropriate behavior
   d) threat of disapproval
   e) ignoring

26. Making the student sit in a corner facing the wall because he threw spitballs at another student. _____

27. Inattention following a student's verbalizations. _____

28. Having the student continue working on arithmetic problems until he finishes them and telling him that only then may he go out to recess. _____

29. Providing special activities for every correct arithmetic problem completed. _____

30. Telling the student that he will be sent to the principal's office if he doesn't stop talking. _____

31. "You have not followed the rules today, Fred. Therefore I am sending you to the time-out room." _____

32. "You have not completed any science problems. You may go to band when you have correctly completed all the problems." _____

33. "Good work, Jane. You have completed your homework assignment and handed it in on time." _____

34. "If you do not finish these problems correctly in five minutes, I am going to make you sit in the corner by yourself." _____

35. I am sorry Mary did not sit still. We will have the party later, if everyone is still. _____

What is the consequence to pinpoints found in the text (not necessarily the one that worked).

PINPOINT	CONSEQUENCE
___ 36. dishonesty	a) Grade assigned without explanation.
___ 37. nail biting	b) Teacher instituted multiple divergent token systems. Some children received paper money which bought surprise gifts at end of day. Other children received candies on various time interval schedules. Some children accumulated points written on notebook. Reinforcers changed constantly.
___ 38. fear in young children	c) Negative practice—students practice inappropriate behavior at specific times (e.g., 8 A.M. for five minutes) in front of mirror. Parent or teacher delivered disapproval responses during sessions.
___ 39. excessive dawdling	d) Teacher ignored all children, made no eye contact, said nothing; only recognized children who raised hands at seats.
___ 40. bothering teacher at desk	e) Incompatible response—object or situation gradually introduced into child's presence while child engaged in fun activity. Gradual approach—child led by degrees, over number of days, to come closer and closer to activity or object made readily accessible to child while other children participated enjoyable.
___ 41. children manipulating parents	a) Large punching bag dummy with red nose installed on playground.

___ 42. standing up walking
around

b) None apply.

___ 43. striking other children
with objects

c) Twofold program to teach
all students discrimination
between possessing ability
and performing before class,
and teach entire class role
playing to deliver approval
feedback to insecure students.

___ 44. aggressive hitting

d) Mothers (1) instructed in
delivery of approval techniques, (2) taught to ignore
inappropriate behavior, and
(3) responded with praise
and affection for appropriate
behavior.

___ 45. embarrassment

e) Adult assigned in vicinity;
child praised and given donut
when playing properly, although when boy hit someone
supervisor hit him back with
same object.

*****

___ 46. boredom

a) School counselor developed
system with parents' cooperation. Every teacher signed
individual daily progress report
(one small sheet) after each
class. Decision of signing
for appropriate social and
academic behaviors based on
teacher's criteria. Allowance,
social engagements, car privileges contingent upon number
of signatures earned each day.

___ 47. school failure

b) Teacher explained to class
that talking during study
time interfered with com-
pletion of work assignments
(this had been done before).

Class discussed importance
of rules for study, agreed
something must be done,
and suggested very extreme
alternatives.

___ 48. disruptive classroom   c) If assignments not completed,
behavior   no recess.

___ 49. arithmetic achievement   d) Disruptive behavior ignored,
appropriate behavior rewarded.
Boy kept after school for
extreme deviations and sent
home on later bus. This put
child with students he did
not know and withdrew peer
attention. Correct behaviors
reinforced by teacher praise
and peer approval (continuously in beginning, more
infrequently later on). Also,
job of blackboard monitor
followed appropriate behavior.

___ 50. disruptive social talking   e) Friday football game instituted, teams chosen, rules
established points, yards,
substitutions, etc., developed
for correct academic responses.
Game played on blackboard
with losing team providing
treat for winners.

PART IV

OBSERVATIONAL MANUAL

CHAPTER 8

Learning Through Observation

It has been stressed repeatedly by those interested in behavioral analyses that data must be collected regarding overt demonstrable behaviors. Often teachers in the field are able to devise their own recording instruments in regard to specific problems to be corrected within their own classroom. In most cases this is preferable, but to sensitize the teacher or potential teacher to individual effects of reinforcement, more elaborate procedures should be used. In addition, researchers must maintain even greater rigor as well as some uniformity in observation data in order that their findings may be transmitted in a systematic manner to others in the area. Regardless of intent or dissemination, observational data must be both accurate and reliable.

CATEGORY DEVELOPMENT

Prerequisites to accurate behavioral observations include mutually exclusive category definitions that are precise enough to allow observers to note and record the behavior reliably. The general rules that are followed in developing observational categories for inappropriate student behaviors are categories that should:

1. Reflect behaviors that interfere with classroom learning by limiting the time (individual or group) students are on-task in the classroom.
2. Involve behaviors that violate rules, written or implied, established by the teacher.
3. Reflect particular behaviors a teacher desires to change (increase or decrease).

4. Refer to overt behaviors that can actually be observed in order to limit the potential for inferences made by the person doing the observing.

5. Be similar in some important way—either topographically (appearing similar) or logically (conceptual class).

6. Be mutually exclusive so that observational recording of one category of behavior will not be confused with another category.

7. Be limited so that the observer can rapidly decide and record the classes of behaviors observed.

Observation that is accurate and reliable requires observers who are extremely proficient in recording procedures. Indeed, recording of behavior should become almost automatic. Therefore careful study of behavioral categories as well as continued practice either in the classroom or with videotape is required.

OBSERVER MATERIALS AND RULES

Each observer should be equipped with (1) a pencil (always better than a pen as corrections are sometimes required), (2) something to write upon (a clipboard is generally best), (3) a means for accurately assessing the passage of small increments of time,* (4) observation sheets with space for the date, time, activity, person or persons being observed, and a section for inferences or other comments, and (5) a pair of sunglasses. Observers should always record all information— never leave any item blank.

Observers need a special signal that identifies them readily to school personnel and also serves as a signal for teachers and students to refrain from interacting with them. Sunglasses are excellent for this purpose. Sunglasses also partially hide the observer's eyes from the teacher and class so that the person being observed is generally unaware of the scrutiny. Teachers should be instructed to refrain from introducing or otherwise referring to the observers when they come into the classroom. Teachers should also be instructed to say nothing and ask no questions of any observer when the sunglasses are over the eyes. When the observer is part of the school staff, for

---

*A stopwatch or watch with a sweep hand is useful. More sophisticated equipment might include electronic recording devices or prerecorded cassette tape signals for observation. Also, two or more observers listening to the same cassette eliminate unreliability due to time differences as the signals can state, "Line one, observe. . . . Record. . . . Line two, observe. . . . Record. . . , and so on. Small timed lights have also been used successfully.

example, a counselor, psychologist, or administrator, the observer will remove the sunglasses before speaking to any of the students or teachers. Thus the sunglasses serve a dual purpose in identifying the observer and signaling to inhibit verbal interaction. Research within many classrooms indicates that observers are effectively ignored by the students in primary classes after about three or four hours of observation, while intermediate and high school classes take about four to eight hours of observation and teachers somewhat longer.

It is axiomatic that observations are not as accurate (valid) prior to the time the class and teacher became accustomed to observers taking data. But, even though interaction patterns are somewhat less frequent during the first phases of observation, the general ratio of approval/disapproval reinforcement is generally similar even during initial observations.

The goal for observers is to become as unobtrusive as a piece of furniture. Teachers should try to be as natural as possible with the class and, except for brief answers to observer's questions prior or subsequent to observation, refrain from interacting with or even mentioning the observers, especially when the class is watching. It is preferred that teachers who are to be observed not have a specific time schedule for the observations. This would only increase initial anxiety and limit observational accuracy. It is recommended that teachers understand the purpose of the observation and be given feedback as soon as possible concerning the results of the observations, preferably immediately following observations.

Observer instruction summary

Observers should be provided with the following instructions:

1. Wear sunglasses when observing. This signals teachers, students, and others that you will not interact with them. During the time of the observation there should be *no* talking or interaction with the teacher and questions or recording problems should be settled before entering the classroom whenever possible. If teacher interactions become necessary, make certain that the sunglasses are removed and that observations cease for a short time. Should a teacher initiate interaction during an observation, generally ignore it until the observation is concluded.

2. Sit silently and as immobile as possible when observing. Change location quietly and only when absolutely necessary. If you are observing a particular student or students who change locations then you may have to change if you are unable to hear the verbal interactions.

3. Your goal as an observer is to become a piece of furniture. Take great care that you do not become a reinforcement variable with reference to the behavior of students or teachers in the classroom.

4. Make no differential responses to students, that is, laughing at wisecracks, answering questions directed toward you, smiling at student's responses, or changing position of head or eyes when addressed. Make the minimal movement necessary to see the student, teacher, or other person you are recording. Social behaviors by students either on entering or leaving the classroom or the school should be ignored as well as behaviors directed toward you while you are in the halls. *Remember,* if ever you decide to talk to another observer, the teacher, or your supervisor, then please remove your glasses.

5. Discussion of any student, by name or otherwise, except with proper school personnel or your immediate supervisor, is a breach of professional conduct.

6. Please conform to the general faculty dress standards of the school in order that your dress does not become a variable and/or interfere with the task of observation.

7. Look only at observation forms during recording intervals and ignore any noises from the person or persons observed.

8. Remain as unsubjective and unbiased as possible at all times. The main objective is for two people watching the same behavior to agree that the same behaviors occurred (reliability). Record what the person does without trying to think what he should have done. Your time will come.

Teacher observation forms

Teacher forms are self-contained and provide for a complete analysis that can later be graphed, summarized, or presented verbally to the teacher who has been observed. Observations of teacher reinforcements following student behavior are more easily understood when the appropriate symbols are related to the two-by-two teacher contingency table (page 219). The teacher observation symbols are placed in the appropriate boxes to facilitate learning. The order of the symbols is identical to the placement on all teacher observation forms; therefore, symbols are directly transferred from the following contingency table to the observation forms whenever an observer is recording teacher reinforcement.

RECORDING PROCEDURES

Before observation begins, all identifying data should be completed. This generally includes recording the name of the teacher(s) and/or student(s) being observed, the date, the time, and name of the observer.

The general activity is recorded at the top of the sheet and the nature of the ongoing classroom (for individual) activity is recorded under the column marked activity. Each time there is a change in activity, such as from reading to math, from group discussion to seat-work, this change should be recorded in the activity column. Activities can be recorded using a number and letter code.

The *first* number recorded in the activity column indicates the number of students with whom the teacher is interacting for that time period. In most classrooms this may change constantly—the teacher may be working with an individual child, then a small group, and perhaps later conduct a class discussion). Record the exact number of students for each line of intervals.

The *second* entry should indicate the content area the teacher is pursuing with the students being instructed. The code indicates only the academic activity of the group or individual with whom the teacher is interacting; other students may be engaged in other activities. An illustrative code that has been used in elementary schools follows:

LA—Language arts M—Mathematics Sc-Science SS-Social Studies PE—Physical Education Mu-Music A—Art R—Recreation Sp—Spelling W—Writing F—Free time, play, student-selected activity, Re-Rest L—Lunch

Behavioral Contingency Interactions: Table 8-1

		SOCIETAL AGENTS BEHAVIOR	
		Approval	Disapproval
STUDENT BEHAVIOR	APPROPRIATE (On-Task - Social and Academic	**YES** (No When No Disapproval) (1)	**NO** (Mistake) (2)
	INAPPROPRIATE (Off-Task - Social and Academic)	**NO** (Mistake) (3)	**YES** (No if Payoff Or When No Approval (4)

Form A: Teacher Observation

Observer_____   Teacher_____
Reliability Observer_____   Grade or Subject_____
No. in Class or Group_____   Date_____
General Activity_____   Time: Start____End_____
Length of Observational Intervals in Seconds_____
Record Intervals in Seconds_____   Page____of_____

TIME	ACTIVITY CODE	(1)	2-RECORD	(3)	4-RECORD	(5)	6-RECORD	COMMENTS
1			As Aa Ds Da / As Aa Ds Da		As Aa Ds Da / As Aa Ds Da		As Aa Ds Da / As Aa Ds Da	
2		O B S E R V E N O W	As Aa Ds Da / As Aa Ds Da	O B S E R V E N O W	As Aa Ds Da / As Aa Ds Da	O B S E R V E N O W	As Aa Ds Da / As Aa Ds Da	
3			As Aa Ds Da / As Aa Ds Da		As Aa Ds Da / As Aa Ds Da		As Aa Ds Da / As Aa Ds Da	
4			As Aa Ds Da / As Aa Ds Da		As Aa Ds Da / As Aa Ds Da		As Aa Ds Da / As Aa Ds Da	
5			As Aa Ds Da / As Aa Ds Da		As Aa Ds Da / As Aa Ds Da		As Aa Ds Da / As Aa Ds Da	
6			As Aa Ds Da / As Aa Ds Da		As Aa Ds Da / As Aa Ds Da		As Aa Ds Da / As Aa Ds Da	
7			As Aa Ds Da / As Aa Ds Da		As Aa Ds Da / As Aa Ds Da		As Aa Ds Da / As Aa Ds Da	
8		O B S E R V E N O W	As Aa Ds Da / As Aa Ds Da	O B S E R V E N O W	As Aa Ds Da / As Aa Ds Da	O B S E R V E N O W	As Aa Ds Da / As Aa Ds Da	
9			As Aa Ds Da / As Aa Ds Da		As Aa Ds Da / As Aa Ds Da		As Aa Ds Da / As Aa Ds Da	
10			As Aa Ds Da / As Aa Ds Da		As Aa Ds Da / As Aa Ds Da		As Aa Ds Da / As Aa Ds Da	
11			As Aa Ds Da / As Aa Ds Da		As Aa Ds Da / As Aa Ds Da		As Aa Ds Da / As Aa Ds Da	
12			As Aa Ds Da / As Aa Ds Da		As Aa Ds Da / As Aa Ds Da		As Aa Ds Da / As Aa Ds Da	
13			As Aa Ds Da / As Aa Ds Da		As Aa Ds Da / As Aa Ds Da		As Aa Ds Da / As Aa Ds Da	
14		O B S E R V E N O W	As Aa Ds Da / As Aa Ds Da	O B S E R V E N O W	As Aa Ds Da / As Aa Ds Da	O B S E R V E N O W	As Aa Ds Da / As Aa Ds Da	
15			As Aa Ds Da / As Aa Ds Da		As Aa Ds Da / As Aa Ds Da		As Aa Ds Da / As Aa Ds Da	
16			As Aa Ds Da / As Aa Ds Da		As Aa Ds Da / As Aa Ds Da		As Aa Ds Da / As Aa Ds Da	
17			As Aa Ds Da / As Aa Ds Da		As Aa Ds Da / As Aa Ds Da		TOTALS:	

TOTALS:
As____ Aa____ Ds____ Da____
As____ Aa____ Ds____ Da____

Form B:Teacher Observation

Observer_____   Teacher_____

Reliability Observer_____   Grade or Subject_____

Number in Class or Group_____   Date_____

General Activity_____   Time Start_____Time End_____

Length of Observation Intervals in Seconds_____

Record Intervals in Seconds_____ Page_____of_____

TIME	ACTIVITY CODE	INTERVALS					Comment
		1 - Record	2 - Record	3 - Record	4 - Record	5 - Record	
1		As Aa Ds Da / As Aa Ds Da	As Aa Ds Da / As Aa Ds Da	As Aa Ds Da / As Aa Ds Da	As Aa Ds Da / As Aa Ds Da	As Aa Ds Da / As Aa Ds Da	
2		As Aa Ds Da / As Aa Ds Da	As Aa Ds Da / As Aa Ds Da	As Aa Ds Da / As Aa Ds Da	As Aa Ds Da / As Aa Ds Da	As Aa Ds Da / As Aa Ds Da	
3		As Aa Ds Da / As Aa Ds Da	As Aa Ds Da / As Aa Ds Da	As Aa Ds Da / As Aa Ds Da	As Aa Ds Da / As Aa Ds Da	As Aa Ds Da / As Aa Ds Da	
4		As Aa Ds Da / As Aa Ds Da	As Aa Ds Da / As Aa Ds Da	As Aa Ds Da / As Aa Ds Da	As Aa Ds Da / As Aa Ds Da	As Aa Ds Da / As Aa Ds Da	
5		As Aa Ds Da / As Aa Ds Da	As Aa Ds Da / As Aa Ds Da	As Aa Ds Da / As Aa Ds Da	As Aa Ds Da / As Aa Ds Da	As Aa Ds Da / As Aa Ds Da	
6		As Aa Ds Da / As Aa Ds Da	As Aa Ds Da / As Aa Ds Da	As Aa Ds Da / As Aa Ds Da	As Aa Ds Da / As Aa Ds Da	As Aa Ds Da / As Aa Ds Da	
7		As Aa Ds Da / As Aa Ds Da	As Aa Ds Da / As Aa Ds Da	As Aa Ds Da / As Aa Ds Da	As Aa Ds Da / As Aa Ds Da	As Aa Ds Da / As Aa Ds Da	
8		As Aa Ds Da / As Aa Ds Da	As Aa Ds Da / As Aa Ds Da	As Aa Ds Da / As Aa Ds Da	As Aa Ds Da / As Aa Ds Da	As Aa Ds Da / As Aa Ds Da	
9		As Aa Ds Da / As Aa Ds Da	As Aa Ds Da / As Aa Ds Da	As Aa Ds Da / As Aa Ds Da	As Aa Ds Da / As Aa Ds Da	As Aa Ds Da / As Aa Ds Da	
10		As Aa Ds Da / As Aa Ds Da	As Aa Ds Da / As Aa Ds Da	As Aa Ds Da / As Aa Ds Da	As Aa Ds Da / As Aa Ds Da	As Aa Ds Da / As Aa Ds Da	
11		As Aa Ds Da / As Aa Ds Da	As Aa Ds Da / As Aa Ds Da	As Aa Ds Da / As Aa Ds Da	As Aa Ds Da / As Aa Ds Da	As Aa Ds Da / As Aa Ds Da	
12		As Aa Ds Da / As Aa Ds Da	As Aa Ds Da / As Aa Ds Da	As Aa Ds Da / As Aa Ds Da	As Aa Ds Da / As Aa Ds Da	As Aa Ds Da / As Aa Ds Da	
13		As Aa Ds Da / As Aa Ds Da	As Aa Ds Da / As Aa Ds Da	As Aa Ds Da / As Aa Ds Da	As Aa Ds Da / As Aa Ds Da	As Aa Ds Da / As Aa Ds Da	
14		As Aa Ds Da / As Aa Ds Da	As Aa Ds Da / As Aa Ds Da	As Aa Ds Da / As Aa Ds Da	As Aa Ds Da / As Aa Ds Da	As Aa Ds Da / As Aa Ds Da	
15		As Aa Ds Da / As Aa Ds Da	As Aa Ds Da / As Aa Ds Da	As Aa Ds Da / As Aa Ds Da	As Aa Ds Da / As Aa Ds Da	As Aa Ds Da / As Aa Ds Da	

Reinforcement Summary

Social Reinforcement

Symbols	Total No. Observed	÷	Total Intervals Observed	=	% Intervals Behavior Observed
As	= _____	÷	_____	=	_____ %
Ds	= _____	÷	_____	=	_____ %
(As)	= _____	÷	_____	=	_____ %
(Ds)	= _____	÷	_____	=	_____ %

Social Approval Ratio: $\dfrac{As}{As + Ds + (As) + (Ds)}$ = —— %

Academic Reinforcement

Symbols	Total No. Observed	÷	Total Intervals Observed	=	% Intervals Behavior Observed
Aa	= _____	÷	_____	=	_____ %
Da	= _____	÷	_____	=	_____ %
(Aa)	= _____	÷	_____	=	_____ %
(Da)	= _____	÷	_____	=	_____ %

Academic Approval Ratio: $\dfrac{Aa}{Aa + Da + (Aa) + (Da)}$ = —— %

$$\text{RELIABILITY} = \frac{\text{Total Agree}}{\text{Total Agree} + \text{Total Disagree}} \_\_ \%$$

Symbols	Number Observed		Same Symbol in Same Interval	
	Observer I	Reliability Observer	Agree	Disagree
As	_____	_____	_____	_____
Ds	_____	_____	_____	_____
(As)	_____	_____	_____	_____
(Ds)	_____	_____	_____	_____
Aa	_____	_____	_____	_____
Da	_____	_____	_____	_____
(Aa)	_____	_____	_____	_____
(Da)	_____	_____	_____	_____
"No Behavior Observed" _____	_____		_____	_____
Total	_____		_____	_____

The *third* code uses roman numerals and indicates the specific student response that is expected:

I—Looking II—Minor Motor (writing) III—Talking IV—Listening V—Major Motor (jumping, walking) VI—Resting

Categories may be expanded by multiple designations or notes in the Comments section.

Teacher observation (Form A)

Learning Activities always start with Form A. During the first interval of each time period (10-second observing and recording intervals have been found to be most useful), the observer should observe and mentally note the ongoing behavior. Observers *do not record the behavior observed at this time.* During the second interval, the behavior observed during the first interval is recorded (marked) on the data sheet. Comments regarding general classroom interaction and/or descriptions of behavior should also be recorded during this time. No observation of behavior occurs during the second interval as this time period is devoted to recording. Observations are continued during the third interval, but are not recorded until the fourth. The same procedure is followed with the fifth and sixth intervals. Thus behavior is observed during the first, third, and fifth intervals and is recorded during the second, fourth, and sixth. Two or more *different* behaviors may be recorded during any one 10-second interval, but, unless specific directions are given to the contrary, only one symbol of the same behavior should appear in each interval box. After observation expertise has progressed (to .80 reliability), behaviors occurring twice during the same interval can be recorded for the appropriate symbol by using numbers or additional marks. All occurrences should be checked or marked in a conspicuous manner. Colored pencils are excellent for this.

Teacher observation (Form B)

Observe and record the behaviors continuously during the first five intervals of each time line (10-second intervals have been found effective) and record comments or rest during the last interval.

RECORDING TEACHER BEHAVIOR

Teacher behavior as well as student behavior is rated with reference to the rules of the classroom. Always attempt to know the general rules for the class and the specific rules for the activity underway.

The ratings of teacher behaviors can perhaps be best conceptualized according to the following scheme, which is essentially the same chart as on page 58 but with two contingencies (withholding approval and threat of disapproval) excluded. Ignoring is also excluded because it cannot be observed.

In demonstrating the reinforcing function of approving and disapproving teacher behavior, a brief review is advisable. Reinforcement must follow student behavior—behavior is a result of its consequences—or there will be no effect upon student behavior. Reinforcement either increases or decreases behavior. When no effect is demonstrated, then no reinforcement has occurred. For example, the attempts of most teachers to elicit student responses by using interest-provoking questions are to be commended; however, for a behavior to be reinforced, the reinforcement must follow the behavior. The behavioral categories are designed to analyze teacher behaviors following responses from students.

When a teacher follows a behavior with approval, this may serve to reinforce the appropriate behavior (Box 1: When you do good things, good things happen to you). When a teacher gives approval following inappropriate behavior, this is regarded as a reinforcement mistake which may increase the rate of inappropriate behavior! This is called an *approval mistake* (Box 3: When you do bad things, good things happen to you).

Disapproval when properly used generally serves to stop or decrease the rate of the disapproved behavior (Box 4: When you do bad things; bad things happen to you). Therefore, the teacher may

Behavioral Contingency Interactions: Table 8-2

		TEACHER BEHAVIOR	
		Approval	Disapproval
STUDENT BEHAVIOR	APPROPRIATE (Social & Academic)	As Aa (1)	Ⓓs Ⓓa (2) (Mistakes)
	INAPPROPRIATE (Social & Academic)	Ⓐs Ⓐa (Mistakes) (3)	Ds Da (4)

be making a mistake if disapproval follows appropriate behavior. This is called a disapproval mistake (Box 2: When you do good things, bad things happen to you).

Disapproval following inappropriate behavior is intended to decrease the inappropriate behavior (Box 4). But, if the student has learned an improper association, the disapproval may function in a different way, depending upon the reinforcement history of the student. Teacher attention may also be reinforcing, and students may work for whatever attention is forthcoming—even disapproval. Disapproving behavior alone without approval for appropriate behavior will often increase the very behavior that the teacher wishes to eliminate. In the lower half of Box 4, the attention serves as a payoff. The upper half of Box 4 shows occasional disapproval is strong enough to stop inappropriate behavior. (When you do bad things, bad things happen to you.) The effects of disapproval following any student behavior probably depend upon the amount of approval to appropriate behavior (Box 1) in relation to the amount of disapproval to inappropriate behavior (Box 4). When the teacher uses more approval to appropriate behavior than disapproval to inappropriate, then both are generally more effective. The contrast between approval and disapproval also serves to enhance the effect of both. When the teacher uses only approval, then students learn that no matter what one does, "good things" happen. When the teacher uses only disapproval, the students learn that no matter what they do "bad things" happen to them.

Approving and disapproving behaviors are not confined to verbal behavior. As human beings we communicate in a variety of ways— by touch, by gesture, by facial expression. Therefore the teacher must be consistent within her/himself as well as with the rules for the particular activity. When the teacher smiles at a student and also verbally disapproves, the teacher is making either a disapproval or an approval mistake. When the teacher frowns while giving verbal approval, the teacher is also making a reinforcement mistake.

Responses available to the teacher to express approval or disapproval are classified in five categories:

1. Words (spoken or written)
2. Physical expressions (facial or bodily)
3. Closeness (nearness or touching)
4. Activities (social or individual)
5. Things (materials, food, awards, or tokens)

The observer should have these categories memorized and analyze teacher behaviors in terms of the responses available. Should the teacher dispense facial approval while hitting, shaking, or forcibly restraining a child, then all applicable categories should be checked depending upon the immediately preceding student behavior. Observers should study in detail the examples of approval and disapproval in Chapter 7.

Academic and social definitions

Approval for academic behavior is easily understood. This category includes what most teachers generally label feedback concerning the correctness of a student's academic response whether oral or written. Academic approval concerns only the correctness of the answer to curricular materials and does not include approval for "working hard" or "trying hard" or getting out materials. Of course, any behavior may be academic if the teacher's goals are to teach the behavior as subject matter. Disapproval for academic behavior involves any means, verbal or physical, of indicating to the student that his answer to the specific activity or question is in error.

Approval for social behavior involves giving approval following any aspect of the student's behavior which gets or maintains the student on-task. This category includes reinforcement for appropriate interaction patterns with either the curriculum materials or other individuals. It does not pertain to the correctness or incorrectness of an academic response.

Disapproval of inappropriate social behavior involves disapproval following a discriminated aspect of the student's behavior that either interrupts or disturbs the learning environment for himself or another person. This is off-task behavior (see Glossary).

It is possible to approve the student's attempts to complete assignments (social behavior) while at the same time disapprove an incorrect academic response—"You are working hard; six responses are not correct." The student may be helped to understand the differences among learning how to "work hard," following instructions, and attempting academic material, even though the product is not as expert as it may become with continued effort. Alternately, some students may have many correct responses but still engage in inappropriate social behavior—"Johnny, all your answers are correct, but you should learn to stay on-task and quit disrupting during seatwork."

Teacher Observation Categories

Aa   Approval for academic behavior is recorded if the teacher indicates the academic work is correct. Academic approval usually involves words, spoken or written. The observer should watch carefully to determine if physical expressions, closeness, activities, or things (see Chapter 7) are specifically paired with correct answers, indicating attention or commendation for the correct answer rather than the "working" itself. Care should be exercised in discriminating between approval directed toward academic work and approval for correct social behavior.

As　　Approval for social behavior is recorded if the teacher gives any approving response paired specifically with appropriate social behavior. This category includes words, physical expressions, closeness, activities, and things directed toward any social behavior (following rules, working, cooperating, getting on-task).

Da　　Disapproval for academic behavior includes any disapproval indicating that a student's response to the curriculum materials was incorrect. Disapproval in classrooms generally involves words, spoken or written (grades), but one should not overlook physical expression, closeness (hitting, grabbing, forcibly holding, putting out of group), or deprivation of activities or things.

Ds　　Disapproval for social behavior given by the teacher follows any disruption of the learning environment that interferes with learning. Disapproval includes words, spoken or written, that reprimand. Disapproval may be of either high or low intensity and includes yelling, scolding, threats, and threatening comments concerning later consequences. Disapproval also includes bodily expressions such as frowning, grimacing, or shaking a fist, closeness such as hitting, slapping, paddling, or other means of corporal punishment, and deprivation of activities or things.

(Aa)　An approval mistake of reinforcement following academic behavior occurs when the teacher indicates the academic response is correct when, in fact, the answer is incorrect.

(As)　An approval mistake of reinforcement following social behavior involves giving approval to inappropriate social behavior. For example, a teacher may touch a student "gently" during or following a misbehavior (closeness) or may reinforce the misbehavior through words, bodily expressions, activities, or things. An approval mistake is recorded when the teacher follows a student's breaking of classroom rules with an approval response (inconsistency). The teacher may verbally recognize a student who is walking around when he is supposed to be in his seat, or the teacher may recognize a student who blurts out an answer (whether correct or incorrect) although the student is supposed to raise his hand for recognition. An approval mistake could also occur if the teacher uses words to dispense group verbal approval (praise) when one or more of the students in the group is off-task.

(Da)　A disapproval mistake of reinforcement following academic behavior is recorded when the teacher indicates the student's academic answer was incorrect when the answer was, in fact, correct.

A disapproval mistake of reinforcement following social behavior is recorded if the teacher uses disapproval when the social behavior was indeed appropriate to the classroom situation. This occurs most frequently when the teacher gives group disapproval and one or more of the students are, in fact, on-task. A disapproval mistake may also occur when the teacher interrupts his work with one student in order to attend another student. Interruptions may lead to a disapproval mistake of reinforcement if the student behavior is disapproved in the process. Disapproval mistakes also occur when the teacher delays too long in using disapproval for inappropriate behavior. For example, a student engages in inappropriate behavior, stops the inappropriate behavior, is working appropriately, and then the teacher disapproves.

Nonreinforcement categories

Any response from the teacher that gives specific directions and requires a response from one or more students in the class is not recorded as either approval or disapproval. Academic instructions pertaining to the academic curriculum that do not require a response from the students are not considered as reinforcement.

Attempts by the teacher to stimulate behavioral responses are extremely common. Often these techniques elicit responses from students that can be reinforced. Questioning, probing, cueing, prompts, illustrations, modelling correct procedures, and so on, seem to be tools of most effective teachers, yet these procedures do not necessarily reinforce behavior. While eliciting techniques may increase reinforcement possibilities for some students, elicitation techniques are less effective with students who lack experience or the ability to stay on-task. Observations concerning reinforcements focus only on behaviors which follow a student's response. The individual teacher must establish goals and ascertain the most effective strategies of presentation to elicit responses that then can be reinforced. This is true especially for those individuals whose reinforcement histories do not include enough background for the academic materials to be self-reinforcing.

Student observation (Form C and Form D)

Classroom behavioral observation focusing on the student is concerned with two major behaviors: (1) on-task or appropriate behavior and (2) off-task or inappropriate behavior. Students' behaviors can be appropriate or inappropriate only with reference to classroom rules and/or the teacher's objectives. Therefore, observers must know the rules of each classroom and differing rules for specific situations before reliable observations can be recorded. It is sometimes necessary

Form C:Student Observation

Observer _____ Student _____
Reliability Observer _____ Teacher _____
No. in class or group _____ Grade or Subject _____ Date _____
General Activity _____ Time: Start _____ End _____
Observation Interval _____ Page _____ of _____
            (seconds)   Record Interval _____
                                (seconds)

TIME	ACTIVITY CODE	(1)	2 - RECORD	(3)	4 - RECORD	(5)	6 - RECORD	COMMENTS
1			+ N M O		+ N M O		+ N M O	
2			+ N M O		+ N M O		+ N M O	
3		OBSERVE NOW	+ N M O	OBSERVE NOW	+ N M O	OBSERVE NOW	+ N M O	
4			+ N M O		+ N M O		+ N M O	
5			+ N M O		+ N M O		+ N M O	
6			+ N M O		+ N M O		+ N M O	
7			+ N M O		+ N M O		+ N M O	
8			+ N M O		+ N M O		+ N M O	
9			+ N M O		+ N M O		+ N M O	
10			+ N M O		+ N M O		+ N M O	
11			+ N M O		+ N M O	OBSERVE NOW	+ N M O	
12		OBSERVE NOW	+ N M O	OBSERVE NOW	+ N M O		+ N M O	
13			+ N M O		+ N M O		+ N M O	
14			+ N M O		+ N M O		+ N M O	
15			+ N M O		+ N M O		+ N M O	
16			+ N M O		+ N M O		+ N M O	
17			+ N M O		+ N M O			

Intervals
Observed

% On - task = _____ (+ %)

% Off - task = 100 − (% On - task) = _____

Totals: + = ____ - ____ = ____ %
N = ____ - ____ = ____ %
M = ____ - ____ = ____ %
O = ____ - ____ = ____ %

to ask teachers what their rules are, since some teachers permit students to stand up, sit on the floor, talk during certain activities, or leave their seats without permission.

Child Categories

On-Task   This category includes verbal and motor behavior that follows the
+   classroom rules and is appropriate to the learning situation. On-task behavior is defined with reference to both the rules of the classroom and the teacher-designated academic activity. If a student is working on the appropriate academic activity and is obeying the rules of the classroom, then the student's behavior is recorded as being on-task. Examples of on-task behavior might include sitting at desk while working, engaging in group games when appropriate, responding to teacher questions (whether or not the answer is correct or incorrect), walking

Form D: Student Observation

Observer_____   Student_____
Reliability Observer_____   Teacher_____
No. in Class or Group_____   Grade or Subject_____ Date_____
General Activity_____   Time: Start_____ End _____
Observation Interval_____   Page_____ of _____
                     (seconds)   Record Interval _____
                                                    (seconds)

TIME	ACTIVITY CODE	INTERVALS					COMMENTS
		1	2	3	4	5	
1		+ N M O	+ N M O	+ N M O	+ N M O	+ N M O	
2		+ N M O	+ N M O	+ N M O	+ N M O	+ N M O	
3		+ N M O	+ N M O	+ N M O	+ N M O	+ N M O	
4		+ N M O	+ N M O	+ N M O	+ N M O	+ N M O	
5		+ N M O	+ N M O	+ N M O	+ N M O	+ N M O	
6		+ N M O	+ N M O	+ N M O	+ N M O	+ N M O	
7		+ N M O	+ N M O	+ N M O	+ N M O	+ N M O	
8		+ N M O	+ N M O	+ N M O	+ N M O	+ N M O	
9		+ N M O	+ N M O	+ N M O	+ N M O	+ N M O	
10		+ N M O	+ N M O	+ N M O	+ N M O	+ N M O	
11		+ N M O	+ N M O	+ N M O	+ N M O	+ N M O	
12		+ N M O	+ N M O	+ N M O	+ N M O	+ N M O	
13		+ N M O	+ N M O	+ N M O	+ N M O	+ N M O	
14		+ N M O	+ N M O	+ N M O	+ N M O	+ N M O	
15		+ N M O	+ N M O	+ N M O	+ N M O	+ N M O	

% On - Task =_____(+%)

% Off - Task = 100 − (% On - Task) =_____%

TOTALS INTERVALS PERCENT
OBSERVED

+ = _____ ÷ _____ = _____ %

N = _____ ÷ _____ = _____ %

M = _____ ÷ _____ = _____ %

O = _____ ÷ _____ = _____ %

to chalkboard when asked, demonstrating activities to others when expected, talking during class discussions, or participating actively in physical education class.

Verbal Noise

Off-task N   Verbal noise is any oral response that breaks the class rules and/or interrupts the learning situation. This category may include inappropriate talking, yelling, blurting out, whistling, humming, screaming, singing, and laughing. The verbalization must be heard for it to be recorded. Simply seeing the student's lips move is not enough. If a child responds to a teacher's question or instruction, then the student is on-task. Further examples of verbal off-task behavior include blurting out an answer instead of raising hand, talking to a neighbor instead of working on materials, and singing during discussion.

Object Noise
Object noise is any audible noise resulting from any behavior on the part of the child that may cause other children to be off-task, such as slamming books, kicking furniture, or rapping a desk.

Motor

M   Motor off-task is any motor response (gross or minor) that breaks the class rules and/or interrupts the learning situation. Some motor behaviors are inappropriate during certain classroom periods but not always at others.

V or I   Should it be important to record differences between gross versus minor motor or verbal noise versus object noise, merely use a different check for each.

Gross Motor
Gross motor behaviors may include getting out of one's seat, turning around at least 90°, running, turning cartwheels, walking around the room, waving arms. Another area of inappropriate gross motor behavior includes behaviors generally labelled "aggressive"—hitting, kicking, pushing, pinching, slapping, striking another person with objects, grabbing another's property, and throwing.

Minor Motor
Minor motor behaviors are only recorded when attention is not directed toward the student's work. If the student is engaged in appropriate activities while he exhibits these small motor behaviors, then his behavior is recorded as being on-task with a check mark on "M" and mention is made of these motor activities in the comment section. Examples of minor motor behaviors include thumbsucking, fingernail biting, fiddling with hair, finger twiddling, chewing on a pencil or other object, and playing with academic materials when not appropriate.

Other or *Passive Off-Task*

O   The student is involved in no interaction or is doing nothing when expected to be involved. Behaviors recorded in this category include daydreaming and staring into space. The students must be engaged in no motor or verbal activity for this category to be recorded. It is important to remember that there are times when doing nothing is not inappropriate, for example, when an assignment is completed and nothing has been assigned. This is very rare as most teachers have activities for all students when one assignment is completed.

Student-teacher interactions (Form E and Form F)

Behavioral studies during the past few years have indicated that the response of the teacher to student behavior maintains a great deal

Form E: Student-Teacher

Observer _____
Reliability Observer _____
No. in class or group _____
General Activity _____
Observation Interval _____ (seconds)

Student _____
Teacher _____
Grade or Subject _____ Date _____
Time: Start _____ End _____
Page _____ of _____
Record Interval _____ (seconds)

TIME	NAME(S)	ACTIVITY CODE	(1)	2 - RECORD	(3)	4 - RECORD	(5)	6 - RECORD	COMMENTS
1	Teacher			+ N M O Aa As Da Ds Aa As Da Ds		+ N M O Aa As Da Ds Aa As Da Ds		+ N M O Aa As Da Ds Aa As Da Ds	
2	Teacher		OBSERVE NOW	+ N M O Aa As Da Ds Aa As Da Ds	OBSERVE NOW	+ N M O Aa As Da Ds Aa As Da Ds	OBSERVE NOW	+ N M O Aa As Da Ds Aa As Da Ds	
3	Teacher			+ N M O Aa As Da Ds Aa As Da Ds		+ N M O Aa As Da Ds Aa As Da Ds		+ N M O Aa As Da Ds Aa As Da Ds	
4	Teacher			+ N M O Aa As Da Ds Aa As Da Ds		+ N M O Aa As Da Ds Aa As Da Ds		+ N M O Aa As Da Ds Aa As Da Ds	
5	Teacher			+ N M O Aa As Da Ds Aa As Da Ds		+ N M O Aa As Da Ds Aa As Da Ds		+ N M O Aa As Da Ds Aa As Da Ds	
6	Teacher			+ N M O Aa As Da Ds Aa As Da Ds		+ N M O Aa As Da Ds Aa As Da Ds		+ N M O Aa As Da Ds Aa As Da Ds	
7	Teacher		OBSERVE NOW	+ N M O Aa As Da Ds Aa As Da Ds	OBSERVE NOW	+ N M O Aa As Da Ds Aa As Da Ds	OBSERVE NOW	+ N M O Aa As Da Ds Aa As Da Ds	
8	Teacher			+ N M O Aa As Da Ds Aa As Da Ds		+ N M O Aa As Da Ds Aa As Da Ds		+ N M O Aa As Da Ds Aa As Da Ds	
9	Teacher			+ N M O Aa As Da Ds Aa As Da Ds		+ N M O Aa As Da Ds Aa As Da Ds		+ N M O Aa As Da Ds Aa As Da Ds	
10	Teacher			+ N M O Aa As Da Ds Aa As Da Ds		+ N M O Aa As Da Ds Aa As Da Ds		+ N M O Aa As Da Ds Aa As Da Ds	
11	Teacher			+ N M O Aa As Da Ds Aa As Da Ds		+ N M O Aa As Da Ds Aa As Da Ds		+ N M O Aa As Da Ds Aa As Da Ds	
12	Teacher		OBSERVE NOW	+ N M O Aa As Da Ds Aa As Da Ds		+ N M O Aa As Da Ds Aa As Da Ds		+ N M O Aa As Da Ds Aa As Da Ds	
13	Teacher			+ N M O Aa As Da Ds Aa As Da Ds					

Totals :

+ = _____ Aa _____ As _____
N = _____ Da _____ Ds _____
M = _____ Aa _____ As _____
O = _____ Da _____ Ds _____

Observer _____
Reliability Observer _____
No. in Class or Group _____
General Activity _____
Observation Interval _____ (seconds)

STUDENT _____
Teacher _____
Grade or Subject _____ Date _____
Time: Start _____ End _____
Page _____ of _____
Record Interval _____ (seconds)

TIME	NAME(S)	ACTIVITY CODE	INTERVAL 1	INTERVAL 2	INTERVAL 3	INTERVAL 4	INTERVAL 5	COMMENTS
1			+ N M O	+ N M O	+ N M O	+ N M O	+ N M O	
	Teacher		Aa As Da Ds	Aa As Da Ds	Aa As Da Ds	Aa As Da Ds	Aa As Da Ds	
			Aa As Da Ds	Aa As Da Ds	Aa As Da Ds	Aa As Da Ds	Aa As Da Ds	
2			+ N M O	+ N M O	+ N M O	+ N M O	+ N M O	
	Teacher		Aa As Da Ds	Aa As Da Ds	Aa As Da Ds	Aa As Da Ds	Aa As Da Ds	
			Aa As Da Ds	Aa As Da Ds	Aa As Da Ds	Aa As Da Ds	Aa As Da Ds	
3			+ N M O	+ N M O	+ N M O	+ N M O	+ N M O	
	Teacher		Aa As Da Ds	Aa As Da Ds	Aa As Da Ds	Aa As Da Ds	Aa As Da Ds	
			Aa As Da Ds	Aa As Da Ds	Aa As Da Ds	Aa As Da Ds	Aa As Da Ds	
4			+ N M O	+ N M O	+ N M O	+ N M O	+ N M O	
	Teacher		Aa As Da Ds	Aa As Da Ds	Aa As Da Ds	Aa As Da Ds	Aa As Da Ds	
			Aa As Da Ds	Aa As Da Ds	Aa As Da Ds	Aa As Da Ds	Aa As Da Ds	
5			+ N M O	+ N M O	+ N M O	+ N M O	+ N M O	
	Teacher		Aa As Da Ds	Aa As Da Ds	Aa As Da Ds	Aa As Da Ds	Aa As Da Ds	
			Aa As Da Ds	Aa As Da Ds	Aa As Da Ds	Aa As Da Ds	Aa As Da Ds	
6			+ N M O	+ N M O	+ N M O	+ N M O	+ N M O	
	Teacher		Aa As Da Ds	Aa As Da Ds	Aa As Da Ds	Aa As Da Ds	Aa As Da Ds	
			Aa As Da Ds	Aa As Da Ds	Aa As Da Ds	Aa As Da Ds	Aa As Da Ds	
7			+ N M O	+ N M O	+ N M O	+ N M O	+ N M O	
	Teacher		Aa As Da Ds	Aa As Da Ds	Aa As Da Ds	Aa As Da Ds	Aa As Da Ds	
			Aa As Da Ds	Aa As Da Ds	Aa As Da Ds	Aa As Da Ds	Aa As Da Ds	
8			+ N M O	+ N M O	+ N M O	+ N M O	+ N M O	
	Teacher		Aa As Da Ds	Aa As Da Ds	Aa As Da Ds	Aa As Da Ds	Aa As Da Ds	
			Aa As Da Ds	Aa As Da Ds	Aa As Da Ds	Aa As Da Ds	Aa As Da Ds	
9			+ N M O	+ N M O	+ N M O	+ N M O	+ N M O	
	Teacher		Aa As Da Ds	Aa As Da Ds	Aa As Da Ds	Aa As Da Ds	Aa As Da Ds	
			Aa As Da Ds	Aa As Da Ds	Aa As Da Ds	Aa As Da Ds	Aa As Da Ds	
10			+ N M O	+ N M O	+ N M O	+ N M O	+ N M O	
	Teacher		Aa As Da Ds	Aa As Da Ds	Aa As Da Ds	Aa As Da Ds	Aa As Da Ds	
			Aa As Da Ds	Aa As Da Ds	Aa As Da Ds	Aa As Da Ds	Aa As Da Ds	

Form F: Student-Teacher

Analysis Form: Student-Teacher Forms E and F

Symbols	Total Number Observed		Total Intervals Observed		Percentage Intervals in which Behavior Observed
+	= _____	÷	_____	=	_____ %
N	= _____	÷	_____	=	_____ %
M	= _____	÷	_____	=	_____ %
O	= _____	÷	_____	=	_____ %

On - Task Percentage (+)_____ %

Academic Assignment _____

Teacher Academic Reinforcement

Symbols	Total Number Observed		Total Intervals Observed		Percentage Intervals in which Behavior Observed
Aa	= _____	÷	_____	=	_____ %
Da	= _____	÷	_____	=	_____ %
(Aa)	= _____	÷	_____	=	_____ %
(Da)	= _____	÷	_____	=	_____ %

Approval Ratio: $\dfrac{\text{Aa}}{\text{Aa} + \text{Da} + \text{(Aa)} + \text{(Da)}}$ (Academic)   = _____   = _____ %

Social Reinforcement

Symbols	Total Number Observed		Total Intervals Observed		Percentage Intervals in which Behavior Observed
As	= _____	÷	_____	=	_____ %
Ds	= _____	÷	_____	=	_____ %
(As)	= _____	÷	_____	=	_____ %
(Ds)	= _____	÷	_____	=	_____ %

Approval Ratio = $\dfrac{\text{As}}{\text{As} + \text{Ds} + \text{(As)} + \text{(Ds)}}$ (Social)   = _ _ _ _ _ _   = _____ %

both of appropriate, on-task behavior and inappropriate, off-task behavior (see Part II).

A common question asked by teachers who refer specific children for counseling or other outside help is: How does the teacher respond to these particular students in the classroom; The Student-Teacher Form is designed to answer this question.

This form is a combination of Form A and the Form C given above. During each interval, the observer checks whether the student is on-task (+) or off-task (N for noise, M for motor, O for other, or Passive) and also indicates the response of the teacher to *this particular child*. Following a series of observations (we suggest at least five be completed during those class periods the teacher considers most troublesome), an analysis can be made of the teacher responses to the particular student. Should the teacher or observer desire to note the differences between the teacher's overall responses to the class and his responses to the particular student, then one mark (e.g., X) can be used for responses to other class members and a different mark (e.g., 1) for the individual in question.

Many studies have been conducted using this form in a variety of ways. It can be expanded to include more than one student by using the student's initial as the recording mark and placing the initial for each student in the appropriate squares over the symbol, using red pencils. The form may also be used to observe from two to five students by using a coded number as the recording mark and writing the actual number in each square. Additionally, the form may be used to observe one child during the first time period (three or five intervals), a second child during the next time period, and so on, then recycling across all children after all have been observed.

The basic form has also been expanded into a series of observation forms which include space for more than one student in each observation block (see Form G). On Form G, three students are observed simultaneously and the teacher's responses are also recorded. For this form, mistakes of reinforcement are recorded as approval mistakes (Am) and disapproval mistakes (Dm), with no distinction between academic as opposed to social mistakes. Should this information be required, a different mark can be used. Thus it is also possible with Form E or other adaptations of it, to record precise student-teacher interactions.

Group on-task/off-task teacher response (Form H)

The average number of students off-task and on-task, expressed as a ratio of students engaged in appropriate or inappropriate behavior compared to the total number of students in the classroom or group

Observer _____
Reliability Observer _____
Students: 1. _____
        2. _____
        3. _____

Teacher _____
Date _____
Time Start _____ Time End _____
Page _____ of _____
Observation Interval _____

TIME	S	INTERVAL 1	INTERVAL 2	INTERVAL 3	INTERVAL 4	INTERVAL 5	COMMENT
1	1	X N M O Aa Da	X N M O Aa Da	X N M O Aa Da	X N M O Aa Da	X N M O Aa Da	
	2	X N M O As Ds	X N M O As Ds	X N M O As Ds	X N M O As Ds	X N M O As Ds	
	3	X N M O Am Dm	X N M O Am Dm	X N M O Am Dm	X N M O Am Dm	X N M O Am Dm	
2	1	X N M O Aa Da	X N M O Aa Da	X N M O Aa Da	X N M O Aa Da	X N M O Aa Da	
	2	X N M O As Ds	X N M O As Ds	X N M O As Ds	X N M O As Ds	X N M O As Ds	
	3	X N M O Am Dm	X N M O Am Dm	X N M O Am Dm	X N M O Am Dm	X N M O Am Dm	
3	1	X N M O Aa Da	X N M O Aa Da	X N M O Aa Da	X N M O Aa Da	X N M O Aa Da	
	2	X N M O As Ds	X N M O As Ds	X N M O As Ds	X N M O As Ds	X N M O As Ds	
	3	X N M O Am Dm	X N M O Am Dm	X N M O Am Dm	X N M O Am Dm	X N M O Am Dm	
4	1	X N M O Aa Da	X N M O Aa Da	X N M O Aa Da	X N M O Aa Da	X N M O Aa Da	
	2	X N M O As Ds	X N M O As Ds	X N M O As Ds	X N M O As Ds	X N M O As Ds	
	3	X N M O Am Dm	X N M O Am Dm	X N M O Am Dm	X N M O Am Dm	X N M O Am Dm	
5	1	X N M O Aa Da	X N M O Aa Da	X N M O Aa Da	X N M O Aa Da	X N M O Aa Da	
	2	X N M O As Ds	X N M O As Ds	X N M O As Ds	X N M O As Ds	X N M O As Ds	
	3	X N M O Am Dm	X N M O Am Dm	X N M O Am Dm	X N M O Am Dm	X N M O Am Dm	
6	1	X N M O Aa Da	X N M O Aa Da	X N M O Aa Da	X N M O Aa Da	X N M O Aa Da	
	2	X N M O As Ds	X N M O As Ds	X N M O As Ds	X N M O As Ds	X N M O As Ds	
	3	X N M O Am Dm	X N M O Am Dm	X N M O Am Dm	X N M O Am Dm	X N M O Am Dm	
7	1	X N M O Aa Da	X N M O Aa Da	X N M O Aa Da	X N M O Aa Da	X N M O Aa Da	
	2	X N M O As Ds	X N M O As Ds	X N M O As Ds	X N M O As Ds	X N M O As Ds	
	3	X N M O Am Dm	X N M O Am Dm	X N M O Am Dm	X N M O Am Dm	X N M O Am Dm	
8	1	X N M O Aa Da	X N M O Aa Da	X N M O Aa Da	X N M O Aa Da	X N M O Aa Da	
	2	X N M O As Ds	X N M O As Ds	X N M O As Ds	X N M O As Bs	X N M O As Ds	
	3	X N M O Am Dm	X N M O Am Dm	X N M O Am Dm	X N M O Am Dm	X N M O Am Dm	
9	1	X N M O Aa Da	X N M O Aa Da	X N M O Aa Da	X N M O Aa Da	X N M O Aa Da	
	2	X N M O As Ds	X N M O As Ds	X N M O As Ds	X N M O As Ds	X N M O As Ds	
	3	X N M O Am Dm	X N M O Am Dm	X N M O Am Dm	X N M O Am Dm	X N M O Am Dm	
10	1	X N M O Aa Da	X N M O Aa Da	X N M O Aa Da	X N M O Aa Da	X N M O Aa Da	
	2	X N M O As Ds	X N M O As Ds	X N M O As Ds	X N M O As Ds	X N M O As Ds	
	3	X N M O Am Dm	X N M O Am Dm	X N M O Am Dm	X N M O Am Dm	X N M O Am Dm	

Form G: Student (S)—Teacher

Form H: Group On-Task/Off-Task Teacher Response

Observer_____ Teacher_____
Reliability Observer_____ Grade or Subject_____ Date_____
No. in class or group_____ Time: Start_____ End_____
General Activity_____ Page_____ of_____
Observation Interval_____ Record Interval_____
                    (seconds)   (seconds)

TIME	ACTIVITY CODE	NO STUDENTS	INTERVALS							OFF-TASK RATIO		
			(1)	2 - RECORD	(3)	4 - RECORD	(5)	6 - RECORD		INTERVALS		
				No. Off- + or – Task Students		No. Off- + or – Task Students		No. Off- + or – Task Students		2	4	6
1			OBSERVE NOW	As Aa Ds Da As Aa Ds Da	OBSERVE NOW	As Aa Ds Da As Aa Ds Da	OBSERVE NOW	As Aa Ds Da As Aa Ds Da		/	/	/
2				As Aa Ds Da As Aa Ds Da		As Aa Ds Da As Aa Ds Da		As Aa Ds Da As Aa Ds Da		/	/	/
3				As Aa Ds Da As Aa Ds Da		As Aa Ds Da As Aa Ds Da		As Aa Ds Da As Aa Ds Da		/	/	/
4			OBSERVE NOW	As Aa Ds Da As Aa Ds Da	OBSERVE NOW	As Aa Ds Da As Aa Ds Da	OBSERVE NOW	As Aa Ds Da As Aa Ds Da		/	/	/
5				As Aa Ds Da As Aa Ds Da		As Aa Ds Da As Aa Ds Da		As Aa Ds Da As Aa Ds Da		/	/	/
6				As Aa Ds Da As Aa Ds Da		As Aa Ds Da As Aa Ds Da		As Aa Ds Da As Aa Ds Da		/	/	/
7			OBSERVE NOW	As Aa Ds Da As Aa Ds Da	OBSERVE NOW	As Aa Ds Da As Aa Ds Da	OBSERVE NOW	As Aa Ds Da As Aa Ds Da		/	/	/
8				As Aa Ds Da As Aa Ds Da		As Aa Ds Da As Aa Ds Da		As Aa Ds Da As Aa Ds Da		/	/	/
9				As Aa Ds Da As Aa Ds Da						/	/	/

TOTALS:

As_____ Aa_____ Cumulative Students Off-Task = _____(A)
Ds_____ Da_____ Cumulative Students Observed = _____(B)
As_____ Aa_____
Ds_____ Da_____ $\frac{A}{B}$ = Percent Off-Task = _____

being observed, usually is important to most classroom teachers. Form H may be used to collect these data. As with all forms, the identification section is completed so that accurate reconstruction of the observational situation is possible.

The activity for the class or group is recorded for each time period, numbered down the left-hand side of the page. The observer then records the number of students in the group who are being observed. This is necessary as the ratio of off-task to on-task students will change depending upon the number being observed. Five students recorded as off-task when a group of five is being observed is 100 percent off-task (0.0 percent on-task), whereas five off-task when twnety are being observed is 25 percent off-task (75 percent on-task). Therefore it is important to record the number of students present for each time interval. Within the record boxes, the upper half is for recording the total number of students off-task and the lower portion is for recording teacher responses.

During interval number 1, the observer scans the group or class and then records the number of students off-task by writing the number in the square under No. Off-Task. In most classrooms the number off-task is less than the number on-task, but if a very disruptive class is being observed, it may be easier to record the number on-task. During the recording interval, the observer also listens carefully to the teacher and mentally notes all teacher responses to the entire class. Then, following the recording of students off-task, the observer marks the teacher symbols in the lower portion of the interval. If, for example, the teacher had given approval for appropriate social behavior, the observer would check As in the lower portion under the number of students who were recorded as off-task. Immediately following the recording of teacher behavior and prior to the next observation interval, the observer records whether any students were added or subtracted from the group being observed during the preceding interval. If any change has occurred, the observer records the number under + or − students.

The observer then proceeds to the next interval and repeats the observational procedure, using exactly the same procedure as during the first interval and making certain to record the number of students in the group being observed who are off-task. When total observations have been completed, the Off-Task Ratios are subsequently recorded for all observation intervals. The area above the diagonal line is used to record the number of students off-task in each observed interval and the portion below the diagonal line to record the number of all students observed during that single interval.

Analysis of the percentage of students off-task represents an average of the percentage off-task during all observed intervals. This is computed by adding each individual fraction from the off-task ratios section and completing the division. If six intervals (two time lines) were observed with the following ratios:

Second interval (No. Students = 20, 5 off-task = 5/20), 3 students left (−3)

Fourth interval (20 − 3 = 17 Students, 4 off-task = 4/17), 10 students came in (+10)

Sixth interval (17 + 10 = 27 students, 8 off-task = 8/27), four students were taken out (No. Students, Line 2, 27 − 4 = 23)

Second interval (10 off-task = 10/23), number of students remained the same (± 0)

Fourth interval (23 + 0 = 23, 6 off-task = 6/23), two students came in (+ 2),

Sixth interval (23 + 2 + 25, 3 off-task = 3/25)

the average percent off-task would be computed as follows:

5/20 + 4/17 + 8/27 + 10/23 + 6/23 + 3/25 =
.25 + .235 + .296 + .435 + .26 + .12 = 1.596/6 =
.266 = 27 percent average off-task.

Calculating on the form:

Cumulative Students Off-task (A) = 5 + 4 + 8 + 10 + 6 + 3 = 36.

Cumulative Students Observed (B) = 20 + 17 + 27 + 23 + 23 + 25 = 135.

A/B = 36/135 = .266 = 27 percent off-task.

The analysis of teacher responses takes place in exactly the same way as when using the Teacher Observation Form. The result is an indication of the average classroom off-task behavior and at the same time shows how the teacher reinforcement for both academic and social behavior may be maintaining the on- or off-task behavior. An interval by interval analysis of the data in terms of increase and decrease across specific intervals can be used in examining results with teachers who desire to become more competent in the application of reinforcement principles in the classroom.

INTERPERSONAL OBSERVATION

Interpersonal observation (Form J)

Sometimes interpersonal behaviors between students need to be observed. This is especially pertinent in newly integrated situations regardless of mode of integration: race, sex, academic ability, schools, aggression, passivity, or other relationships between one, two, or any group of people.

Interpersonal behaviors are most frequently expressed by means of verbal or motor expression. Verbal behaviors include any oral response of either an approving or disapproving nature by the person being observed, directed toward any designated person(s). Verbal responses primarily include words spoken, but also comprise yelling, whistling, humming, screaming, and laughing. Verbalizations must be heard for the observer to record the behavior.

Form J: Interpersonal Observation

Person (s)_____ Teacher_____
Observed_____ Grade or Subject _____ Date_____
Observer 1_____ Activity_____
Reliability Observer_____ Time Start_____ Time End_____

TIME	ACTIVITY	Interval 1					Interval 3					Interval 5				Analysis			
		V	V	M	M		V	V	M	M		V	V	M	M	COMMENTS SYMBOL FREQ. %			
		x↓o	o↓x	x↓o	o↓x		x↓o	o↓x	x↓o	o↓x		x↓o	o↓x	x↓o	o↓x	Vx → o₍a₎ ___ ___			
																Vx → o₍d₎ ___ ___			
1																Vo → x₍a₎ ___ ___			
2																Vo → x₍d₎ ___ ___			
3																Mx → o₍a₎ ___ ___			
4																Mx → o₍d₎ ___ ___			
5																Mo → x₍a₎ ___ ___			
6																Mo → x₍d₎ ___ ___			
7																			
8																Reliability			
9																		Agree	Disagree
10																x → o₍a₎ ___ ___			
11																x → o₍d₎ ___ ___			
12																o → x₍a₎ ___ ___			
13																o → x₍d₎ ___ ___			
14																Total ___ ___			
15																			
16																			
17																Total Agree ___			

$$\frac{\text{Total Agree}}{\text{Total Agree + Total Disagree}} = \text{___}$$

REACTION_____
_____
_____
_____
_____

Motor behavior includes both gross and minor motor behaviors as well as bodily and facial expressions. Touching, hitting, pushing, slapping, and striking with objects are motor behaviors, as well as patting and tapping. Bodily expressions such as raising hands or holding fists may also be included.

This observation form provides two basic designations for persons being observed (X and O) and a method of recordings the direction of the behavior (X toward O or O toward X). These X and O symbols may designate any individual or number of individuals.

Interpersonal Categories

Vx O_a Any verbal behavior (words spoken) initiated by the student designated· by the X subsymbol (white-black, male-female, friend-protagonist), directed toward the student designated by the O subsymbol, and defined as approval. (See teacher approval category.)

Vo X_a Any verbal behavior (words spoken) initiated by the student designated by the O subsymbol, directed toward the student designated by the X subsymbol, and defined as approval. (See teacher approval category.)

Vx O_d Any verbal behavior (words spoken) initiated by the student designated by the X subsymbol, directed toward the student designated by the O subsymbol, and defined as disapproval. (See teacher disapproval category.)

Vo X_d Any verbal behavior (words spoken) initiated by the student designated by the O subsymbol, directed toward the student designated by the X subsymbol, and defined as disapproval. (See teacher disapproval category.)

Mx O_a Any motor (definition of student categories) behavior (bodily expression or closeness) initiated by the student designated by the X subsymbol, directed toward the student designated by the O subsymbol, and defined as approval. (See teacher approval category.)

Mo X_a Any motor (definition of student categories) behavior (bodily expressions or closeness) initiated by the student designated by the O subsymbol, directed toward the student designated by the X subsymbol, and defined as approval. (See teacher approval category.)

Mx O_d Any motor (definition of student categories) behavior (bodily expressions or closeness) initiated by the student designated by the X subsymbol, directed toward the student designated by the O subsymbol, and defined as approval. (See teacher disapproval category.)

Mo X_d Any motor (definition of student categories) behavior response (bodily expressions or closeness) initiated by the student designated by the O subsymbol, directed toward the student designated by the X subsymbol, and defined as disapproval. (See teacher disapproval category.)

If we assume that a teacher desires to observe the approval and disapproval behaviors directed toward a particular pupil who does not appear to respond to interpersonal contingencies, the observer could designate this child as X and all other children as O. Observations are then recorded in the appropriate squares underneath the symbols by placing either an A (approval) or D (disapproval) in the square and a number to indicate the number of children who received or dispensed the particular behavior. Suppose that three children stuck out their tongues at a retarded student. The observer would record a D in the first interval under $M_{o \to x}$ and following the D write a small "3." Should the observer desire to record the particular response the word "tongue" could be written under the comments section. Anyone analyzing the report would then know that three children engaged in motor disapproval toward the particular pupil.

It is thus possible to observe one or more students at any time. In a newly integrated high school class, for instance, the teacher wished to know the number of approving and disapproving responses directed toward members of each group by all members of the group. In this case, the X would be one group and the O would designate the other group. The observer would record the number of responses in each square as well as the symbol A or D. This particular example of recording would indicate the total number of approval or disapproval responses, whether motor or verbal or both, of an entire group in each interval. Similar procedures can be used for any number of questions involving interpersonal responses in classrooms, recreation areas, cafeterias, playgrounds, and so on.

The precise designation of persons being observed depends upon the questions of interest to the persons who are responsible for asking such questions. Should more than two groups or persons be of interest, it is necessary to attach a subsymbol to the A and D. For example, the responses of male and female faculty (two groups) toward male and female students could be of interest. In this case, the A receives a subscript. Thus X represents faculty and O represents students. Responses of an approving nature by males is recorded A_m and by females A_f. These kinds of distinctions may, of course, be expanded, but it is suggested that no more than four groups be observed at any one time as it becomes much more difficult with each additional subscript.

Interpersonal observation (Form K)

Precise observations of group interactions are possible with the use of Form K: Interpersonal Observation. Through the analysis of the categories, group totals, individual reactions, and individual or group reactions to a teacher or group leader may be analyzed.

Categories include Verbal, Contact, and Expressions of an approving nature; Verbal, Contact, and Expressions of a disapproving nature; and Neutral interactions.

Observer Name _____ Date _____ Time _____ End _____

Activity _____ Location _____ Reliability Observer _____ Number in Group _____

Page _____ Of _____ Subject Name _____ Subject Number _____

Observation Interval _____ Record Interval _____

	Record A												Record B												Record C												Line Totals											
	APR			NEU			DISAPR					APR			NEU			DISAPR					APR			NEU			DISAPR					APR			NEU			DISAPR		
	V	C	E	V	C	O	V	C	E			V	C	E	V	C	O	V	C	E			V	C	E	V	C	O	V	C	E			V	C	E	V	C	O	V	C	E
1																																									
2																																									
3																																									
4																																									
5																																									
6																																									
7																																									
8																																									
9																																									
10																																									

Page Totals

Form K: Interpersonal Observation

It is recommended for this type of recording that one observer record each participant and indicate the direction of the recorded behavior. For example, if there were eight participants, all would be numbered and the observer watching No. 1 would record each behavior and indicate whether it was directed toward any other participant by recording the other participants' number(s) under the appropriate symbol. Recording in this manner requires a great deal more time for reliability training than the more simple observation codes (twelve to eighteen hours of training).

Should one desire to reconstruct a precise matrix of behavioral interactions, it is necessary to employ some mechanical means of keeping all observers in the same interval at the same time. A prerecorded tape may be used for this purpose. The taped voice begins by warning the observers prior to the first observation and then states "Get ready. . . . Line one. . . . Observe." This is followed by fifteen seconds of blank tape whereupon the taped voice continues; "Record." The recording interval usually constitutes five seconds of blank tape and the recorded voice then continues, "Observe," with fifteen seconds of blank tape, and "Record," with five seconds of blank tape, until four intervals have been recorded. The recorded voice will then state, "Line Two . . . Observe." The taped voice takes little time to prerecord and keeps all observers on-task while reducing unreliability when observers lose their place. Thus these time indicators given every minute allow few problems with observers and eliminate recording in the wrong interval.

Behavioral Definitions

The following behavioral definitions used in analysis of a series of "encounter and personal growth groups" indicate that the categories of Approval, Disapproval, and Neutral are sufficient for almost all interpersonal interactions.

Symbol
V   Verbal: One continuous, audible, meaningful phrase or idea.

Approving Verbal. Verbal communication that indicates either a compliment or caring, correctness, acceptance, or agreement that is unbroken by a different thought or idea.

Examples: Words

yes	fantastic
good	terrific
nice	swell
great	marvelous
fascinating	exactly

charming
commendable
delightful
brilliant
fine
uh-huh

Apr
V
positively
go ahead
yeah
all right
correct
excellent
that's right
perfect
satisfactory
absolutely
keep going
beautiful
wonderful

of course
cool
groovy
likeable
wonderful
outstanding
exciting
interesting
pleasant
delicious
fabulous
splendid
thoughtful
remarkable
cheerful
friendly
elegant
well thought out

Examples: Sentences

I like you.
I respect you for that.
I agree. •
I approve.
I'm glad you're here.
You make us happy.
That shows thought.
How charming.
We think a lot of you.
You're very pleasant.
You're so outgoing.
Yes, please continue.
A good way of putting it.

You are very friendly.
You have a nice _____
That's interesting.
Show us how.
You're doing better.
That's very good.
I'm proud of you.
That's logical.
You're polite, nice courteous, etc.
You have (a) nice eyes, smile,
    personality, etc.
I like your clothes.

Disapr
V
Disapproving Verbal. Audible communication of disagreement, dislike, disinterest, nonacceptance, or incorrectness that is unbroken
by a different thought or idea

Examples:

Impractical
Work faster
Try to understand.
Do your best.
Unclear explanation
Don't you want to do things
    right?

That's ridiculous, meaningless, ab-
    surd, bad, nonsense.
Too vague
Try harder.
That's not right.
Incorrect
You should be ashamed.

It can't be that difficult.

You're too slow.

Stop talking.

Pay attention.

Don't

Wrong

Stupid

Think for a change.

Use some thought.

No, that's not what I said.

You don't understand because
 you don't listen.

You're gutless.

You'd better get on the stick.

You must be confused.

I don't see your point.

You know better than that.

That's not clear.

I dislike you.

I dislike that.

Don't make excuses.

Listen to me.

Leave her alone.

You're dull.

It's hopeless for you.

You're worthless.

You're rude.

Don't laugh at me.

That's childish.

That wasn't the right thing to do.

You haven't been paying
 attention.

People never change

Neutral Verbal. By exclusion, all other verbal behavior.

Examples:

Neu
V

I went to the store today.

It sure is hot and humid
 outside.

It is going to rain.

I have two kids.

It sure is pretty today.

I went home yesterday.

E

Expressions: Muscular movements of the face or body that express interpersonal meaning.

Approving Expression. Communication by movement of caring, correctness, acceptance, or agreement directed toward some person(s).

Examples: Facial

Apr
E

smiling

winking

nodding

raising eyebrows

fawning kiss

opening eyes

slowly closing eyes

laughing

chucking

widening eyes

wrinkling nose

blinking rapidly

giggling

whistles

cheering

licking lips

smacking lips

rolling eyes

Examples: Bodily

clapping hands

raising arms

grabbing

bouncing

shaking head

shrugging shoulders

expansive movement of hands

taking a fast breath

signaling OK.	opening hands
cocking head	embracing hand or finger to face,
rubbing stomach	hair, head
thumbs up	"right-on" sign

Disapr
E

Disapproving Expression. Communication by movement of dislike, disinterest, nonacceptance or incorrectness directed toward some person(s)

Examples: Expression

frowning	clicking tongue
curling lip	pointing finger
furrowing brows	putting hand behind ear
lowering eyebrows	grimacing
shaking finger or fist	sniffing
squinting eyes	tightening jaw
wrinkling forehead	sticking out tongue
puckering lips	snickering
pounding fist	turning head away
laughing at	letting out breath
shaking head	kissing
turning away	fingers in front of lips
gritting teeth	shaking head no
biting lips	showing teeth
closing eyes	pulling in bottom lip

None

Neutral Expression. Not recorded .

Contact: The touching of any parts of the bodies of two or more people

Apr
C

Approving Contact: The touching of another person which expresses caring, correctness, acceptance, or agreement. Examples:

hugging	nudging
patting	holding
kissing	leaning against
touching	caressing

Disapr
C

Disapproving Contact: The touching of another person which expresses dislike, disinterest, nonacceptance, incorrectness (determined by intensity). Examples:

hitting	restraining
grabbing	kicking
pushing	shoving

Neu
O

Neutral contact. Recorded as neutral other. Unintentional contact or passive behavior.

General Instructions: All behaviors should be recorded even if they occur simultaneously. If a person being observed makes a comment, smiles, and touches someone else, then a mark would be placed under verbal, expression, and contact. In addition, all behaviors should be recorded even if they are contradictory. A smile is always recorded as an approval. Sarcasm when it can be recorded is disapproving.

If a behavior begins prior to the record time and its meaning cannot be determined, then record the behavior as neutral. Two or more unbroken statements of the same type (either approving, neutral, or disapproving) are recorded as one unit of behavior. A broken statement is one which is interrupted; a pause is not considered as a break.

The direction of the behavior (toward another member of the group) is sometimes difficult to assess and observe correctly. If the direction of the behavior is unknown, record the behavior under the appropriate symbol by using a question mark. When the behavior is directed toward the group (four or more persons is considered as the group), a G should be used in the appropriate box.

During each observation interval, the observer should be prepared to answer the following questions with recorded data:

Did a vocalization (verbal behavior) occur? If the answer is yes, determine whether it was approving, disapproving, or neutral.

Was there an expression other than neutral? If so, then determine whether it was approving or disapproving.

Was there physical contact? If yes, then determine whether it was approving, disapproving, or neutral.

Should behaviors occur that do not fit any of the category definitions, implied by the above questions during the observation interval, put an X in the Neutral Other category.

General observation (Form L)

Form L: General Observation is an overall model for record keeping. As most teachers realize, behavioral principles are of little use unless accurate records are kept. Behaviors are defined (pinpointed) in precise behavioral terms and then observed by checking occurrences of the defined behavior during the planned recording interval. Consequences are applied systematically and recorded, then the behavior is again measured (recorded) in order to evaluate the effect of the consequences.

The specific behavior to be observed is determined and written on the pinpoint line. The person or persons to be observed are indicated together with the person who is going to do the observation

Form L: General Observation

PINPOINT_____ Person(s) observed_____

Observer(s)_____ Location _____

Time of observation_____ Desire that behavior increase decrease _____

I (we) will conduct_____ observations per_____ every_____ for_____
(number)   (min-hr-day)   (day-wk)   (day-wk)

before consequating takes place

Observation interval_____Time between obs._____
(sec-min-hr-day)   (sec-min-hr-day)

RECORD Each occurrence of Pinpoint		CONSEQUATE Consequences following occurrence of behavior					EVALUATE Each occurrence of Pinpoint		
Date	Obs. No.		Date	Obs. No.	Approval	Dis- approval	Other	Date	Obs. No.	

Total = _____
No. Obs.= _____
Average = _____

Totals = _____ _____ _____

When_____
(appropriate)

When_____
(inappropriate)

Total =_____
No. Obs.=_____
Average =_____

Comments _____

for_____
(time-times)
Then these approvals
will follow:
a._____
b._____
c._____

Then this
disapproval
will follow:
a._____

SUMMARY

Record total_____
Evaluate total_____
Record average_____
Evaluate average_____
Increase_____
Decrease_____

(teacher, students, themselves, other pupils, teacher aides). The recording times for observations are determined, and whether the behavior is to be increased or decreased is noted by circling the appropriate word. Next the observer makes a contract with himself or the teacher to insure that a sufficient number of observations (baseline recording) take place prior to the application of consequences.

The Record section includes dates, observation number(s) and a space for checking, or marking in any way, each occurrence of the behavior observed. It is recommended that observations take place over at least a five-day period and/or that ten observations be made to insure that an accurate representative measure of the behavior has been achieved. The teacher then determines what consequences are to be applied (approval and/or disapproval) and fills in the lower portion of the consequate section. During the Record phase, the teacher has sufficient time to determine just what potential reinforcers are to be used and when these consequences are to be applied (schedule of reinforcement.) The observer records the number of approvals and/or disapprovals. A record of the pinpointed behavior is generally achieved automatically and this gives a preliminary check to see if the behavior is increasing, decreasing, or not changing. However, it is suggested that a teacher apply consequences for two weeks before taking additional observations to evaluate the effectiveness of the program.

Following the application of consequences for two weeks, the observer records in the Evaluate section using exactly the same procedure as was employed during the Record phase. The Summary indicates the effectiveness of the procedures by comparing the Record average with the Evaluate average.

Following completion of Form L, it is generally necessary to maintain the appropriate behavior through effective use of reinforcements. When the environment of the child changes, it is expected that the responses of the child will also change. Self-motivation (response to internal reinforcement) is achieved only after extensive structuring across many different situations. Continual reevaluation and application of appropriate contingencies is almost always necessary.

OBSERVATIONAL ANALYSIS

Observational information should include all necessary identification as well as a complete summary. Observational forms include an analysis section (on the back or front) which should be completed.

Frequency: All discrete observational symbols recorded (marked or written) should be counted across all intervals and the total number written on the line opposite the appropriate symbol.

Percentages: After recording the frequency of various behaviors, the relative frequency with which each rated behavior has occurred should be computed. It may be desirable to express observational findings in terms of the percentage of observational intervals in which a given behavior was recorded, rather than dealing only with frequency.

The percentage of occurrences for each discrete symbol is found by dividing the total number of times a symbol was recorded by the total number of intervals over which observation was conducted. For example, let us assume that Aa is recorded four times in a 15-minute observation, three 10-second observations being made each minute. The numerator in this case is four. The denominator is found by multiplying the number of minutes in the observation period (15 minutes) by the number of observation periods per minute (three). In this example, the denominator is 45. When the necessary division is made, it is found that during .088 or .09 or 9 percent of the intervals observed, an approval for academic behavior was recorded. In the same manner, percentages may be obtained for all other symbols.

Percentages for any symbol or combination of symbols may be graphed across time intervals such as subject periods, times a day, days, or weeks. Such a graph will supply information as to whether the behavior(s) being observed are increasing, decreasing, or remaining the same. Applications of specific consequences may be indicated and changes in behavior noted.

Reliability Computation

Observer reliability concerns the amount of agreement/disagreement on the part of various observers when observing the same behaviors at the same time. In behavioral observation it is very important to determine the measure of agreement between two observers. This is expressed as a percentage—how often do two observers watching the same behavior record it as same behavior? In this way it is possible to check the accuracy of any classroom observation.

While it is important to assess interobserver reliability, it is also usually not practical to have two observers at all times. Reliability training can be conducted and then one may assume that reliable observation is achieved. Generally a reliability coefficient of .80 is considered a minimal average. After training, reliability should be assessed often to be certain there is not a systematic change in one or more observers. It has been determined that when reliability checks occur 20 percent of the total observation time with subsequent observer feedback, then observers remain reliable. Of course, some particular projects may require additional reliability checks.

When calculating observer reliability, each discrete symbol is listed separately. For computation, use the reliability section of the observer form and record the number of times observer 1 and the reliability observer agree for each symbol in the same time intervals. Thus if As behavior has been checked on both forms in the third interval of the second time period and the first interval of the fourth time period, then two agreements would be recorded for the As category. Similarly, if Da behavior occurred in the second interval of the first time period, the third interval of the tenth time period, and the first interval of the fifteenth time period, on both observer forms, then three agreements would be recorded for the Da symbol. To compute reliability, systematically check each symbol on both forms in every interval for agreements.

The next stage is to record the number of times both observers *disagree* for each symbol. When each observer has a different symbol checked in the same interval, disagreement is recorded under both symbols. For example, if a Ds behavior occurred on one observation sheet and a Da behavior occurred on the other sheet, both in the first interval of the third time period, then a disagreement would be recorded for each symbol (Ds and Da). This procedure is continued across the entire observation with the total number of agreements and disagreements being recorded for each symbol.

Nothing is also a category and can be recorded with a horizontal line through the interval. This category may be included in reliability calculations. However it is better that reliability approaches .80 using defined categories only.

In the final stage, sum the total number of agreements and total number of disagreements for all symbols. Next, divide the sum of the total number of agreements by the sum of total agreements plus total disagreements in order to obtain a percentage of reliability; as shown:

$$\frac{\text{Total Number Agreements}}{\text{Total Number Agreements plus Disagreements}} = \frac{\text{Percentage}}{\text{Reliability}}$$

While there are many different formulas to compute reliability, the above is both stringent and manageable enough to be used with all observers.

Observer reliability for group off-task student behavior uses the same basic rationale and is calculated as follows:

$$\frac{\dfrac{(N - [n_1 - n_2])}{N} + \cdots + \dfrac{(N - [n_1 - n_2])}{N}}{O} = \underline{\hspace{2cm}}\%$$

where N = total number of students under observation in each interval, and

n_1 = number of students observed off-task by the first observer.

Observational Summary

Accurate recording, assessment of social behavior, and subsequent remediation seem to be the most important considerations when students are referred for inappropriate behavior. Unfortunately, when many students are referred they are taken out of the environment where the problem is occurring (the classroom) and are administered tests by a professional who only rarely observes the child in the classroom. The use of a combination of observational procedures (including tests), when analyzed properly, are generally more beneficial to teachers. However, cursory nonsystematic observation does not appear to be any better than other types of nonspecific evaluation. The environmental situation must be carefully analyzed (baseline) by rigorous observation and a specific plan designated for implementation. Discussions may then be held with appropriate personnel and procedures determined to alter the student's inappropriate responses. Diagnostic evaluation, whether by tests or observation, seems limited unless remedial steps are planned and implemented in the classroom where the maladaptive behaviors occur.

Complete analysis of a child's problem requires that the person who is to interpret the results know the implications of the results. If a teacher is told that a child who was referred for observation engages in 50 percent inappropriate behavior, what conclusion can be drawn? Obviously the conclusion must be based upon answers to some of the following questions: Were the inappropriate behaviors of a passive variety or active interference with other children? What behaviors of the teachers or peers served to maintain or reinforce the inappropriate behavior? Was the activity during which the student was observed of such a nature that the whole class was approaching 50 percent off-task behavior? What constitutes the baseline of appropriate behavior for this class during these particular activities? How many observations of other members of the class have been taken under similar circumstances? Were the behaviors of an interpersonal nature? What is the academic achievement level of the student during this activity? Is the academic material geared to the student's level? What is the level of off-task behavior in other activities with the same teacher? Different teachers? What reinforcers are important to the particular student? Does the teacher use appropriate rewards for this student as well as others?

An analysis of answers to these and similar questions is generally necessary if the student is to be helped to achieve his/her highest potential.

STUDY GUIDE FOR CHAPTER 8

Questions:

1. Explain why it is *not* possible to observe ignoring.

2. What observation form would be most useful in observing student/ teacher interactions? Why?

3. What would you expect within a classroom if the teacher gives an extremely high amount of approval to appropriate *academic* behavior but makes approval social mistakes?

4. What would you expect within a classroom where the teacher pays a great deal of attention to appropriate *social* behavior but ignores most academic behavior?

5. Why is it necessary to observe in small amounts of time if one is observing interpersonal and very subtle interactions?

6. Do you believe that it is more damaging (in the long run) for the teacher to make approval mistakes or disapproval mistakes? Why?

7. Why is it necessary to observe a student if the teacher can already tell what the student's problem is?

8. Why is it necessary to compute reliability? How valid are observations without some reliability check?

9. What would you list (from your own observations) as the most important positive aspect of the teaching/learning situation? What was the most negative aspect?

10. Is it possible from your observation to ascertain why it is that some children are "liked" more by some teachers? Is it because the children are "nice?" Is it because teachers treat them with approval and therefore they become that way?

LEARNING ACTIVITY 15—
OBSERVATIONAL EVALUATION

Instruction:

Study carefully Chapter 8, paying special attention to the definitional categories. Complete all answers on the Observational Evaluation. Small discussion groups provide an excellent method to check the accuracy of the test responses and in addition develop a general competency in the application of observational rules prior to actual classroom observation.

Part I: For each category listed below, please put the appropriate symbol to the right of the category.

Teacher reinforcement categories

1. Approval Mistake (Social) _____

2. Disapproval (Academic) _____

3. Approval (Social) _____

4. Approval Mistake (Academic) _____

5. Disapproval Mistake (Social) _____

6. Instructions _____

Student categories

7. Verbal (Noise) Off-Task _____

8. Motor Off-Task _____

9. On-Task _____

10. Passive Off-Task _____

Part II: Below are listed the rules for Mrs. Jones' classroom. Using these rules, check the appropriate space(s) as to how the specific behaviors should be categorized.

Rules for specific activity

1. Work quietly (no talking).

2. During this period work individually on math in your seat.

3. Raise your hand to receive help.

4. You may get materials without permission.

5. Sign in and out on the list for going to the restroom without asking permission.

Part II A. You are observing the students. Record behaviors using the observational code:

	On-Task	Off-Task N M O	None Apply
11. One student is talking to his neighbor.			
12. Student is quietly writing spelling words.			
13. Student is staring out the window while chewing on his pencil.			
14. Student is working in seat on math.			
15. Student lies on floor working on math.			
16. Student is staring out of window.			
17. Student signs list to go to restroom, but does not ask teacher's permission.			
18. You can see the student talking to his neighbor, but you cannot hear him.			
19. Student is turned 45 degrees in his seat.			
20. Student turns around 90 degrees and talks to his neighbor.			
21. Student hits his neighbor.			
22. Student calls out to teacher.			
23. Student staring at floor.			

	On-Task	Off-Task N M O	None Apply
24. Teacher asks student a question and student responds with an incorrect answer.			
25. Student gets up to get materials.			
26. On the way back from getting materials, the student stops and talks with another student.			
27. A child puts up his hand and looks around the room.			
28. A student is talking to himself.			
29. A student is gently drumming his desk while working on math.			
30. A student is asking a fellow student about an assignment.			

Part II B: Teacher Behaviors
            Record teacher behaviors using the following code:

Aa Approval—Academic   As Approval—Social
Da Disapproval—Academic   Ds Disapproval—Social
(As) Approval Mistake—   (As) Approval Mistake—Social
        Academic
(Da) Disapproval Mistake—   (Ds) Disapproval Mistake—Social
        Academic   — No Behavior Rated

If more than one code applies, use the following order of importance:

  1. Mistakes of Reinforcement
  2. Approval
  3. Disapproval

31. "That's a correct answer but sit down while working." _____

32. "That's good you raised your hand for help." _____

33. Teacher asks student to respond.   _____

34. "Sit up straight. You look sloppy."   _____

35. Teacher gently places hand on student while
    telling him to sit down.   _____

36. "The whole class is doing well." (Two students
    off-task)   _____

37. Student blurts out answer and teacher says,
    "That's correct, Jimmy."   _____

38. "I don't want to hear another word for the
    next ten minutes."   _____

39. Teacher calls on student who is quiet but does
    not have hand up. (Student behaving appro-
    priately except that his hand is not up.)   _____

40. Student is out of his seat and taps teacher on
    shoulder. Teacher says, "Sit down, Johnny. I
    will not talk to you unless you raise your hand."   _____

41. Student is out of seat and touches teacher. The
    teacher puts his arm on shoulder and says, "Sit
    down. I will not talk to you unless your hand
    is raised."   _____

42. "No, Johnny. That is not the right answer."   _____

43. "This class is just not working." (Two students
    are working.)   _____

44. "Except for Linda and Jane, who are working
    very nicely, the rest of you are behaving
    abominably. Sit down and stop talking."   _____

45. The teacher responds to a student's answer to
    a question by repeating the student's answer.   _____

46. The teacher inadvertently marks a correct
    answer as incorrect.   _____

47. "Johnny, you're always raising your hand to
    answer. Let someone else answer for a change."   _____

48. "Johnny, stop copying Jimmy's paper."   _____

49. "That's almost right."   _____

50. The teacher puts her arm around a student and
    says, "These problems are all correct," when
    in fact, two are incorrect.   _____

LEARNING ACTIVITY 16–CLASSROOM OR
ROLE-PLAYING OBSERVATIONS

The purpose of observing others is to sensitize teachers or potential teachers to the behaviors of both teacher and students in order to more effectively choose appropriate approval and disapproval techniques that are in line with personal value decisions.

Using the observational chapter, definitions of categories, and observational forms, observe for four 20-minute (50 time intervals) periods. Use Teacher Observation Form A for one period, Individual Student Form C for one period, Student-Teacher Form E for one period, and Classroom On-Task-Teacher Response Form H for one period.

Participants (students) should be assigned observational tasks in groups of two. Following completion of each of the four observations, reliability should be computed and results discussed. Instructors may assign films, videotapes, or actual classroom observation or have some participants role play while others observe.

Accuracy of observations is critical for appropriate discriminations to occur. Observers should remember to fill in every part of the observational forms including Feelings and Reactions in the comments section or on the back of the form. Interpretations and inferences are important for learning but should not be confused with the behavior observed in the classroom.

CHAPTER 9

An Introduction to Behavioral Terminology

This introduction to terminology is included to serve as a transition from the present volume to the published research found within scientific journals dealing with aspects of behavior modification. Indeed, the entire growth of behavior modification represents a scientific approach to the control and/or modification of behavior.

Behavior refers to the way people react to their environment and what they do to their environment. The behavior modifier generally classifies behavior as operant and respondent. *Respondent behavior* refers to behavior which is involuntary, elicited, or automatic; for example, the eyeblink, sneezing, coughing, and so on. *Operant behavior* refers to behavior which is voluntary and purposeful. Most human behaviors and behaviors labeled as "doing" are considered as operant, e.g., walking, talking, driving. Operant behavior or responses are often a function of more than one stimulus (anything that activates the organism). These responses are modified primarily through their environmental consequences, that is, what happens in the external environment after the behavior occurs. All that is needed to bring about respondent behavior is the proper stimulus. For instance, the touch of a hot iron causes one to jerk the hand away. Behavior modification concerns itself *only* with the external aspects of these behaviors—the observable and the measurable.

The goal of behavior modification is to predict and influence the behavior of an individual organism through scientific laws and procedures. *Laws* are statements concerning the empirical scientific relationship between independent and dependent variables. The *dependent variable*—the response—is the behavior the scientist is interested in controlling. The *independent variable(s)* represents events or occurrences within the environment, or things that will effect change in *dependent variables.* This is the variable that is manipulated or treated with consequent changes on the dependent variable noted. The relationship between these two represents the cause-and-effect relationship in behavioral science. Thus, behavior modification functions on a scientific basis. The cause-and-effect relationship constitutes the primary realm of concern for the behavioral technician. In essence, behavior modifiers maintain that behavior is a result of its consequences. Therefore, if the independent variable (cause) is known and its effect on the dependent variable is known, the behavior modifier is in a more certain position to control and predict behavior.

Behavior modification employs a variety of techniques to change maladaptive behaviors. Some selected principles underlying the use of these techniques and a glossary of key terms follow. A synthesis of techniques used in behavior therapy is given as a means of familiarizing the layman with the approaches, procedures, and principles of several of the most widely used techniques.

The first technique is used primarily to manipulate respondent behavior. Respondent behavior is often accompanied by an emotion of fear which represents a conditioned response to pain. When the emotional component becomes paired with the respondent behavior, *respondent conditioning* is said to have occurred. Technicians employing this technique view many psychological disturbances (maladaptive behavior) as a result of this type of learning. The basic principle of respondent conditioning may be summarized as follows:

After a *neutral stimulus* (which will not normally bring a specific response, e.g., a tone does not cause one to blink the eye) has been paired with an *unconditioned stimulus* which elicits an *unconditioned response,* then the neutral stimulus will also elicit that response or a part of that response. The neutral stimulus now becomes known as the *conditioned stimulus.* For example, a tone is paired with a puff of air near the eye, an eye blink occurs. After several pairings, the tone alone will elicit an eye blink *(conditioned response).*

Related to this principle is the concept of *stimulus generalization* which plays a role in conditioned emotional reactions. Stimulus generalization refers to the fact that stimuli similar to a conditioned stimulus will also elicit the *conditioned response.* The conditioned response is the response which is brought about by the conditioned stimulus (CS) alone. If the CS was a tone in "C", a tone of A or E might also bring about the conditioned response (CR).

The respondent conditioning paradigm is a model for the development of most learned emotions, the learned guilts, and angers that bring individuals to clinics or to other sources for treatment. According to basic learning principles, conditioned respondents can be eliminated through two processes, extinction and counterconditioning.

Extinction occurs when the conditioned stimulus is presented over and over again without further pairing with the unconditioned stimulus. The conditioned response begins to diminish and finally ceases to occur at all. When the conditioned response no longer occurs, extinction has taken place. Just as the process of conditioned respondents follows the laws of stimulus generalization, so does the principle of extinction. *Generalization of extinction* is the process wherein, once extinction has occurred, similar stimuli also will not elicit the conditioned response.

A second approach to the modification of maladaptive behaviors employs the principle of *counterconditioning:* there are certain responses that do not "go together," that are incompatible; if one occurs, the other will not. For example, one cannot experience intense "hate" and "love," or excitement and tranquility, at precisely the same time. The concept of structuring an incompatible response is employed by many behavior modifiers in treating conditioned respondents. In essence, counterconditioning is accomplished by selecting a response incompatible with fear, usually something pleasurable to the individual, and gradually introducing some aspect of the conditioned stimuli that no longer evokes the fear reaction. If both techniques are used, the combined forces of reconditioning and extinction at each step will eventually result in the elicitation of a pleasurable response, in place of fear, when the conditioned stimulus is presented.

Desensitization, aligned with counterconditioning, is a very popular technique employed by behavior modifiers. Desensitization is probably successful because of the principle of incompatible behavior, that is, if a response that prevents anxiety can be made to occur in the presence of the anxiety-evoking stimuli, new responses will then be learned. In systematic desensitization, the response that prevents anxiety is usually complete relaxation, and the "anxiety-evoking stimuli" are the fears and phobias that represent a part of or the essence of the maladaptive behaviors of the individual.

Desensitization consists of eliminating the fears and phobias through extinction, as well as reconditioning the former anxiety-stimuli to the response associated with complete relaxation. This process generally involves three basic operations: (1) training muscle relaxation; (2) the construction of anxiety hierarchies (specific stimuli arranged from least to most anxiety provoking); and (3) counterposing relaxation and anxiety-evoking stimuli from the hierarchies.

The modification of operant behaviors is also based on scientific principles. In order to more clearly understand how operant maladaptive behaviors are modified, a brief overview of how operant behaviors are acquired and maintained is necessary. *Positive reinforcement* (any stimulus that, when it follows a response, will increase the strength or maintain the occurrence of that response) is perhaps the most important aspect of operant modification.

When an operant response is strengthened after it has been succeeded by a positive reinforcer, *operant conditioning* has taken place. Examples of positive reinforcers (*primary,* which are necessary for survival, and *secondary,* which have been learned) are food, water, rest, elimination, sex, attention, praise, money, and so on (see Part III). Operant conditioning occurs when a reinforcing stimulus is made contingent upon a response. For example, one works for a week and then receives a paycheck, one does an assignment and then receives a grade. A conditioned operant response is eliminated by terminating the contingency between that response and the reinforcing stimulus. This process is called *operant extinction.* When the response-reinforcement contingency is no longer in effect, the rate of the response gradually declines and finally ceases. The concepts of *shaping* and *schedule of reinforcement* are important aspects of operant conditioning. The process of *shaping* refers to the reinforcing of successive approximations to a desired behavior until a specific behavior is performed. Schedule of reinforcement simply refers to the temporal arrangement of reinforcement.

Positive reinforcement is of primary importance in effective modification of maladaptive behavior, but there are many situations in which ascertaining an effective reinforcer is not immediately feasible. This poses a problem; however, the use of the *Premack Principle* is one way to overcome this impasse. It has been asserted that, if some specific behavior is more probable than another, then the more probable behavior may be used to reinforce and strengthen the less probable behavior. A contingency is established between the more highly probable behavior and the less probable one (for example, if you finish your math, then you may go to recess).

Operant behaviors are also modified through the use of aversive stimuli. An *aversive stimulus* refers to any stimulus that an organism will escape from, avoid, or terminate; a stimulus causing pain or discomfort. Responses to aversive stimulus may take three possible forms: (1) *Escape behavior* occurs when the individual does something to terminate or actually remove the aversive stimulus. (2) *Avoidance behavior* takes place when the individual does something to postpone or prevent pending aversity. (3) *Punishment* occurs when an aversive stimulus is received as a consequence of a response.

Negative reinforcement is the process whereby the response that is immediately followed by the termination of an aversive stimulus becomes conditioned. In other words, a response that terminates aversity will increase in frequency or strength. The stimulus used in negative reinforcement must be "naturally" aversive to the individual, such as electric shock, or aversive as a result of conditioning.

Maladaptive operant behaviors are modified through the use of punishment, another type of aversive stimulus. The operation of punishment is constituted by either of two events: (1) the individual receives an aversive stimulus as the consequence of a response; or (2) a positive reinforcer is withheld or withdrawn as a consequence of an individual's response. Both of these events result in the suppression or decrease in the probability of the response that produced punishment. This suppression enables the behavior modifier to condition other responses, which are viewed as potentially more "desirable," to the individual's behavior repertoire. Usually these more desirable responses are incompatible with the punished responses, hopefully increasing the probability that they will be emitted on future occasions.

Remaining variables in the control of operant behavior concern *deprivation, satiation* and the function of *discriminative stimuli.* The strength or probability of an organism's behavior can be increased or decreased either by depriving the individual of an appropriate stimulus, or by satiating the subject with the reinforcing stimulus. A discriminative stimulus is defined as a stimulus that sets the occasion for reinforced responding: a signal indicating that after the response reinforcement may follow. Thus the probability of the occurrence of an operant response can be made functionally dependent upon the presence or absence of this discriminative stimulus.

In summary, perhaps the most important contribution of the behavior modification movement is its emphasis on an operationally defined, readily observed, and easily measured dependent variable: behavior.

GLOSSARY OF BEHAVIORAL TERMINOLOGY

Abscissa: The horizontal reference axis on a graph (chart). In behavior modification the abscissa is usually labeled with a scale that represents the passage of time in some form such as minutes, days, observations, or trials.

Accountability: Providing an objective demonstration in measurable terms of the effectiveness of given programs. Ex: An increase in reading scores following the introduction of contingency contracting with students.

Adaptation: The gradual reduction of responses or responsiveness as an organism adjusts to the introduction of new stimuli into the environment. Ex: Sensory adaptation to a bright light; students tuning out a teacher's loud (or soft) commands when there is no contrast.

Adaptation Period: The phase (time period) in any behavioral program during which the subject (or subjects) adjusts to any novel stimuli that have been introduced into the environment. Ex: The time necessary for a class to adapt to observers prior to collection of baseline data.

Adaptive Behavior: Behavior that serves to insure survival or is considered appropriate in specified societal contexts such as school.

Addiction: A condition in which cessation of reinforcement (usually physiological) produces physical or psychological problems of abstinence.

Applied Research: Research that is directed toward an analysis of variables that can be effective in improving behavior under study. Applied research is often conducted in natural settings.

Approval: Any observable endorsement of behavior.

Aversive Control: The withdrawal or presentation of an aversive stimulus, which then maintains or increases the frequency of a response. Three types of aversive control exist.

1. Escape, in which the organism terminates the aversive stimulus after is has begun.
2. Avoidance, in which the organism postpones the beginning of aversive stimuli.
3. Punishment, in which responses are followed by an aversive stimulus.

Aversive Stimulus: Any stimulus that an organism will escape from, avoid, or terminate.

Back-Up Reinforcer: An object or event that has already demonstrated its reinforcing effect on an individual that is received in exchange for a specific number of tokens, points, or other more generalized reinforcers.

Baseline: A stable, usually recoverable, performance (five or more observations) upon which the effects of experimental variables can be assessed. (Record phase.)

Behavior: Any act of an organism, either internal or external, that can be observed and/or measured. Any behavior may have one of four relationships to the environment.

1. Dependent, when the event *must,* by nature of the situation, occur following the behavior. Ex: Because the water must cease running from the faucet when the handle is turned, the subsequent cessation of the flow of water is said to be dependent upon behavior of turning the handle.
2. Contingent, when the event does follow the behavior but *need not* do so. Reinforcement is generally contingent upon behavior. After reinforcement has occurred a contingency is said to have been established. Ex: If one is asked to turn off the water and does so, the behavior is said to be contingent.
3. Superstitious, because behavior has nothing to do with the reinforcer. Ex: The fondling of a "good luck piece" does not cause "good luck" but is occasionally reinforced with chance good fortune.
4. Random, when the behavior has no logical relationship to the environment and all stimuli are neutral. Ex: Tuneless whistling while daydreaming.

Behavior Modification: The changing of behavior (increasing or decreasing frequency of occurrence) using a combination (schedule) of reinforcement (positive and/or negative) and/or nonreinforcement. Generally represents the programmed use of techniques based on scientifically derived principles of learning to produce observable changes in behavior.

Behavior Therapy: The application of learning theory techniques for the purpose of changing maladaptive behavior.

Behavioral Approach: An approach in which values and/or ideas, in order to be considered, are operationally defined into directly observable and measurable behaviors. The assumption is made that most behavior, including behavior defined as abnormal, is learned.

Behavioral Contrast: A phenomenon that may occur if a behavior is placed on one reinforcement schedule under one stimulus condition and on another schedule under a different stimulus condition. In such a situation a decrease in the rate of the behavior under one stimulus-correlated condition may be accompanied by an increase in the rate under the other stimulus-correlated condition.

Behavioral Dimensions: Measurable descriptive characteristics of behavior such as frequency, intensity, duration, and topography.

Behavioral Goal: The specification of the set of responses to be emitted by the subject at the completion of a given behavior modification program. Usually the criteria for achievement of the goals and conditions under which the responses are to be emitted are also specified. When limited to academic instruction, this is often referred to as the behavioral objective.

Chaining: A series of two or more responses joined together into a complex behavioral sequence by stimuli which act as both discriminative stimuli and conditioned reinforcers. For instance, discriminative stimulus–response–reinforcement–response to reinforcement–reinforcement for last response–etc. Therefore one operant response leads to another in a linking of the three-term paradigm (discriminative stimulus, response, reinforcement) which permits the development of a series of operants of indefinite length. Ex: Child is offered candy–takes candy and says "Thank you"–Child given a smile and "You're welcome"–Child engages in eye contact and smiles–Child is given a hug.

Cognitive Behavior Modification: The application of behavioral principles and techniques of behavior therapy to problems of a primarily cognitive nature. Most behavior therapists are presently concerned with cognitive as well as overt behaviors.

Conditioned Aversive Stimulus: (See Conditioned Stimulus.)

Conditioned Reflex: A reflex that is elicited by a formerly neutral stimulus that has been paired with the naturally eliciting stimulus.

Conditioned Reinforcer: Some stimuli acquire the power to reinforce (strengthen or maintain) behavior through being paired with the delivery of primary, or stronger conditioned reinforcers, within the experience of the organism. These are called secondary or conditioned reinforcers. Ex: Money is useless, unless one can exchange it for goods. To many people, however, money is a *conditioned reinforcer* because *it* has become the reward.

Conditioned Stimulus: A formerly neutral stimulus that has been paired with an unconditioned stimulus or a reinforcing stimulus (either positively or negatively) and has taken on the reinforcing properties of the stimulus with which it has been paired.

Conditioning: A neutral stimulus may acquire reinforcing properties through temporal association with another reinforcer. This process is called conditioning. (See Operant Conditioning and Respondent Conditioning.)

Confounding Variables: Variables that are operating in an experimental study, which make the effects of the experimental manipulation on the independent variable difficult to evaluate precisely.

Consequate: To apply consequences (reinforcement) following the occurrence of behavior.

Contingency: The relationship between the behavior of an organism and environmental events (generally reinforcing) that follow the behavior and either increase or decrease the probability of similar behavior in the future.

Contingency Contract: A written contract specifying subsequent behavioral contingencies between persons involved. Ex: Completion of school assignments will result in money and special privileges from parents and free time in school.

Contingency Control: The ability to manipulate the environmental consequences of a given behavior in order to achieve a specific behavioral goal.

Contingent: The relationship between a specific response and environmental consequence is said to be contingent if the consequence follows the behavior and subsequently has the effect of increasing, maintaining, decreasing, or eliminating behavior. (See Contingency.)

Continuous Field: A continuum of stimuli.

Continuous Response: A response that does not have a clearly discriminable beginning or end.

Criterion: Specification of a predetermined level of behavioral performance that is to be achieved. Criteria are used to specify goals and to evaluate the success of behavioral programs.

Cue: A stimulus used to help an individual remember to produce any specified response which may then be reinforced. (See Discriminative Stimulus.)

Dependent Variable: A phenomenon that varies in any way (appears, disappears, or changes) as a function of any application, removal, or variation in other variables (independent). A dependent variable is usually monitored or measured in behavior modification studies.

Deprivation: The removal of the occurrence of a stimulus.

Differential Punishment: The extinguishing of certain behaviors while others are being reinforced. (See also Differential Reinforcement.)

Differential Reinforcement: The strengthening of certain behaviors while others are being extinguished. A programmed contingency whereby specified responses are reinforced while others are not. (See also Differential Punishment.)

Differential Reinforcement of High Rates (DRH): A schedule that involves the selective contingent reinforcement of a grouping of responses that occur in rapid succession. High rates are differentially reinforced while low rates are not.

Differential Reinforcement of Low Rates (DRL): A schedule in which responses that are spaced relatively far apart in time are selectively reinforced. Low rates are differentially reinforced while high rates are not.

Differential Reinforcement of Other Behaviors (DRO): A procedure in which a reinforcer follows any response an individual makes, except for one particular response. Thus, the individual receives scheduled reinforcement except when he engages in a particular specified behavior. This procedure results in a decrease of the specified behavior.

Disapproval: Any observable consequence to behavior defined negatively by the organism receiving it.

Discrete Stimuli: Separate presentation of stimuli.

Discriminative Stimulus (S^d): An environmental event that sets the occasion for responses that are followed by reinforcement. The probability of the response is high only when certain environmental events (discriminative stimuli) are present. Whenever the discriminative stimulus (S^d) is present, specific responses may then be reinforced. (See Stimulus Control.)

Eliciting Stimuli: Environmental events that regularly precede responses. They elicit relatively fixed and stereotyped responses. Ex: The bell in Pavlov's classic dog experiment.

Emotion: A complex response elicited and occasioned by environmental conditions and composed of both operants and respondents. Ex: Love or sadness.

Environment: The sum total of an organism's surroundings (stimuli).

Errorless Discrimination Procedure: Teaching the acquisition of a discrimination by carefully arranging a sequence of discriminative stimuli so that only correct responses are occasioned.

Event Sampling: An observational procedure in which the frequency or duration of a specific discrete behavior, such as times tardy or number of pages completed, is recorded over a specific extended period of time. The specific time interval may be, for instance, a classroom period or day.

Extinction: A procedure in which the reinforcement for a previously reinforced behavior is discontinued. The process whereby a conditioned response is reduced to its preconditioned level or strength, often approaching or reaching zero magnitude or frequency. The process of extinction in the case of respondents involves continuing presentation of the conditioned stimulus without any further pairing with the unconditioned stimulus. With operant responses, extinction results when responding is no longer followed by reinforcement.

Fading: The gradual removal of discriminative stimuli such as cues and prompts.

Fixed Interval Reinforcement: (See Schedules of Reinforcement.)
Fixed Ratio Reinforcement: (See Schedules of Reinforcement.)
Frequency: The number of occurrences per given time period.
Functional Analysis: The determination of the external variables of which behavior is a function. (See also Functional Relation.)
Functional Relation: A relation in which the occurrence of event B consistently follows the occurrence of event A or is dependent upon the previous occurrence of event A.
Functional Relationship: A lawful relationship between two variables. In behavior modification, a dependent variable and a given procedure are functionally related if the behavior systematically varies as a function of the application of the procedure.
Generalization: Responding to two or more discriminatively different stimuli as if they were the same. Generalization involves the following components:

1. Stimulus Generalization—the spread of the effects of reinforcement (or of other operations) in the presence of one stimulus to other stimuli that differ from the original stimulus along one or more dimensions.
2. Response Generalization (induction)—the spread of effects of reinforcement to responses outside of a specific response may be accompanied by other responses that are similar but not identical to the reinforced response.
3. Generalization Training—a procedure designed to facilitate the occurrence of generalization.

Generalized Reinforcer: A conditioned reinforcer that is effective over a wide range of deprivation conditions as a result of having been paired with a variety of previously established reinforcers.
Habituation: A gradual decline in the magnitude of a respondent over repeated occurrences. Ex: A nurse's aversion to the sight of blood decreases as she is exposed to repeated viewings of open wounds.
Imitation: Matching the behavior of a model.
Incompatible Behavior: Any two or more behaviors that, by the very nature of one, cannot exist with the other. Sometimes the term is used to include not only behavior that cannot occur simultaneously with another, but also behavior that interferes with other behavior. Ex: Speaking and being quiet.
Incompatible Response: A response whose occurrence precludes the simultaneous occurrence of another response. Ex: A musician cannot be both flat and sharp at the same time.
Inconsistency: Not applying the previously specified consequences to the occurrences of a behavior, applying the consequences when

the behavior has not occurred, applying inappropriate consequences (approval following inappropriate behavior or disapproval
for appropriate behavior), or applying appropriate and inappropriate consequences simultaneously.

Independent Variable: The factor purposely manipulated in a behavior modification program to ascertain its relationship with
the dependent variable. Sometimes thought of as the "cause"
of the "effect" on the dependent measure.

Intermittent Reinforcement: (See Schedules of Reinforcement.)

Interresponse Reinforcement: The amount of time that passes between two responses.

Interval Reinforcement: (See Schedules of Reinforcement.)

Latency: The time between the occurrence of the stimulus and the
occurrence of the response.

Learning History: The sum of an individual's behaviors that have
been conditioned or modified as a result of environmental events.

Link: Each unit of a chain, composed of a discriminative stimulus,
response, and a reinforcer.

Modeling: A technique whereby the behavior that is to be taught
is demonstrated for the learner and any semblance of the goal
behavior is initially rewarded. The criterion for reinforcement
is then gradually increased until the goal behavior is obtained.
Sometimes no shaping is required.

Multiple Baseline Design: An experimental design (usually single-
subject) that involves:

1. Obtaining base rates on several dependent behaviors
2. Applying the independent variable to one of the dependent
   behaviors until it is substantially changed while the other dependent behaviors are left free to vary
3. Applying the independent variable to a second dependent
   variable as in No. 2 above. This procedure is continued until
   it is demonstrated that each behavior systematically changes
   when the independent variable is applied to it.

Negative Reinforcer: A stimulus whose removal, if paired with
the occurrence of a behavior, will increase the probability of
occurrence of the behavior. Many times the term aversive stimulus is used in place of negative reinforcer. (See also Aversive
Control.)

Negative Transfer: (See Transfer.)

Neutral Stimuli: All those environmental events that at any given
moment, do not elicit any behavior change, whether they precede,
accompany, or follow responses.

Off-Task: Any behavior that interferes or is incompatible with previously defined situational expectations.

On-Task: Behavior consistent with definitional classes of behavior previously defined.

Operant: A behavior emitted by an organism that operates on or changes the environment in a very particular way.

Operant Behavior: Operants have the potential to produce stimulus events that alter the behavior's future occurrence. Operant behavior is behavior that is controlled by consequences. Operant behavior is mediated by the central nervous system and involves, primarily, the skeletal musculature. Operant responses act on, and interact with, the environment and are controlled and modified by the principles of operant conditioning. Operant responding includes not only the gross motor movements of the organism but also its verbal behavior. Most of the daily, ongoing behavior of the individual as he interacts with his environment and other people is operant in nature.

Operant Conditioning: The changing of the frequency of an occurrence of a behavior by modifying the consequences of that behavior.

Operant Level: The strength of an operant before any known reinforcement; the unconditioned level of an operant (response), or the rate at which responses occur before they have been reinforced. Generally, baseline or base rate recording is a record of the operant level.

Operant Reinforcement: The potential of operants to produce events which will strengthen their future occurrence; following operant behavior with consequences of a reinforcing nature.

Ordinate: The vertical reference axis on a graph. In behavior modification, the ordinate is usually labeled with a scale that measures the dependent behavior, for example, frequency, percentage of responses, or rate.

Oscillation: Alternation of emotional reponses usually found during the process of extinction.

Pairing: The act of associating one stimulus with another.

Pavlovian Conditioning: (See Respondent Conditioning.)

Pay-Off: That which rewards the occurrence of a behavior.

Positive Reinforcement: A stimulus that, when presented as a consequence of a response, results in an increase or maintenance of that response.

Premack Principle: The principle that contingent access to high frequency behaviors serves as a reinforcer for the performance of low frequency behaviors.

Primary Reinforcers: Reinforcing stimuli that have the effect of maintaining or perpetuating life, such as food, water, elimination, and warmth.

Probe: A phase in a behavior modification experiment designed to test the effect of a given procedure. A reversal is a probe since it removes the behavioral procedure for a brief period of time to test the procedure's effects. (See also Reversal Procedure.)

Programmed Instruction: The selection and arrangement of educational content based upon principles of human learning.

Prompt: An auxiliary discriminative stimulus that is applied to help occasion a given response. Prompts are usually faded before the terminal goal is judged as having been achieved.

Punishing Stimulus: A contingent stimulus that, when presented, results in a reduction in the occurrence of the dependent behavior.

Punishment: The potential of all operants to produce events which will *weaken* their future occurrence. There are two broad types of punishment:

1. Positive punishment—those events that will weaken an operant's future occurrence by the *presentation* of stimuli; and
2. Negative punishment—those events that will weaken an operant's future occurrence by the *removal* of stimuli.

Rate of Responding: The number of occurrences per unit time of the response.

Ratio Reinforcement: (See Schedules of Reinforcement.)

Reflex: A physical response (behavior) mediated by the autonomic nervous system.

Reinforcement: The contingent use of a stimulus resulting in an increase or maintenance of behavior. All operants have the potential to produce events that will strengthen their future occurrence. There are two broad types of reinforcement:

1. Positive reinforcement—those events that will strengthen an operant's future occurrence by the *presentation* of stimuli; and
2. Negative reinforcement—those events that will strengthen an operant's future occurrence by the *removal* of stimuli.

Reinforcement Density: Frequency or rate with which responses are reinforced. The lower the ratio or shorter the interval required by a given reinforcement schedule, the denser the reinforcement.

Reinforcement History: The sum total of an organism's past.

Reinforcer: A stimulus, the contingent use of which results in the increase or maintenance of the dependent behavior. The stimulus will increase the probability of the response which precedes it (see Approval, Disapproval, and Reinforcement).

Reinforcing Incompatible Behavior: A behavioral procedure that increases the occurrence of a behavior or behaviors that cannot coexist with another, usually "undesired," behavior.

Reliability: Refers to consistency of measurement. It is usually calculated by comparing how well two or more independent observers agree among themselves. It is often calculated and reported in percentages by dividing the number of agreements by the number of agreements plus disagreements and then multiplying the fraction by one hundred. Reliability measures should be reported for each phase of a single-subject design.

Replicate: To repeat an experimental procedure or finding.

Respondent: A regular response from all normal organisms of the same species to the same eliciting stimulus. Ex: Salivation.

Respondent Behavior: All respondents are a function (elicited or maintained) of antecedent stimulus events.

Respondent Conditioning (Classical or Pavlovian Conditioning): The process whereby eliciting stimuli increase the frequency of respondents (usually a physiological change). A neutral stimulus, when associated repeatedly with an unconditioned stimulus which reliably elicits a specific response, comes to elicit a "new" response, which is similar to some respect to that produced originally by the unconditioned stimulus.

Response: A physical reaction in time and space to an environmental event, generally synonymous with behavior and, in behavioral research, both observable and measurable (fines, etc.)

Response Cost: A procedure in which there is contingent withdrawal of specified amounts of available reinforcers.

Response Differentiation: The process whereby reinforcement alters some specific property of an operant such as its duration, intensity, or topography; a procedure that reinforces a subset of specific behavior, conforming to specified behavioral dimensions.

Reversal Procedure: A technique that involves the removal of the procedure in order to test the effectiveness of the procedure. For instance, one frequently utilized experimental design involves: (1) obtaining a base rate of the dependent variable; (2) applying the independent variable until a substantial change in the dependent variable is recorded; (3) the reversal, a discontinuation of the independent variable and a reintroduction of the conditions in effect during the baseline period, until a substantial reversal in the value of the dependent variable is obtained; and (4) a reapplication of the independent variable to reinstate the change (Often abbreviated as ABAB design.) Such a procedure is used to demonstrate a *functional relationship* between the *independent* and *dependent* variables.

Satiation: The process whereby a reinforcer temporarily ceases to strengthen an operant. A reduction in performance occurs generally after a large amount of reinforcement.

Scallop: A pattern on a response record that is characterized by a sequence of positively accelerating curves.

Schedule of Reinforcement: The rule followed by the environment in determining which among the many occurrences of a response will be reinforced. Schedules include three general types—ratio, interval, and mixed.

1. **Ratio Schedule of Reinforcement:** A schedule in which reinforcement is made contingent upon the emission of a number of responses before one response is reinforced. One version is the Fixed Ratio (FR) schedule, when a specific number of responses must occur prior to the reinforced response. For example, an FR-3 schedule indicates that each third response is contingently reinforced. The other type is the Variable Ratio (VR) schedule, when a variable number of responses must occur prior to the reinforced response. The number of responses usually varies about a specified average. For example, a VR-6 means that six performances on the average are required prior to each reinforcement.

2. **Interval Schedule of Reinforcement:** A schedule in which reinforcement is made contingent upon the passage of time before the response is reinforced. It could be a Fixed Interval (FI) schedule, when a particular response is scheduled for reinforcement following the passage of a specific amount of time, and that time is held constant. For example, an FI-3 indicates that reinforcement follows the first occurrence of the primed response after three minutes have passed. Or one might establish a Variable Interval (VI) Schedule in which a variable time interval must occur prior to the reinforced response. The time interval usually varies within a specified average. For example, a VI-6 indicates that an average of six minutes passes before the primed response receives contingent reinforcement.

3. **Mixed Schedules of Reinforcement:** Combinations of interval and ratio schedules. Most school and home reinforcement of necessity is mixed.

Shaping: Taking the behaviors that the organism already has in his repertoire and reinforcing those that are similar to the goal behavior, gradually requiring that the organism's behavior be more and more similar to the goal behavior to be reinforced. This is continued until the goal behavior is obtained. New behaviors may be developed by systematic reinforcement of successive approximations toward a specified goal. (See also Successive Approximations.)

Single-Subject Experimental Designs: Research designs developed for evaluating the effects of one or more independent variable(s) on the behavior of a single organism.

Social Reinforcer: A conditioned reinforcing stimulus mediated by another individual within a social context.

Spontaneous Recovery: The reappearance of a response—previously eliminated by means of an extinction procedure—following a time interval without any intervening reinforced responses.

Stimulus: An environmental event.

Stimulus Change: A behavioral procedure that employs discriminative stimuli, or stimuli that occasion or inhibit specific behaviors.

Stimulus Control: After an operant has been reinforced in the presence of a particular stimulus a number of times, that stimulus comes to control the operant. Control of this sort is achieved when responses are reinforced in the presence of a specified stimulus and not others and the stimulus controls the probability that the response will be emitted.

Stimulus Delta (S^Δ): A stimulus in the presence of which a given response is not reinforced. This kind of discriminative stimulus, like S^d, is said to be established when, after several pairings with the occurrence or nonoccurrence of reinforcement, its presence or absence is accompanied by reliable changes in response.

Stimulus Deprivation: The process whereby the reinforcing power of a stimulus is restored by depriving the organism of it for a period of time.

Stimulous Discrimination: The process whereby an operant is emitted only in the presence of certain stimuli.

Stimulus Generalization: Responding to similar stimuli that approximate the original stimulus.

Stimulus Overload: When a response decreases in frequency because of too large a frequency or magnitude of reinforcement, stimulus overload has occurred.

Subject Confounding Variables: Subject characteristics (demographic, previous learning history, and present behaviors) that have not been controlled in an experiment but may effect changes in the occurrences of the dependent variable. Single-subject designs control for subject confounding variables by comparing the subject's performance under one condition with his performance under other conditions.

Subset of Behavior: The group of simple response components that compose a more complex behavior.

Successive Approximations: Behavioral elements or subsets, each of which more and more closely resembles the specified terminal behavior. (See Shaping.)

Superstitious Behavior: Behavior that is not based on contingencies that are actually in existence but is reinforced by chance. Ex: A child might wish on a star for a bicycle and believe that his wish caused him to get it for his birthday.

Supplementary Reinforcers: Reinforcers used in addition to the major contingent reinforcer.

Target Behavior: A behavioral goal.

Terminal Behavior: The behavior that is achieved at the end of a behavior modification program. The terminal behavior is described according to all its relevant behavioral dimensions and is usually assigned a criterion by which an acceptable level of performance is to be judged.

Tic: An habitual spasmodic movement of particular muscles.

Time Sampling: A direct observational procedure in which the observer records the presence or absence of the behaviors to be changed, within uniform time intervals. For example, an observer may observe for 10 seconds and record during the following 5 seconds the occurrence or nonoccurrence of the subject's behavior. This procedure may continue for a specified 30 minutes each day. Observers may sample any predetermined time periods.

Time Out: Time out from positive reinforcement is a procedure in which access to the sources of various forms of reinforcement are removed for a particular period, contingent upon the emission of a response. The opportunity to receive reinforcement is contingently removed for a specified time. Either the behavior individual is contingently removed from the reinforcing environment or the reinforcing environment is contingently removed from him for some stipulated duration.

Time Out Room, Time Out Booth: A facility that is arranged in such a manner that the individual placed therein has little likelihood of receiving reinforcement from the environment. The place in which time out from positive reinforcement occurs.

Token Reinforcer: An object that can be exchanged at a later time for another reinforcing item or activity. The extent to which tokens are reinforcing or take on the properties of a generalized reinforcer is dependent on the individual's experience and on what back-up items are available.

Topography: The physical nature of the responses which compose the operant. Ex: How hard the lever was pushed, by which hand, and how long a time it stayed depressed, the movement of the body during observed motor off-task.

Transfer: The effect that learning a task has on the learning of another task. If having learned the first task facilitates learning the second task, it is called *positive* transfer; if learning the first task interferes with learning the second task, then it is called *negative* transfer.

Unconditioned Reinforcer: When a stimulus can reinforce a behavior without the organism having had any previous experience, the reinforcer is said to be a primary or unconditioned reinforcer. Ex: The smell of food produces salivation.

Unconditioned Response: A response which nearly inevitably follows a specific stimulus. This is the *unconditioned* stimulus of that response.

Unconditioned Stimulus: (See Unconditioned Response.)

Variable Interval Reinforcement: (See Schedules of Reinforcement.)

Variable Ratio Reinforcement: (See Schedules of Reinforcement.)

STUDY GUIDE FOR CHAPTER 9

Questions:

I. True or False

1. _____ A negative reinforcer will decrease the behavior.

2. _____ In classical conditioning, food is the conditioned stimulus for salivation.

3. _____ Removal of tokens for inappropriate social behavior in a class is an example of response cost.

4. _____ A consequence is noncontingent if it decreases a specific behavior.

5. _____ Successive approximation of speech might initially include reinforcement of any vocalization.

6. _____ Observer reliability is the measurement of agreement between independent observers.

7. _____ A schedule of reinforcement refers to the type of primary or secondary reinforcers used in the shaping process.

8. _____ A multiple baseline controls for subject confounding variables.

9. _____ Negative transfer refers to a lack of stimulus generalization.

10. _____ Replication is an important aspect of behavioral research.

11. _____ The multiple baseline design is generally an example of a single-subject design.

12. _____ Placement in a juvenile detention house may be a time-out procedure.

13. _____ Punishment will frequently result in escape and avoidance behavior.

14. _____ The effectiveness of behavioral techniques may be accountable without data.

15. _____ A rising baseline is an indication of the operant level of a behavior.

16. _____ A classroom with continuously available record player, TV, and games may cause "stimulus overload."

17. _____ Money is a back-up reinforcer.

18. _____ Laws are statements concerning empirical scientific cause-and-effect relationships.

19. _____ A teacher giving a high amount of approval is responding to a "a good class."

20. _____ One of the most important contributions of behavior modification is its emphasis on operationally defined dependent variables.

II. Circle the answer that best completes the statement:

21. One process through which a conditioned respondent can be eliminated is:

    a) desensitization
    b) negative reinforcement
    c) punishment
    d) extinction
    e) positive reinforcement

22. A student being reinforced for any behavior except for hitting other students is on a _____ schedule of reinforcement.

    a) continuous
    b) variable interval
    c) DR
    d) DRO
    e) FR

23. Criterion are generally used in behavioral programs to:

    a) decide what to teach
    b) structure the program in sequential steps
    c) provide the student with feedback
    d) evaluate the program
    e) all of the above

24. Programmed instructional texts use:

    a) positive reinforcement
    b) an errorless discrimination procedure
    c) learning principles
    d) fading techniques
    e) all of the above

25. Behavior is the result of:

    a) mental ability
    b) a person's emotional state
    c) its consequences
    d) premeditation
    e) all of the above

26. Counterconditioning refers to:

    a) desensitization
    b) confounding of certain behavior modification principles
    c) structuring incompatible responses
    d) two of the above
    e) three of the above

27. Counting the number of problems completed during a 20-minute math period is an example of:
   a) time sampling
   b) continuous response measurement
   c) event sampling
   d) variable interval observation
   e) a continuous field

28. Removal of tokens until a behavior increases is an example of:
   a) response cost
   b) DRL
   c) punishment
   d) negative reinforcement
   e) two of the above

29. If a teacher adjusts his teaching to compensate for a student's learning the teacher's behavior is a _____.
   a) respondent behavior
   b) operant behavior
   c) positive reinforcer
   d) neutral stimulus
   e) conditioned reflex

30. A child who acts similarly to a parent has usually acquired those behaviors through _____.
   a) transfer
   b) modeling
   c) stimulus generalization
   d) adaptation
   e) discriminative stimuli

III. Complete the following statements:

31. Singing a song, hitting a ball, participating in class discussion are all examples of _____ behavior.

32. The process of causing a student to transfer from a specific situation to another similar situation is called _____.

33. To decrease piano performance anxiety _____ may be used to recondition anxiety-stimuli.

34. The use of rock music listening time as a reinforcer for increasing math scores is often an example used to illustrate the _____ principle.

35. Rewarding a child with frequent large quantities of food will probably result in _____.

36. Spanking a child after a child misbehaves is an example of _____ if the child's misbehavior decreases.

37. A parent gives a child weekly allowance contingent on completion of assigned work tasks. The dependent variable is _____.

38. All teaching involves the establishment of _____ where there previously existed nondiscrimination.

39. Reinforcement should be contingent; however, a consequence of a behavior could be contingent but not _____.

40. The principles of behavior are functional. This is true because the behavioral principle operating can only be defined by the _____ of that consequence.

LEARNING ACTIVITY 17–
SPECIFYING A SHAPING PROCEDURE

Choose one learning (academic) task in your specific subject area:
_____

Specify the following for the above task:

Terminal behavior:

Criterion for measuring terminal behavior:

A shaping procedure for learning including at least five steps:

An example of contingency contracting with the student:

LEARNING ACTIVITY 18–
DETERMINING BEHAVIORAL PRINCIPLES

Read the following excerpts and determine which principles are being used in the underlined passages.

A four-year-old hyperactive child attends a session where the objective is to stay in the area of activity. A large hula hoop is placed on the floor and is a cue for working since all activities take place inside of the hoop. (1) The child's favorite songs are tape recorded and played while the child has two feet in the hoop. Music is turned off when at least one foot is out of the hoop. (2) By the end of six weeks the child knows that when he sees the hoop it means that two feet should be placed inside of it. (3) Then the volume of music is gradually decreased (4) until the child can stay in the hoop without the aid of the music.

1.
2.
3.
4.

A four-year-old girl is learning to sing a song. The music teacher sings the first line first while the child listens. (1) A different musical note is associated with each word syllable of the song. (2) When the child repeats the verse correctly, the teacher smiles (3) but when the child simply babbles, the teacher stops the music, sits back, and waits 10 seconds before continuing. (4) At this point, the teacher decides that there are too many mistakes and that the song must be taught differently. The teacher decides to sing the first line leaving out the last word, then leaving out the second to the last word and last word (5) and continues in this manner. After every single response (6) from the child the teacher lets her know how she has done. (7) Thus the song has been taught so that each step is progressively learned. (8)

1.   5.
2.   6.
3.   7.
4.   8.

CHAPTER 10

Introduction to Behavioral Workshops

The learning activities contained in this chapter were specifically developed for use in in-service workshops. Many variations of these activities are possible: media additions or supplementary activities may be used in lieu of or in addition to the live classroom observations. Five to seven hours of prerecorded videotapes and movies are used by the authors for in-service sessions. In-service workshops have been conducted with varying lengths of instruction lasting from two hours, to two weeks. Considerations of time availability and specific goals are important. Every hourly time period and attendant learning activity can be developed in a variety of ways (e.g., contingency managed discussion groups, students as aides, lectures, group work on activity, videotape feedback). Adaptations of the activities may facilitate whatever predetermined objectives are deemed important. Individual participation is paramount and actual doing as opposed to passivity cannot be overemphasized.

The following outline for learning indicates specific learning activity numbers found at the end of each chapter.

BEHAVIORAL TECHNIQUES FOR CLASSROOM USE

Objectives

General and specific objectives are intended to involve participants in learning behavioral techniques (applied behavior analysis principles) for potential classroom use. Objectives are formalized as follows:

General Objective: Participants will become familiar with behavior modification. *Specifically,* participants will:

1. Pinpoint specific social/academic behaviors
2. Develop skills in observational techniques
3. Learn how to use approval/disapproval reinforcers across time, in specific time intervals, to shape desired classroom behavior
4. Develop techniques to evaluate classroom effects following application of specific consequences

Outline of learning topics

Each topic in the following outline serves as the basis for one hour of instruction, (lecture, interview, group discussion, classroom application, videotape or film viewing, observation, or in-class activity). This particular sequence of instruction and activities is a direct outgrowth of experience gained in conducting workshops and classes. However, many variations in the sequencing of specific topics and attendant learning activities are possible in any class or workshop. In addition, participants may be involved in additional readings that can also serve as a basis for quizzes, discussions, and examples for additional applications.

A. Introduction: Values and behavior modification
   1. Pretest on behavioral principles, such as a test covering Part I to be administered the first hour: When possible an observational evaluation of classroom behavior prior to taking a course or workshop can serve to document actual in-class behavior as a baseline from which subsequent change may be evaluated.
   2. Orientation and explanation of evaluation procedures: Assignment of study guide and explanation of time logs (Learning Activity 6, page 45), and assignment of outside reading.
   3. Definitions of behavioral terms: An overview of behavioral models dealing with teaching and learning
      a) *Pinpoint:* The behavioral objective toward greater specificity
      b) *Record:* An actual record of observed behavior
      c) *Consequate:* The teaching strategy (use of approval/disapproval reinforcers)
      d) *Evaluate:* The effect of the reinforcement (is the behavior better, same, or worse?)
   4. Values and behavior modification: An understanding of the differences between teachers' (or society's) values and the techniques used to achieve these values (Learning Activity 1, page 15)

    5. Values/Techniques differentiation: Discussion of differential techniques to achieve similar values or the use of identical techniques to achieve opposing values (Learning Activity 2, page 16)

B. *Pinpoint:* Specifying observable behavior

    1. Attributes of a pinpoint: A pinpointed behavior must be (1) observable and (2) measurable (counted). Why are *observable* and *measurable* academic and social behaviors necessary for effective behavioral change?

    2. Translation of values/ideas into behaviors: Ideas must be translated into observable and measurable behaviors which are specific enough to be taught (Learning Activity 5, page 42).

    3. Behaviors actually define ideas: Participants list all behaviors that pertain to more than one idea within Learning Activity 5.

    4. Pinpoint ranking exercise: Participants structure values into specific behaviors to increase skill in determining methods of recording observable behaviors (Learning Activity 11, page 175).

    5. Discussion of ranking exercise: Small group discussion of Learning Activity 11 generally increases skills in helping participants determine behaviors that are both observable and measurable.

C. *Record:* Observational training

    1. Recording classroom behavior: Recording specific behaviors of teacher-student interactions; observational instructions, definitions, and forms, based upon an introduction of the 2 × 2 Behavioral Interaction Table 1 (page 219).

    2-3. Observation of teacher reinforcement: Recording of classroom behaviors involving teacher-student interaction patterns based upon Behavioral Interactions Table 1 and observational definitions. A teacher training film designed to teach observation of teacher-student reinforcement is used by the authors (available from Florida State University). Videotape of simulated classroom observation may be substituted.

    4-5. Observation of student behavior: Recording of student on-task and off-task behavior. The authors use film or videotape specifically developed to teach student behavior. Role playing or other simulated classroom observation may be substituted.

D. *Record:* Actual classroom observation

    1-4. Classroom observation: Participants record on observation forms (Chapter 8). Participants observe two teachers and two

students (on-task, off-task) as well as two student-student interaction patterns and classroom off-task. Observational order:
  a) Student
  b) Teacher
  c) Human relations: Student-student
  d) Classroom off-task
  e) Student
  f) Human relations
  g) Classroom off-task
  h) Teacher

5. Observational evaluation: Participants evaluate observation techniques (Learning Activity 15, page 255).

E. *Record:* Reliability

  1. Correction or observational evaluation: Group or small group discussion of Learning Activity 15.

  2-3. Computation of reliability: Reliability is computed from classroom or videotape observations with discussion and feedback (see Chapter 8).

  4. Inconsistency: Analysis of existing teacher/student behavioral patterns. Discussion of the effect of teacher inconsistency (mistakes of reinforcement) in the classroom (see Behavioral Interaction Tables, pp. 58 and 219). The authors use a videotape which illustrates a classroom starting with 95 percent of students on-task. Then the teacher reinforces academic behavior but makes approval mistakes for social behavior. In only nineteen minutes the class becomes 95 percent off-task. The teacher then uses contingent social approval and restores the original level of on-task behavior within five minutes.

  5. Approval versus disapproval: A model is developed to illustrate specific effects of differential reinforcement in the classroom. The authors use a film that shows a teacher using high approval for 10 minutes, high disapproval for 10 minutes, and so on, to pinpoint the effects of approval versus disapproval.

F. *Consequate:* Cause-and-effect relationships

  1. The effect of reinforcement across time: Using participants' essays (How is time important in modifying behavior? Learning Activity 9, page 78), a gambling model is constructed to illustrate the effects of partial reinforcement.

  2. The effect of partial reinforcement: Discussion of gambling model followed by participants' writing four pinpoints (Learn-into Activity 9)

3. Reinforcement principles applied: Participants gather in small groups and read selected pinpoints from Part II (pages 82–172) and discuss cause-and-effect relationships.

4-5. Ecology and reinforcement: Human ecology and discrimination of reinforcement. What controls are available to societal agents in order to influence student behavior? (See Learning Activity 3, page 29).

G. *Consequate:* Choice of reinforcers

1. Consequate evaluation: Participants take Consequate Evaluation Test, correct and discuss it within groups (Questions Chapter 6, page 173).

2. Structuring potential reinforcers: Participants fill in logical consequates for the pinpointed behaviors to indicate that there are many different ways to consequate behaviors (Learning Activity 13, page 198).

3. Categorization of reinforcers: Participants state reasons for selecting specific reinforcers and categorize all reinforcers listed for the preceding pinpoints into:
   a) Words
   b) Closeness
   c) Bodily expressions
   d) Activities
   e) Things

4. Consequating personal behaviors: Participants pinpoint specific personal behaviors and develop a specific plan to consequate.

5. Success and failure of reinforcement: Participants write short behavioral analysis (pinpoint model) of personal classroom problems and state how reinforcement principles apply (Learning Activity 12, page 176).

H. *Developing Responses:* Classroom presentations

1-5. On-site school activities: Two live twenty-minute presentations and four teacher observations of other participants, working in groups of three (Chapter 8, page 215).

I. *Developing Responses:* Role playing

1-2. Human relations: Small group discussions to separate values from techniques applied to teacher-teacher interactions toward more positive human relations. Compute positive/negative inter-actions—rotate record keeper (Learning Activity 4, page 29).

3. Structuring personal responses: Write pinpoints and consequate strategies for human relations problems arising from previous small group discussion.

4–5. Role-playing demonstration: Participants present six-minute role-playing illustrations of an essay from Chapters 1–5. Participants work with other class or workshop members (Learning Activity 19, page 301).

J. *Developing Responses:* Summary of techniques

1–3. On site school activities: Each participant takes charge of a classroom for two twenty-minute mini-presentations. Participants work in groups of three and complete four teacher observations of other participants as they take over classrooms for minipresentations.

4. Analyzing classroom observations: Compute and discuss reliability for preceding observations.

5. Summary of workshop or class: A summary of behavioral models dealing with teaching and learning—Pinpoint, Record, Consequate, Evaluate. Discussion of personal projects, and sharing of results. Evaluation of workshop or class (Learning Activity 20, page 303) is generally comprised of subjective verbal reports, although verbal reports provide only limited information. Therefore actual on-site, in-class, pre- postobservations should be conducted whenever possible.

Additional assignments

In addition to the Learning Activities described above, other assignments to supplement lectures and discussions are generally included in most classes and, of course, should be chosen to implement the specific objectives of the workshop director or class instructor. Some additional assignments that are illustrative of many which could be beneficial are listed by major scheduled topics.

A. Introduction: Values and behavior modification

1. Read or reread Chapters 1–5 and complete in detail the Study Guide Questions.
2. Write a short one- or two-page essay on the question: Why is it important to pinpoint specific social and academic behaviors?
3. Maintain time logs for all activities (Learning Activity 6, page 45).

B. Pinpoint: Specifying observable behavior

1. Study in detail the examples listed in Part II.
2. Write a short essay discussing the difference between values as opposed to behaviors.
3. Complete Time Log.

C. Record: Observational training

1. Study Observational and Reliability Summary in Chapter 8 and compute category percentages.
2. Detail subjective observations of teaching techniques employed during observations.
3. Complete time log.

D. Record: Actual classroom observation

1. Write a one-page essay on the topic: What is the relationship between teacher behavior and student behavior?
2. Explain the necessity for using various forms for observing behavior.
3. Complete time log.

F. Record: Reliability

1. Explain the necessity for impartial, unbiased, reliable observations in the evaluation of teaching.
2. Write a short essay on: The effects of teacher inconsistency.
3. Complete Time Log.

G. Consequate: Cause-and-effect relationships

1. Study again selected examples in Part II, paying close attention to the notes.
2. Write an essay on the importance of analyzing cause-and-effect relationships in human interactions.
3. Complete Time Log.

H. Consequate: Choice of reinforcers

1. Explain how a teacher could get identical results using two different "methods."
2. Write a short essay on the effectiveness of using behavioral principles to consequate one's own behavior.
3. Complete Time Log.

I. Developing Responses: Classroom presentations

1. Explain why actual teaching is different from classroom discussions about teaching.
2. Write a short essay indicating how observation increases teaching effectiveness.
3. Complete Time Log.

I. Developing Responses: Role-playing

   1. List how one may use reinforcement principles in developing personal responses and outline a plan for your own on-site classroom activity.
   2. Write an essay on the topic: Why is it easier to analyze and explain another's behavior than one's own?
   3. Complete Time Log.

J. Developing Responses: Summary of techniques

   1. Prepare summary charts and graphs for your group's observations of each other from on-site classroom observations or role playing.
   2. Write a critical appraisal concerning the use of reinforcement techniques in classroom teaching. Specifically indicate how this learning will be applied in your classroom, home, or life.
   3. Complete Time Log.

Establishing a training sequence

A series of workshop presentations including observational feedback with a variety of teachers led to the conclusion that merely hearing about, or even learning to repeat the principles of behavioral classroom management (90 percent accuracy on criterion tests over behavioral techniques and practical examples) was not an effective method of changing classroom behavior. A series of observational studies based upon comparison of pretraining with posttraining-in-class observations of teachers from kindergarten through high school in 13 counties led to questioning the traditional learning sequence. The traditional learning sequence generally involves understanding principles as opposed to emphasizing actual participation. Using hindsight, it should be clear that behaviorists especially should not be deluded into thinking that there is some magic in the learning of "words," even if the words are behavioral and substantiated by test papers indicating a 90-percent criterion level. However, this is a difficult lesson to learn—especially by those who have been reinforced for many years to memorize, analyze, and repeat theories and facts. The results cited led to additional studies designed to assess at least some of the questions raised during the 13 workshops concerning amount of time necessary for change, particular sequences of training, and necessity for periodic feedback.

Effects of training sequence

In another training workshop, it was determined that the sequence of training should be investigated. By now it had been decided that there were main components for this particular method of teacher training. The components included:

1. Teachers receiving or reading about principles and concepts of behavioral analysis
2. Teachers using role playing, with feedback, to practice developing approving and disapproving behaviors
3. Teachers functioning as teachers within classrooms monitored by those conducting the workshop

It should be remembered that the common teacher-training sequence within teacher-training institutions of higher learning is as follows: Theory is presented in lectures and texts, principles are applied and analyzed in miniteaching or microteaching situations, and, lastly, the teacher goes out into the classroom as an intern under the watchful eye of an experienced teacher who is to give the new teacher feedback and extend practical effectiveness in the classroom. The question was posed as to what would happen if the sequence of presentation were varied.

The traditional sequence was contrasted with two varying sequences using a series of volunteers. Observations included three hours of baseline observation, then the workshop followed by postobservation. The sequence of presentation that resulted in the greatest change varied from the traditional sequence. The largest observed gains were demonstrated by teachers who followed this sequence:

1. Four hours of self-critical videotape feedback based on observational categories
2. Four hours of discussion of the principles of applied behavior analysis in a practical way
3. Four hours of role playing and actual practice in the principles involved

The second most beneficial sequence was:

1. Role playing and practice
2. Videotape observation
3. Discussion of principles

The least effective sequence was:

1. Discussion of principles
2. Role playing and practice
3. Self-evaluation

This study involved 16 teachers who received training and 6 control teachers who received no training. All 22 teachers taught K–3 in three rural county schools. Preobservation included three data points with a minimum reliability on every point of 85 percent. Six teachers participated in each of two workshop sequences while four teachers participated in a third sequence, with six teachers receiving no workshop experience. Half of the teachers had participated in a 24-hour introductory workshop in behavior modification the preceding year, which made it possible to check effectiveness concerning the carryover from the previous workshop as well as observe any additional results.

Six weeks were used for presentations, in three two-week subsections. Each of the three training groups spent two weeks in each of the three methods used in training, for four meetings each with a minimal meeting time of six hours in each section. In sum, all of the 16 teachers received a minimum of 18 hours of instruction and training. Six teachers, serving as controls, received no training during this period. The three groups were as follows:

1. Discussion of Principles. A copy of *Teaching/Discipline: Behavioral Principles Toward A Positive Approach*, was provided each teacher. A programmed text, based on selected portions of the book, was also utilized. This method was basically the traditional academic, theoretical approach.

2. Practice and Role Playing of Principles. Each teacher was instructed in what was being observed in her classroom performance by use of her own preobservation records. Behaviorally, her teaching actions were pinpointed and discussed. Learning principles were discussed. Particular situations of problems in the classroom were role played by the instructor and teachers. Application of the principles involved was subsequently explained, discussed, or clarified.

3. Self-evaluation and Observation. Prior to each group session, a 10 to 15-minute videotape was made of each teachers' actual classroom situation and her teaching, including the controls. These individual teacher tapes served as the basis for the four meetings for each group. Each was observed and evaluated in terms of the behavioral principles involved. Each was discussed, and alternate ways of applying the principles were presented.

Each of the microgroups received essentially the same instruction and experience in each procedure, limited only by the differences of the teachers involved in each subsection and the instructor's ability of exact replication. Each method of training was received by each group, but in different sequences. A total of three instructors were used, each one presenting the same procedure three times, once for each group.

All 22 teachers were women. Roughly half had had less than three years teaching experience, half had had four or more years. They ranged in age from 21 to 56. The county system had participated in an in-service workshop in methods of classroom management the previous summer. No observations were taken but all county teachers participated. One-half of the 22 teachers participating in the present study had previously attended the former workshop, the others had not. All 22 teachers had degrees from colleges or universities in the Southeastern United States. Eight of the teachers were currently taking courses toward a Master's degree; two had earned their Master's degree. Three were recent graduates and were unmarried, four were divorced or separated, and the remainder were married. Seventeen had children of their own. Number of children per teacher ranged from one to ten; ages of children from 18 to 29 years. Thus, it was assumed that these teachers represented a cross section of most kindergarten through third-grade elementary teachers in the United States.

Results on preobservations indicated the infusion of behavior principles into the county system from the previous workshop sessions. The control group in this case might have functioned as an indicator of the benefits of an additional session six months after the initial session or the amount of communication for training teachers. The initial approval average for the 11 naïve teachers was a great deal higher than would have been expected on the basis of observations of many other teachers prior to experience in the use of behavioral principles and almost identical to the teachers who had 20 prior hours of workshop experiences. Average approval ratio for those without the workshop was 68.2 percent and for those with the workshop 64.6 percent. The average approval ratio for those given the additional experience increased from 64.6 percent to 89.1 percent (N = 16) while the average approval ratio for those not receiving the additional workshop increased from 68.1 percent to 77.9 percent. Fourteen of the 16 teachers participating increased approval ratios, while five of the six controls also increased their approval ratios. It appears that, when the majority of teachers in an elementary school are in a workshop, the principles are communicated and modeled from the teachers receiving the workshop to those who are not. Further research needs to be completed to ascertain the critical mass necessary for behavioral principles to be used by the other teachers.

The absolute frequency of approval, disapproval, and mistakes of reinforcement indicate changes during the course of the workshop.

The workshop participants increased the average absolute percentage of approvals from 12.8 percent to 20.6 percent, decreased the average disapproval observed from 4.7 percent to 2.0 percent, and decreased the average mistakes of reinforcement from 2.3 percent to 0.5 percent. The control teachers increased their average observed approvals from 15.2 percent to 20.8 percent and decreased mistakes of reinforcement from 2.9 percent to 1.5 percent; however, there was not an average decrease in the use of disapprovals and the control teachers increased from 4.2 percent to 4.4 percent.

Exactly one-half of the workshop group (N = 6) and one-half of the control group had received the prior summer's experience. When the results are broken down in this manner, it may be asked whether these teachers were contributing most of the change in either the experimental or control group. The results indicate very little difference between those who had received the prior workshop and those who had not. The major difference apparent in the differing sequences of training appears to be an increase in the overall dispensing of approvals. The approval ratios following training were not very disparate (92.4 percent, 90.9 percent, and 84.3 percent). The real differences appear to be in the increase in approvals for sequence 2 from 11.7 percent prior to the workshop to 28.2 percent following the workshop experience. These results indicate the importance of allowing the teacher to learn the observational categories early in instruction rather than later, if the purpose is to increase the overall reinforcement activity level. It will be noted that the teachers in sequence 1 decreased overall reinforcement from a preworkshop level of 20.9 percent (approval plus disapproval plus mistakes) to a level following the workshop of 18.6 percent. Sequence 3 decreased the overall reinforcement level from 21.8 percent to 18.1 percent while sequence 2 (the group starting with self-observation and evaluation of videotapes) increased from 16.7 percent to 31.0 percent. While mistakes of reinforcement were less than 1 percent in all three groups, the overall use of disapproval was significantly less in group two. The exact effect of an increased frequency of reinforcement is not yet clear and needs further research. However, modification of further workshops to include instruction and training on specific observational categories was initiated as a result of this study.

WORKSHOP DEVELOPMENT AND OBSERVATIONAL RESULTS

A two-week in-service workshop conducted for 32 teachers comprising the entire staff of a rural elementary school supplied the opportunity to develop aspects of the workshop instructional model. This workshop was especially designed to ascertain the effects of continual observational feedback to teachers involved. The major focus of the workshop involved (1) learning behavioral principles, (2) learning observational categories pertaining to classroom reinforcement, and (3) role playing and practicing techniques to be employed later in the classroom. The focus was on a practical approach that could help teachers handle problems expected in the opening of a newly integrated school with a great disparity in both the academic abilities and the socioeconomic status of blacks and whites.

The major innovation within this workshop was the long-term observational recording and the graphic feedback given to teachers. Teachers were observed on the average of three times per week during the entire school year and were provided observational graphs indicating their percentages of approval to appropriate behavior, disapproval to inappropriate behavior, and mistakes of approval and disapproval reinforcement. Concurrent recording of the behavior of 84 students was also completed throughout the year. The amount of inappropriate behavior (off-task) was recorded for those students selected by their teachers. The selection was determined by observing students whose behavior interfered with learning (their own or another's). Results of observations for both teachers and students were reported to the teacher approximately once a week in small group sessions.

Preobservations prior to workshop experiences were not possible in this study, so a sample of comparison teachers were matched on age, race, socioeconomic status of classroom, grade level, years of teaching experience, years since degree awarded, and number of children in the class. This matching was continued during the next two school years and observations completed over an extended period of time. Since observers are constantly being trained and a series of teacher workshop experiences are continually in progress, an almost precise matching was possible except for the variable concerning socioeconomic level of students. Therefore, four additional teachers were matched with 4 of the original 28 so that socioeconomic ability could be averaged across two classrooms with teachers similar in all other aspects.

During this same school year, it was also possible to work with another project that included only first-grade teachers working in predominately black classrooms. Very similar workshop experiences were conducted by the same personnel. Each project was supervised by an on-the-job psychologist who was responsible for observational scheduling and graphic and verbal feedback sessions for teachers, as well as periodic videotaping for self-evaluation.

The results and comparisons between teachers who had behavioral workshops in two separate counties and the matched teachers indicated the effectiveness of the combination workshop-follow-up procedures as shown in Table 10–1.

The approvals, disapprovals, and mistakes of reinforcement indicated by the comparison teachers match very closely the average approval ratio for most teachers observed prior to workshop experiences in behavioral techniques. It should be noted, however, that the project teachers who were being observed approximately three times per week and given videotape feedback and weekly graphic feedback for the first one-half of the school year were spending on the average 19.9 percent of their time in reinforcement behaviors with an approval ratio of 84.4 percent and less than 1 percent mistakes of reinforcement. The effect on the three students whom they considered to be potentially the most disruptive was quite dramatic. The average off-task behavior for the 84 students observed as 24.4 percent. This should be placed in perspective by indicating that, in most well-controlled classrooms where a great deal of academic learning is accomplished, the average off-task is approximately 20 percent for the entire classroom. Thus, in a school which had a complete socioeconomic range of students, 60 percent white and 40 percent black, in the first year of integration and a potentially disruptive student body, the behavior of students referred by teachers was very close to the average in other well-controlled classrooms. However, in the comparison classroom, the average off-task student behavior for the 96 referred students was approximately the same for most referred students. (It has been our experience that, when a student approaches 50 to 60 percent off-task, he is generally well known to teachers, counselors, principals, and other referring agencies in the community and school system.) Students engaging in this much disruptive behavior will usually have a lengthy evaluation in their cumulative folder and also will have received some label from school professionals (brain damaged, hyperkinetic, learning disabled, retarded, emotionally disturbed). The average off-task behavior for the comparison teachers' classrooms was 59.9 percent. Of course, teachers generally seek out professionals because they do in fact have behavior problems in their classes and this result is not generalizable to all classrooms under all situations.

The second major point of this study concerned differences between the approval ratio of the comparison teachers (23.2 percent) and the mistakes of reinforcement (5.2 percent). The comparison teachers were using reinforcement (disciplining) 30.1 percent of the time, which was 10.2 percent more often than the teachers who participated in the workshop. However, the off-task percentage for their

Table 10–1 Reinforcement of Student Behavior With and Without Workshops and Feedback in Behavioral Techniques

	Approval	Disapproval	Mistakes of Reinforcement	Total Reinforcement	Approval Ratio	Percent Off-Task Student Behavior
Project Leon County, Florida N = 28, K-6 Observations = 1,408	16.8	2.5	0.6	19.9	84.4	24.4*
Comparison Teachers Southeastern United States N = 32, K-6 Observations = 1,042	7.0	17.9	5.2	30.1	23.2	59.5*
Project II Orange County, Florida N = 15; First grade Observations = 492	41.0	4.0	0.9	45.9	89.3	18.3*

**The average off-task behaviors are recorded for these students whom the teacher referred as children with problems.

‡The average off-task behavior were recorded for the entire classroom.

*The average reliability across all 3,352 observations was 88 percent, with a range from 73 percent to 100 percent, computed by comparing each symbol within each interval and dividing total agreements by total agreements plus disagreements.

referred children was over half as low (24.4 percent compared to 59.9 percent) when compared to the workshop–trained teachers. This effect appears to be based upon the lower ratio of approval responses and the higher rate of reinforcement mistakes. The differential effects of increasing approvals and/or decreasing mistakes need to be experimentally isolated; however, it is clear that a combination of high approval with low mistakes of reinforcement has a greater effect on pupil behavior with less interaction by the teacher.

Results of this project are also instructive in that these first grade teachers were instructed to maintain higher levels of approvals to see if there would be an attendant decrease in off-task behavior. This proved to be the case, as the classroom averages were 18.3 percent, which was slightly lower than the K–6 comparison teachers. The precise effects of almost continuous approval need to be ascertained. The attendant decrease from approximately 24 percent to 18 percent may not be worth the additional 26 percent increase in intervals during which reinforcement is administered.

The foregoing study was primarily concerned with reinforcement following social behavior and did not deal with academic reinforcements for correct or incorrect materials. Naturally, there were individual differences among teachers. However, all 28 of the workshop teachers maintained an approval ratio that averaged approximately 80 percent, ranging from 53 percent to 100 percent.

TEACHERS AS BEHAVIORAL CONSULTANTS

An important aspect concerning the use of behavioral principles to promote the arrangement of an environment where effective learning can take place requires the local system to continue follow-up after the initial training. The best situation appears to be an hierarchical model of training that allows the consultant "to work himself out of a job" and let the local school district personnel conduct all future training sessions.

An excellent prototype was begun in a large public school system. Pupil personnel within the staff development section of this county system chose approximately 35 counselors, teachers, and administrators to participate. Two workshop directors assisted by 13 persons conducted an in-service workshop for these people, directed toward preparing them to conduct similar workshops with teachers within the county system. Teachers had been assigned to work in schools that had been recently integrated. The particular program focused on *A Behavior Modification Workshop in Human Relations* and was designed to involve teachers in practical techniques directed toward classroom management and human relations problems. Experience in the practical application of behavioral techniques within actual classes, including videotaped analysis, theoretical discussions, and role playing, prepared participants to conduct similar workshops with other county personnel. Following the initial prototype two-week workshop, observational data on all participants was gathered by the 13 behavioral specialists. Data included white-black interactions, small group interactions, scores on tests, and classroom observations. Data were analyzed and the 35 persons were assigned on the basis of the data to teams of two or three. Each team conducted two workshops for 20 to 30 local teachers. The directors and assistants correlated the training and assisted the county personnel. This expansion model resulted in the training of over 750 teachers during the six-week time period. Subsequently, these local county personnel have also conducted over 20 additional workshops without additional training or contact from the consultants, except for consultants providing a videotape library and some additional materials.

Since the initial expansion workshops, local personnel have conducted regular 30-hour workshops with approximately 25 teachers per group, thus reaching directly over 500 additional teachers.

Long-term results

Preceding workshops were tailored to the needs of individual schools or districts but generally included the following three-phase program:

1. Preobservations of participating teachers (baselines). Three to five observations are considered minimal; however, more extensive observation is sometimes limited by available funds. This problem has been solved in some school systems by training local personnel in observation techniques.

2. Workshop experience. Research indicates that a four-day program can have long-lasting effect, especially if followed by periodic feedback and help in the classroom. Lasting results are difficult to maintain with a one- or two-day introduction or four or five days spread out throughout the year.

3. Postworkshop observations with graphic and/or videotape feedback to the individual teacher followed by random intermittent checks with teachers. The best postworkshop experience involves allowing the teacher to observe classroom interaction behavior via videotape with immediate observational analysis.

Three workshops that were conducted over the past few years have at least one-year follow-ups on results of teacher workshop experience. Concerning the effect of these teacher behaviors on students, it should be observed that the average percent of students on-task was 81.8. Every teacher was able to maintain an average on-task percent much higher than most untrained teachers. Average on-task student behavior of about 80 percent is generally considered to represent a well-controlled classroom. Comparisons between trained and untrained teachers matched on teaching experience and grade level indicates the effectiveness of the training procedures. This effectiveness is apparent in both the increase of appropriate student classroom behaviors as well as increasing the positive, or approval, behavior of the project teachers. There is a direct relationship between the positive teacher ratio and the amount of inappropriate student behavior. Generally, the higher the positive teacher ratio, the greater is the student's responsiveness to the learning situation. Behavioral improvement seems to be directly related to the amount of attention teachers give to appropriate academic and social behavior.

LEARNING ACTIVITY 19–ROLE-PLAYING
ESSAYS FROM PART I

Participants work in groups of four to six and produce a skit to be presented to other participants which demonstrates principles covered in a single essay from Chapters 1 through 5. Each group is assigned one essay, such as "Is the World Fair?" pages 00–00, or "Who has the Responsibility?" pages 00–00, and other participants are not told which essay was assigned to another group. Thirty minutes preparation time should be sufficient to outline the skit, assign responsibility for props, decide who is going to play what roles, and practice.

Groups present skits and the others, those not presenting, use the following form, recording the name, date, and presentation number, and rate the presentation on all categories. Following the presentation, they attempt to determine which essay was being presented.

Following all presentations, the results of ratings should be given to participants and several aspects of the presentation discussed: What was the level of the role-playing situation? Was the approval/disapproval representative of the classroom level? Did the approval/disapproval "fit" the situation? Did it seem unnecessarily contrived? Was the skit creative?

INDIVIDUAL PRESENTATION RATING

Observer Name_____

Date_____

Group_____

Presenter No._____

Essay_____

A. Model	1 Fair	2 Below Average	3 Average	4 Above Average	5 Excellent
Specificity of behavior (pinpoint)					
Recording possibilities					
Consequences (logical?)					
Evaluation possibilities					
B. How points got across					
Communication of principles					
Organization					
Presentation (gestures, voice)					
C. Potential for consequences in classroom extensions					
Approval					
Disapproval					
D. Overall rating					

E. Comments

LEARNING ACTIVITY 20–
SUBJECTIVE VERBAL REPORT

Complete the following Evaluation Form. Attempt to be as objective as possible.

Instructor(s)   Course or Workshop Name

Date

The following statements are designed to allow you to help evaluate your experiences. Please answer each item honestly. *Do not put your name on this paper.*

Read each statement and indicate your agreement or disagreement by writing the appropriate number from the scale in the blank provided at the right.

Answer Scale

1	2	3	4	5	6	7
Disagree Strongly	Disagree	Disagree Slightly	Undecided	Agree Slightly	Agree	Agree Strongly

1. The general objective was accomplished.   1. _____

2. Each specific objective was accomplished.   2. _____

3. A schedule of specific topics and activities was provided.   3. _____

4. There was at least one activity for each specific objective.   4. _____

5. Activities were appropriate for the specific objectives.   5. _____

6. Materials were supplied to   6. _____
   implement activities.

7. Instructor(s) stimulated   7. _____
   appropriate participation.

8. Instructor(s) know(s) the   8. _____
   subject.

9. Feedback to participants was   9. _____
   directed toward specific objectives.

10. I intend that my teaching   10. _____
    will improve as a result of this
    course.

11. I intend to try new methods   11. _____
    and techniques in the classroom.

12. Other participants have   12. _____
    profited by this experience.

13. I would recommend that   13. _____
    most other teachers or pro-
    spective teachers take this
    course.

The amount of new material I learned from this experience (Circle appropriate choice) was: (a) 0–20%; (b) 21–40%; (c) 41–60%; (d) 61–80%; (e) 81–100%.

Comments:

What did you like about this course or workshop?

What did you dislike about this course or workshop?

LEARNING ACTIVITY 21—FEEDBACK FROM EXPERIENCED TEACHERS

In both practice and research the authors are dedicated to the improvement of education at all levels and in all specialties. Thus, we share some of the same values expressed by teachers in many divergent programs throughout teaching and related professions. Most of the specific techniques and principles found in this book came from teachers—beginning teachers, special education teachers, elementary, secondary, vocational-technical, and college teachers; teachers for gifted, for emotionally disturbed, for physically handicapped, and for children with learning disabilities; art, music, speech and hearing, home economics, and physical education teachers; content area specialists, subject matter specialists, and resource specialists; pre-school, child development, and nursery school teachers; social workers, counselors, and school psychologists; more especially *older teachers* whose long-term experiences have too long been ignored or repudiated by those very students who through scholarly denunciation attest to the effectiveness of their past learning.

In a continuing effort to learn of effective and ineffective practices in teaching, the authors sincerely encourage written responses from teachers. We would like information concerning techniques, materials, special projects, and any conceivable procedure used in teaching social and/or academic behaviors. Written responses will be used toward the goal of improving education through research application, and continuous dissemination. Teachers who share this concern please send responses to:

Steve Mathews, Series Editor
Allyn and Bacon, Inc.
470 Atlantic Avenue
Boston, MA 02210

References

Example
number

1 Jersild, A. T., and Holmes, F. B. "Methods of Overcoming Children's Fears" *Journal of Psychology* 1 (1935): 75–104.

4 Reynold, N. J., and Risley, T. R. "The Role of Social and Material Reinforcers in Increasing Talking of a Disadvantaged Pre-school Child." *Journal of Applied Behavior Analysis* 1 (1968): 253–62.

5 Harris, F. R.; Johnston, M. K.; Kelly, C. S.; and Wolf, M. M. "Effects of Positive Social Reinforcement on Regressed Crawling of a Nursery School Child." *Journal of Educational Psychology* 55 (1964): 35–41.

8 Brown, R., and Elliott, R. "Control of Aggression in a Nursery School Class." *Journal of Experimental Child Psychology* 2 (1965): 103–107.

10 Allen, K. E.; Hart, B.M.; Buell, J. S.; Harris, F. R.; and Wolf, M. M. "Effects of Social Reinforcement of Isolated Behavior of a Nursery School Child." *Child Development* 35 (1964): 511–518.

12 Harris, F. R.; Wolf, M. M.; and Baer, D. M. "Effects of Adult Social Reinforcement on Child Behavior." *Young Children* 20 (1964): 8–17.

13 Kobasigawa, A. "Inhibitory and Disinhibitory Effects of Models on Sex-appropriate Behavior in Children." *Psychologia* 11 (1968): 86–96.

Example
number

15 O'Leary, K. D.; O'Leary, S.; and Becker, W. C. "Modification of a Deviant Sibling Interaction Pattern in the Home." *Behavior Research and Therapy* 5 (1967): 113–120.

16 Hawkins, R. P.; Peterson, R. F.; Schweid, E.; and Bijou, S. W. "Behavior Therapy in the Home: Amelioration of Problem Parent-child Relations with the Parent in a Therapeutic Role." *Journal of Experimental Child Psychology* 4 (1966): 99–107.

17 Madsen, C. K. and Geringer, J. "Choice of Televised Music Lessons versus Free Play in Relation to Academic Improvement." *Journal of Music Therapy* 13 (1976): 154–162.

20 Zeilberger, J.; Sampson, S. E.; and Sloane, H. N., Jr. "Modification of a Child's Problem Behaviors in the Home with the Mother as Therapist." *Journal of Applied Behavior Analysis* (1969): 47–53.

21 Wahler, R. G.; Winkel, G. H.; Peterson, R. F.; and Morrison, D. C. "Mothers as Behavior Therapists for Their Own Children." *Behavior Research and Therapy* 3 (1965): 113–124.

22 Dickinson, D. J. "Changing Behavior with Behavioral Techniques." *Journal of School Psychology* 6 (1968): 278–283.

23 Kennedy, W. A. "School Phobia: Rapid Treatment of Fifty Cases." *Journal of Abnormal Psychology* 70 (1965): 285–289.

24 Baer, P. E., and Goldfarb, G. E. "A Developmental Study of Verbal Conditioning in Children." *Psychological Reports* 10 (1962); 175–181.

25 Becker, W. C.; Madsen, C. H., Jr.; Arnold, C. R.; and Thomas, D. R. "The Contingent Use of Teacher Attention and Praise in Reducing Classroom Behavior Problems." *Journal of Special Education* 1 (1967): 287–307.

27 Hall, R. V.; Lund, D.; and Jackson, D. "Effects of Teacher Attention on Study Behavior." *Journal of Applied Behavior Analysis* 1 (1968): 1–12.

29 Schutte, R. C., and Hopkins, B. L. "The Effects of Teacher Attention on Following Instructions in a Kindergarten Class." *Journal of Applied Behavior Analysis* 3 (1970): 117–122.

30 O'Leary, K. D., and Becker, W. C. "Behavior Modification of an Adjustment Class: A Token Reinforcement Program." *Exceptional Children* 9 (1967): 637–642.

Example
number

32 Patterson, G. R. "An Application of Conditioning Techniques to the Control of a Hyperactive Child." In *Case Studies in Behavior Modification,* edited by L. P. Ullman and L. Krasner. New York: Holt, Rinehart and Winston, 1965, pp. 370–375.

34 Madsen, C. H., Jr.; Becker, W. C.; Thomas, D. R.; Koser, L.; and Plager, E. "An Analysis of the Reinforcing Function of Sit-down Commands." In *Readings in Educational Psychology,* edited by R. K. Parker. Boston: Allyn and Bacon, 1968.

35 Madsen, C. K. "The Effect of Music Subject Matter as Reinforcement for Correct Mathematics." *Council for Research in Music Education* 59 (1979): 54–58.

36 Holland, C. J. "Elimination by the Parents of Fire Setting Behavior in a Seven Year Old Boy." *Behavior Research and Therapy* 7 (1969): 135–137.

37 O'Leary, K. D., and Becker, W. C. "The Effects of the Intensity of a Teacher's Reprimands on Children's Behavior." *Journal of School Psychology* 7 (1968): 8–11.

38 Ellison, D. G.; Barber, L.; Engle, T. L.; and Kampwerth, L. "Programmed Tutoring: A Teaching Aid and Research Tool." *Reading Research Quarterly* 1 (1965): 77–127.

41 Madsen, C. H., Jr.; Becker, W. C.; and Thomas, D. R. "Rules, Praise and Ignoring: Elements of Elementary Classroom Control." *Journal of Applied Behavior Analysis* 1 (1968): 139–150.

42 Ferritor, D. E.; Buckholdt, D.; Hamblin, R. L.; and Smith, L. "The Non-effects of Contingent Reinforcement for Attending Behavior on Work Accomplished." *Journal of Applied Behavior Analysis* 5 (1972): 7–17.

46 Doubros, S. G., and Daniels, G. J. "An Experimental Approach to the Reduction of Overactive Behavior." *Behavior Research and Therapy* 4 (1966): 251–258.

48 Holmes, D. S. "The Application of Learning Theory to the Treatment of a School Behavior Problem: A Case Study." *Psychology in the School* 3 (1966): 355–358.

57 Hall, R. V.; Panyan, M.; Rabon, D.; and Broden, M. "Instructing Beginning Teachers in Reinforcement Procedures Which Improve Classroom Control." *Journal of Applied Behavior Analysis* 1 (1968): 315–328.

Example
number

61 Chadwick, B. A., and Day, R. C. "Systematic Reinforcement: Academic Performance of Under-achieving Students." *Journal of Applied Behavior Analysis* 4 (1971): 311-319.

62 Grandy, G. S.; Madsen, C. H., Jr.; and DeMersseman, L. M. "Effects of Individual and Interdependent Contingencies on Inappropriate Classroom Behavior." *Psychology in the Schools* 10 (1973): 488-493.

63 Hall, R. V.; Cristler, C.; Cranston, S. S.; and Tucker, B. "Teachers and Parents as Researchers Using Multiple Baseline Designs." *Journal of Applied Behavior Analysis* 3 (1970): 247-255.

64 Polirstok, S. R., and Greer, R. D. "Remediation of Mutually Aversive Interactions Between a Problem Student and Four Teachers by Training the Student in Reinforcement Techniques." *Journal of Applied Behavior Analysis* 10 (1977): 707-716.

70 Bailey, J. S.; Wolf, M. M.; and Phillips, E. L. "Home-based Reinforcement and the Modification of Pre-delinquent Classroom Behavior." *Journal of Applied Behavior Analysis* 3 (1970): 223-233.

73 Hall, R. V.; Panyan, M.; Rabon, D.; and Broden, M. "Instructing Beginning Teachers in Reinforcement Procedures Which Improve Classroom Control." *Journal of Applied Behavior Analysis* 1 (1968): 315-328.

79 Davison, G. C. "Self-control through 'Imaginal Aversive Contingency' and 'One-downmanship' Enabling the Powerless to Accommodate Unreasonableness." In *Behavioral Counseling: Cases and Techniques,* edited by J. D. Krumboltz and C. E. Thoresen. New York: Holt, Rinehart and Winston, 1969, pp. 319-327.

80 Madsen, C. K., and Forsythe, J. L. "The Effect of Contingent Music Listening on Increases of Mathematical Responses." *Research in Music Behavior* edited by C. K. Madsen, R. D. Greer, and C. H. Madsen, Jr. New York: Teachers College Press, 1974.

81 Kirby, F. D., and Shields, F. "Modification of Arithmetic Response Rate and Attending Behavior in a Seventh-grade Student." *Journal of Applied Behavior Analysis* 5 (1972): 79-84.

84 Madsen, C. K., and Madsen, C. H., Jr. "Music as a Behavior Modification Technique with a Juvenile Delinquent." *Journal of Music Therapy* 5 (1968): 72-76.

Example
number

85 Marlowe, R. H.; Madsen, C. H., Jr.; Bowen, C. E.; Reardon, R. C.; and Logue, P. E. "Severe Classroom Problems: Teachers or Counsellors." *Journal of Applied Behavioral Analysis* 11 (1978): 53–66.

88 Miller, L. K. "A Note on the Control of Study Behavior." *Journal of Experimental Child Psychology* 1 (1965): 108–110.

100 Schwitzgebel, R. L., and Kolb, D. A. "Inducing Behavior Change in Adolescent Delinquents." *Behavior Research and Therapy* 1 (1964): 297–304.

101 McSweeny, A. J. "Effects of Response Cost on the Behavior of a Million Persons: Charging for Directory-Assistance in Cincinnati." *Journal of Applied Behavior Analysis* 11 (1978): 47–51.

Index